The Majesty of Chicago Jazz

The Majesty of Chicago Jazz

Twenty-Five Visionaries Who Define the City's Sound

HOWARD REICH

The University of Chicago Press
Chicago and London

The University of Chicago Press, Chicago 60637
The University of Chicago Press, Ltd., London

Published 2026
Printed in the United States of America

35 34 33 32 31 30 29 28 27 26   1 2 3 4 5

ISBN-13: 978-0-226-84644-6 (cloth)
ISBN-13: 978-0-226-85235-5 (ebook)
DOI: https://doi.org/10.7208/chicago/9780226852355.001.0001

Library of Congress Cataloging-in-Publication Data

Names: Reich, Howard author
Title: The majesty of Chicago jazz : twenty-five visionaries who define the city's sound / Howard Reich.
Description: Chicago ; London : The University of Chicago Press, 2026. | Includes bibliographical references and index.
Identifiers: LCCN 2026009847 | ISBN 9780226846446 cloth | ISBN 9780226852355 ebook
Subjects: LCSH: Jazz musicians—Illinois—Chicago | African American jazz musicians—Illinois—Chicago | Jazz—Illinois—Chicago—History and criticism | LCGFT: Essays | Reviews
Classification: LCC ML3508.8.C5 R45 2026 | DDC 781.650977311—dc23/eng/20260223
LC record available at https://lccn.loc.gov/2026009847

♾ This paper meets the requirements of ANSI/NISO Z39.48-1992 (Permanence of Paper).

Authorized Representative for EU General Product Safety Regulation (GPSR) queries: **Easy Access System Europe**—Mustamäe tee 50, 10621 Tallinn, Estonia, gpsr.requests@easproject.com
Any other queries: https://press.uchicago.edu/press/contact.html

For the memory of Jack Fuller, the Chicago Tribune editor who appointed me jazz critic.

And for Pam Becker, my wife and companion on our magical journey through music and life.

CONTENTS

PREFACE

Jazz Without Chicago?

Imagine—if you can—jazz without the music that erupted first in Chicago.

That means jazz without the revelations of two New Orleans visionaries who achieved their artistic pinnacles here in the Roaring '20s: Jelly Roll Morton and Louis Armstrong.

Morton and His Red Hot Peppers proved in Chicago that the rambunctious spirit and freely improvised methods of New Orleans' bands could be captured not only in Morton's meticulously penned scores but also in the hothouse of the recording studio. Classic Red Hot Pepper records such as "Black Bottom Stomp" and "Doctor Jazz" defined an era and provided a template for generations of ensemble composers to come.

Armstrong's airborne flights in his Hot Five and Hot Seven recordings in the same town, same time, gave jazz not only its first great star but incontrovertible proof that a brilliantly conceived solo could hold as much allure as Morton's intricately crafted compositions. Standing front and center on the bandstand—white handkerchief in hand—Armstrong created a vision of jazz as a soloist's art, his spotlight eventually to be taken up by Miles Davis, Charlie Parker, Dizzy Gillespie, John Coltrane and other immortals.

Why did Morton, Armstrong and their Crescent City peers flock to Chicago? In part because the 1917 shuttering of New Orleans' celebrated Storyville vice district—a cauldron of the new music—meant musicians needed to find work elsewhere. Chicago provided the nightspots, recording studios, publishing houses and national radio broadcasts that would bring their art to the world.

But that's just the start of Chicago's contributions to an art form revered around the globe and still widely identified with this city.

Consider the classically tinged work of cornetist Bix Beiderbecke; the ebullient spirit of cornetist Jimmy McPartland and the Austin High Gang; the coast-to-coast popularity of clarinetist-bandleader Benny Goodman; and the piano innovations of Earl Hines (who famously duetted with Armstrong), Nat "King" Cole (a piano wizard long before he became a popular singer), Ahmad Jamal (whose experiments still sound radical today) and Herbie Hancock (who fearlessly stretched the definition of jazz).

The otherworldly exhortations of Sun Ra and his Arkestra in the 1950s led to the revolutions of the Association for the Advancement of Creative Musicians (AACM) in the '60s. AACM breakthroughs in instrumentation, improvisation, composition, costumery and entrepreneurship resonate through our culture to this day, not least in the ever-increasing popularity of what we inadequately call "world music."

Without all this—and without the music chronicled in the pages to come—would we really be talking about jazz at all?

I came into this miracle of music-making quite fortuitously. At 16, I ventured with a high school friend to a spot on North Lincoln Avenue where legendary Chicago impresario, Joe Segal, was presenting Sun Ra and his Arkestra. We had no idea what we were in for. As Ra volubly chanted "space is the place," we beheld a large jazz orchestra jolting the room, while fire-eaters, dancers and shamans bounded through the crowd.

So this was jazz?

That indelible experience drew me to subsequent encounters with Segal's Jazz Showcase, in the 1970s ensconced in the lower level of the Happy Medium on North Rush Street. I savored the velvet ribbons of sound that Teddy Edwards unspooled on his tenor saxophone; I marveled as tenor giants Zoot Sims and Al Cohn thundered at each other from opposite sides of the stage, one sonic blast answered in kind by the next.

Though practically overwhelmed by this music, I did not imagine that my access to it soon would expand exponentially. For in 1978, a few years after graduating from Northwestern University's School of Music as a piano performance major, I began writing about music for the Chicago Tribune, a privilege that would stretch 43 years, until I retired from the paper (but not from writing) in 2021. I spent the last 32 years of that tenure as the newspaper's staff jazz critic, the last such position on any major paper in the U.S.

When you're covering jazz for a leading metropolitan daily, you get to hear as many concerts and interview as many musicians as you wish. If Northwestern had versed me in music theory, history, performance and ear training, Chicago's jazz clubs and concert halls offered extraordinary proximity to a singularly American art form. This was my long-running, post-graduate education, in which I could ask the world's greatest musicians to detail how they create, develop and hone their work, and why.

The process yielded thousands of articles on jazz, and I've tried to cull some of the most telling of them for this book. Specifically, by focusing on the visionaries who pushed the art forward in Chicago, I hope to give a sense of what the city where I was born has given to the world.

By limiting myself to 25 such artists, I was able to include some—but, of course, not all—of the most influential. For after Morton and Armstrong, Chicago somehow produced an unending line of innovators, from tenor saxophone wizards Johnny Griffin and Von Freeman to iconoclastic singer-songwriters Oscar Brown Jr. and Patricia Barber; from AACM founders Muhal Richard Abrams and Kelan Phil Cohran to MacArthur "genius" grant winners Reginald Robinson and Ken Vandermark.

For each artist I've included two articles, often a profile paired with a review or appreciation (the articles by and large appear exactly as they were originally published, with a few exceptions to eliminate repetition; anything written after 2021 appears only in this book). By way of introduction, I've opened with "Hotter Near the Lake," an exploration of how and why jazz took root here, and "Revolution in Sound," a look at the pivotal contributions of the AACM.

Of course, limiting the collection to those two introductory pieces and 25 artists leaves out many figures (more about that in the epilogue).

Even so, I wish for this collection to give readers a sense of the groundbreaking character of the jazz that has come out of Chicago, a city primed for innovation by Morton, Armstrong and their New Orleans brethren.

Ever since, Chicago has been a breeding ground for musical experimentation, and its audiences have expected nothing less.

Which is why listeners around the world still treasure the majesty of Chicago jazz.

On Chicago Jazz: Hotter Near the Lake

Sept. 5, 1993

> *Chicago always sounded like the most glamorous place in the world to me when I heard the guys in Frank Holliday's poolroom talking about their travels . . . they told very romantic tales about nightlife on the South Side. By the time I got there in 1930, it glittered even more . . . the Loop, the cabarets . . . city life, suburban life, luxurious neighborhoods—and the apparently broken-down neighborhoods where there were more good times than any place in the city.*
>
> —Duke Ellington in "Music Is My Mistress" (Da Capo, 1973)

There was a time in Chicago when you simply could not escape the glorious sounds of jazz. As Duke Ellington discovered, the good times were abundant, and the music literally never stopped.

On busy streets and in crowded neighborhoods, hot swing rhythms and gritty blue melodies provided the backdrop for city life. On the South Side of Chicago, out on the West Side, up on the far reaches of the North Side and, of course, all through the Loop, it was the unbridled sound of jazz that seemed to make the good times possible.

In gin joints, jazz clubs, showrooms, theaters, plush hotels, seedy backrooms, penthouses overlooking the city and street corners where you could dance to music roaring from open windows on hot summer nights, the tune was modern, the beat was jazz.

On the eve of the Chicago Jazz Festival, which runs Friday through Sunday in Grant Park, it's worth remembering that, from the dawning of this century until at least the mid-1950s, Chicago reveled in a

Jazz Age far longer and richer than any F. Scott Fitzgerald might have imagined when he coined the phrase. For if Fitzgerald's Jazz Age was an era of flappers and society bands that flourished in the 1920s, before the Crash, Chicago's Jazz Age was the real thing—a noisy, raucous, dangerous era when mobsters, musicians, socialites and working people danced past dawn to the rhythms of America's only original art form.

Though popular mythology holds that jazz was born and nurtured in New Orleans, the less romantic fact remains that the seeds for jazz—and for Chicago's Jazz Age—were planted across America at the turn of the century and earlier. In the ragtime parlors of St. Louis, on riverboats docked at ports along the Mississippi, in the South Side theaters of Chicago and, of course, in the vice dens of New Orleans, a new, rambunctious, thoroughly American music began to emerge late in the 19th Century.

Significantly, it was to Chicago where the proselytizers of the new music—the piano professors and New Orleans improvisers and riverboat trumpeters—gravitated early in this century. No less than ragtime kings Scott Joplin and Tom Turpin, keyboard wizard Tony Jackson and self-proclaimed "inventor of jazz" Jelly Roll Morton had moved here, with hundreds of other inspired, African-American artists soon to follow.

"In Chicago at that time you could go anywhere you wanted regardless of creed or color," Morton once said, in explaining his move north from New Orleans. "This is why most famous musicians went to Chicago. That was not true of Kansas City. I came to Kansas City in the year 1911. I had been to Chicago much earlier. Kansas City did not have one decent pianist. The people were prejudiced also in St. Louis."

Just as important, Chicago was hungry for the party music that later would be christened jazz. Having savored the rhythmically mesmerizing West African drumming that was the sensation of the World's Columbian Exposition in Chicago in 1893, the city was ready to embrace jazz, as well as the musicians who played it, as no other city in America did.

"Consequently," wrote Rudi Blesh and Harriet Janis in "They All Played Ragtime" (Oak Publications), "much of the talent was drained from St. Louis and from Kansas City as well, from New Orleans, Louisville, Memphis, Little Rock, Oklahoma City, and a score of other places, as well as from the hinterlands of the deep South and the old 'Wild-Goose Nation' of Texas. . . . These men isolated themselves in Chicago's South Side."

The new talent played cakewalks and ragtime in spots as far South as the Pekin Temple of Music, which was thriving at 27th and State Streets as early as 1905, and as far north as the Green Mill, which was alive with music at Lawrence and Broadway as early as 1907. In long-forgotten rooms such as the Elite No. 1, at 3445 S. State St., and the Elite No. 2, at 31st and State, the new influx of artists was busily setting the stage for Chicago's Jazz Age.

By 1916, Tony Jackson, whom Jelly Roll Morton had called "maybe the best entertainer the world has ever seen," had published his beguiling tune "Pretty Baby," thereby creating a gigantic hit and giving Chicago's Jazz Age an unforgettable theme song.

Three years later, New Orleans cornetist Joe "King" Oliver was playing in the Dreamland Ballroom, at 3518–20 S. State St., and the Jazz Age was on in earnest.

"Chicago was a tremendously exciting and wide open place back then, especially on the South Side," recalls Danny Barker, the octogenarian New Orleans guitarist who had first come to Chicago in 1921.

"There was a place called the Pleasures Inn [on 31st Street] where this man would appear dressed up in drag and sing under the name Gloria Swanson. And he didn't sing like any soprano, or any Lily Pons either.

"And people would watch him and listen to him all night, stumbling up the stairs in the morning, when the sun would hurt their eyes. And then they'd hurry to try to catch a cab home.

"And there was a place called Jack Johnson's Cabaret [42 W. 31st St.], which had these gold spittoons—or at least they were supposed to have been gold," Barker continues. "And they had a cat working there whose job was just to take care of spittoons."

Of course, in this heyday of Prohibition, gangster-operated gin joints and speakeasies flourished, with live jazz as the musical backdrop.

"They would disguise these speakeasies in different ways," recalls 80-year-old Chicago musician Franz Jackson, who worked all manner of establishment in the '20s.

"One place I played was disguised as a Chinese restaurant—they were supposed to be selling Chinese food there, of all things.

"But the cops were always raiding them, and they would round up the musicians and put us on the wagon. Sometimes I'd spend a night in jail sleeping on my instrument case.

"The next morning they'd let you out, and you didn't have to do any serious time, but they did take your fingerprints—this was over at 35th and Indiana.

"You'd get paid every night, which was a good thing, because sometimes the place you played in one night would get blown up or burned to the ground before the next night [by mobsters who kept shifting locations for selling their illegal booze]. That's how you learned never to leave your instrument anyplace overnight."

That Chicago's mobsters held a passion for jazz, and the drink-and-be-merry mood it enhanced, no doubt helped the proliferation of the music and the venues that featured it.

"You see, Al Capone, the gangster, made the beer and the whiskey and all that stuff—so he opened up so many of the joints in Chicago," Doc Cheatham, an 88-year-old trumpeter who spent the Roaring '20s in Chicago, once told this writer.

"In those joints, he could sell his stuff. He had nice cabarets and after-hours joints all over the place. Everywhere there was space, he rented it, had music in there and kept bringing in musicians from New Orleans."

Though the nightspots proliferated in various neighborhoods in the city, it was the South Side, specifically along State Street between 31st and 35th, that was the beating heart of Chicago's Jazz Age.

"That stretch, from 31st to 35th on State, was called the Stroll," says Richard Wang, a music professor at the University of Illinois at Chicago Circle. "It was the center of the whole Black entertainment industry during the 1920s and somewhat into the '30s.

"The Dreamland was there, the Vendome Theater [3145 S. State St.], the Grand Theater [3110–12 S. State St.], plus clubs and restaurants and an incredible amount of music and entertainment centered along a four- to five-block stretch."

Amid all the music that made the Stroll come alive, though, the clarion sound of Louis Armstrong's trumpet was pre-eminent.

Armstrong first had come to Chicago in 1922 to play in King Oliver's band but had left shortly thereafter, apparently hoping to find greater glory in Fletcher Henderson's New York swing band than Oliver had allowed him here.

By the mid-'20s, however, Armstrong was back in Chicago, this time intent on conquering the city, which is precisely what he did.

"It was Louis' wife Lillian [Hardin, a noted jazz pianist in her own right] who advised him to leave Fletcher Henderson and come back to Chicago," remembers Cheatham, a friend of Armstrong's since the mid-'20s.

"He wasn't making any money with Fletcher Henderson, so he came back to Chicago, and when he did, I never have seen so much publicity in all my life.

"Trucks and loudspeakers [blasting] 'Armstrong this' and 'Armstrong that.'

"At one point, Louis came to me, when I was working at the Dreamland, and he asked me to go over to the Vendome Theater to play [fill in] for him. And he was so big that you couldn't even get standing room in that place the whole time he was there.

"But there were other greats in Chicago then too. Jimmie Noone [originally from New Orleans] was one of the greatest clarinet players in the world, a beautiful player, he had a lot of technique, he knew what he was doing—Benny Goodman [a Chicagoan] learned all he learned from Jimmie Noone. Almost every night Benny Goodman and Bix Beiderbecke would be up there listening to Jimmie Noone.

"Bix was terrific too—he brought a new style to jazz, new chords, but his trouble was the fact that Louis came to Chicago right immediately behind him and washed him out.

"So when he was up against Louis, he couldn't get too far, even though he could be a beautiful player."

In many ways, Armstrong epitomized Chicago's Jazz Age in the '20s, his brash confidence, miraculous high notes and ever-rising popularity helping to put both the city and its music on the international map.

By the 1930s, the scene had shifted, for theaters such as the Vendome no longer required live music to accompany talkies. The era of silent movies virtually had ended in 1927 with Al Jolson's "The Jazz

Singer," which had made a terrific splash with its sporadic, sung numbers.

So the center of musical activity now moved to 47th Street and South Park Way (now Martin Luther King Drive), where spots such as the Savoy Ballroom, Regal Theater and Grand Terrace Ballroom featured big jazz bands for dance shows and live radio broadcasts.

"All through the '30s and '40s, there was a thriving jazz scene down on the South Side," remembers Von Freeman, at 70 still Chicago's reigning tenor saxophonist.

"I'd go to the Regal as a kid and listen to the Count Basie Band, which had Lester Young on tenor; to Duke Ellington's Band, which had Ben Webster on tenor and Johnny Hodges on alto. You'd hear the big bands of Jimmie Lunceford and Andy Kirk—they'd all come through town and play the Regal, and that's where you learned what saxophone playing was all about.

"And the music kept moving farther south. I'd play at Dave's Cafe, which became the Rhumboogie, at 55th Street just off South Park Way, and there was the original Club DeLisa, at 55th and State.

"Even so, there still was a bunch of clubs down around 39th Street too. There was so much jazz it was amazing."

Indeed, "at 64th and Cottage Grove, there was the fabulous Pershing Hotel," recalls drummer and jazz scholar Charles Walton, who for years visited the hotel's Pershing Lounge, Pershing Ballroom and El Grotto supper club.

"Then there was the Sutherland Hotel, at 47th Street, which had the Sutherland Lounge; there was Cabin in the Sky, a club between 63rd and 64th Streets, on Cottage Grove, that Ethel Waters had put up money for.

"There were clubs all around. On 63rd was the Kitty Kat, where John Young and Ahmad Jamal would appear. And there was the Cotton Club, at 63rd and Cottage Grove, where Sun Ra used to rehearse when he was still known as Sonny Blount. That place would be going from 7 in the morning to 4 in the morning, and people like Clifford Jordan and Johnny Griffin played there, got famous there.

"But it was more than just a bunch of jazz rooms—it was like a real community. We jazz musicians would hang out together. When we got off at 4 o'clock in the morning, we'd go hang out at restaurants and watch the breakfast shows.

"A club wasn't just a place you went to hear music. Back then, to a lot of people it was like a home away from home. People came in there because they knew each other."

Because Chicago was deeply segregated along North-South lines, because musicians were divided by race into two unions, the South Side emerged as a mighty hub of Black culture, life and, of course, jazz.

Yes, there were other clusters of activity in Chicago. As early as 1926, the Blackhawk restaurant, downtown at 139 N. Wabash Ave., was featuring big bands such as the Coon-Sanders Orchestra in its dining room, "and we had Ted Weems with his orchestra and a boy singer named Perry Como, who was earning $128.60 a week," recalls Don Roth, son of the restaurant's founder.

"Our neighbors had plenty of music too. There was the College Inn at the Sherman House, which also had the Panther Room, where the swing bands played. Art Kassel led a big band at the Bismarck Hotel, and they had a live radio feed too."

Through the '30s downtown jazz rooms such as the Band Box, at Randolph and Dearborn Streets, and the nearby Down Beat proliferated. And in the '40s the Blue Note, at Clark and Randolph Streets, drew international names to Chicago's seemingly limitless nightlife tableau.

Many of the big, touring white bands played in Uptown, where singer Anita O'Day grew up and got her start; and a few clubs, such as the Silhouette, turned up on the Far North Side along a jazz strip on West Howard Street.

But, even with the spread of jazz and big band music across the city, the focal point remained the South Side.

"If you lived almost anywhere on the South Side, within 10 or 15 minutes of your house you could hear some of the best jazz in the world," UIC's Wang says, "and you could even get there by streetcar.

"At 63rd and Cottage Grove, you could stand there while waiting for a streetcar going to the Loop, and there was a club right on the corner. And this place served hot dogs in the summer to people waiting for the streetcars. They had this window that they always had open, so while you were eating your hot dog and waiting for the streetcar, you always could hear the musicians playing inside."

Like a soundtrack for life in the city, jazz rang out from sunup to sunup.

"One of the things that made that scene so great in the '20s, '30s, '40s—and even the early '50s—was that a band would be booked into a club for five, six, seven nights a week," Wang adds. "If a traveling band would come to town, they'd often spend, say, a week at Club DeLisa, two weeks at the Band Box, and so on.

"Well, this way, they could put together packages of traveling musicians who had good reputations, fine players who could go from city to city, but they could plan on several weeks, or even months, on location in a certain town.

"For the listener, if you knew that Coleman Hawkins was in town, you knew he'd be there for two or three weeks, and you could drop in on him any night you wanted, or every night. And because so many of those South Side clubs were clustered together, it was really easy to hear music. You'd buy a beer in one place, then sneak it under your jacket and walk it over to the next place and work your way down the street hearing almost every great name in jazz.

"Of course, that was a time when this city was more together in its culture. Public transportation was *the* way of getting around, most people did not have cars, and it was generally safe and efficient to take the streetcars."

No one can say exactly when or where or why Chicago's Jazz Age began to dim, though some facts seem inescapable. By the mid-'50s the jazz scene became a victim of television, suburban migration, the rise of the automobile, expressways, changing musical tastes and a myriad of other factors.

"It all began to change around the time Charlie Parker passed—1955," says tenor saxophonist Freeman, referring to a particularly dispiriting moment in the history of jazz, when the music lost its primary leader and symbol. "The bottom just dropped out, especially on the South Side."

With Chicago's two musicians' unions, which had been separated by race, merged into a single union in 1966, suddenly the North Side opened up to African-American artists, who leapt at the opportunity to play more lucrative, North Side jobs.

But there were even greater forces at work.

"It was really in the '50s that the adults surrendered their musical values to the teenagers," Wang says. "With the Baby Boom, the teenagers became the prime purchasers of entertainment and recordings," and so rock 'n' roll supplanted jazz as the popular music of the day.

Yet jazz in Chicago survived even through the bleak years of the '60s and '70s. If a posh, downtown supper club such as the London House, at Michigan Avenue and Wacker Drive, would be shuttered in favor of a Burger King, the music itself would find a home in a variety of rooms along North Rush Street, North Wells Street and in the pioneering South Side concerts of the AACM (Association for the Advancement of Creative Musicians).

Today, only the Green Mill still stands from the earliest days of jazz in Chicago, but the enduring success of Joe Segal's Jazz Showcase (founded in 1947), as well as Andy's, The Bop Shop, HotHouse, Cotton Club, Pops for Champagne, New Apartment Lounge and other spots suggest that jazz still contributes to the pulse of life in this city.

Of course, it always has, since the first, awakening moments of Chicago's Jazz Age.

On the AACM: Revolution in Sound

March 1, 2015

They changed the way we think about music.

Fifty years ago, a group of South Side jazz musicians found themselves backed against a wall. Clubs were closing, radio stations were going pop, America's musical interests were shifting elsewhere: toward youth-oriented rock 'n' roll.

If these Chicago jazz artists had given in to inevitably changing musical tastes, jazz might have devolved into a nostalgia bath or succumbed to the commercial excesses of the fusion era that followed. Instead, the Chicago musicians who half a century ago created the Association for the Advancement of Creative Musicians, or AACM, invented original musical languages, created intriguing new instruments, crafted novel ways of penning scores and otherwise defied long-standing presumptions about how music was supposed to be made.

Because their work was steeped in the rituals of ancient Africa, as well as certain traditions of early New Orleans music, the AACM artists managed to convey a vast sweep of Black cultural history—even as they were reinventing an art form. And though they didn't necessarily intend it, their breakthroughs opened the door to new ways of creating, staging and perceiving music.

Chicago and the rest of the musical planet will be celebrate the AACM's 50th throughout this year, a fitting response considering this organization's global profile and impact.

Pioneering AACM artists such as Muhal Richard Abrams, Henry Threadgill (a future Pulitzer Prize winner), Roscoe Mitchell, Anthony Braxton (a MacArthur Fellowship winner) and Wadada Leo Smith (a future Pulitzer Prize finalist) command international followings, as do AACM figures such as Nicole Mitchell, Kahil El'Zabar and George Lewis (another MacArthur Fellow).

If early AACM bands such as the Art Ensemble of Chicago and Threadgill's Air carried the organization's banner to acclaim in Europe and beyond in the late 1960s and '70s, subsequent groups such as Nicole Mitchell's Black Earth Ensemble, Ernest Dawkins' Live the Spirit Ensemble, Dee Alexander's Evolution Ensemble and El'Zabar's Ritual Trio continue to do so today.

But even an admirer of this majestic history might reasonably ask what exactly is the AACM? An organization? An attitude? A series of cultural practices?

Surely it's all of those, but also something more.

"It's really kind of a spirit thing," says Kelan Phil Cohran, a founder of the organization and, at 87, an active musician in Chicago and around the world.

"It was—and is—about creating your own artistic presence. That was the primary goal. Nothing has value other than that."

The idea of forging a singular sound and musical personality always has been central to jazz, dating back to its first great composer-intellectual, Jelly Roll Morton, and its first genius improviser, Louis Armstrong.

But the AACM founders in Chicago conceived fiercely individualistic approaches to music under duress, for their world was imploding in the early 1960s.

"Chicago musicians had been employed seven days a week—we couldn't get a day off," recalls Cohran, who came to Chicago in 1953, when jobs were plentiful.

"And gradually, by degrees, it went down and down, until there was no work at all."

Club dates, dance-band gigs, R&B sessions and the like were evaporating in the early 1960s, because of shifting musical fashions, changing population patterns and discriminatory enforcement of cabaret licensing laws, as George Lewis outlines in his definitive study, "A Power Stronger Than Itself: The AACM and American Experimental Music" (University of Chicago Press).

In response, the South Side musicians organized.

If clubs wouldn't hire them, they would present concerts themselves. If conventional jazz idioms of an earlier era were losing the public's attention, they'd create music they wanted to hear, whether there was an audience for it or not.

In 1962, Abrams formed the Experimental Band that included saxophonists Fred Anderson, Joseph Jarman and Roscoe Mitchell and drummers Jack DeJohnette and Steve McCall (drawing inspiration from Sun Ra's Arkestra).

This was the cauldron from which the AACM would emerge, a gathering of musical free-thinkers eager to break free of bebop, hard bop, cool and other stylistic boxes into which jazz had been packaged, sold and confined.

By 1965, Abrams, Cohran, McCall, pianist Jodie Christian and recording secretary Sandra Lashley signed the articles of incorporation for the AACM, officially launching what would become a revolution in sound.

"We figured there was no place for us to be showcased, no place to be heard," Anderson told me in 1990, as the AACM was preparing to celebrate its 25th anniversary (he died in 2010 at age 81).

"Most of the clubs weren't too keen on booking the latest new music, and there weren't even that many clubs to begin with. So we decided to showcase ourselves, build an organization that would feature us, instead of waiting around for someone else to do it.

"It was really tough at first. Any time you're breaking ground and playing original music, you can expect resistance. But that was no problem, because the Chicago guys were used to that."

The Art Ensemble of Chicago was the first to trumpet the new movement around the world, conquering Europe in the late 1960s with its free-flowing improvisations, unconventional instrumentation, Afrocentric garb and African-inspired face-painting.

Nothing like this had been heard or seen in jazz, inspiring sold-out concerts and wide critical acclaim in Europe and, eventually, back home in the U.S.

Threadgill's band Air similarly seduced audiences foreign and domestic with its unusual melodic material and its translucent ensemble textures, inspiring a galvanic shift in audience expectations of what jazz could be.

"We had no idea the AACM would catch on as it did," Abrams told me in 1990. "We certainly didn't establish it to be some kind of important institution.

"We weren't looking for notoriety, or anything. If we had, it probably wouldn't have turned out that way.

"We simply were turning to each other for support, and that was all it took. The resources were within us."

No doubt the AACM wasn't the first such enterprise.

The Underground Musicians' Association, UGMA, in Los Angeles, and the Jazz Composers Guild, in New York, slightly predated it.

Something was in the air. But none of these groups, or others that followed, attained the impact and longevity of the AACM.

Exactly why the AACM flourished artistically—notwithstanding virtually no financial support from foundations or corporations—is open to debate. The ingenuity and virtuosity of the musicians, as well as Chicago's long-standing taste for the jazz avant-garde, surely were essential.

But there's another reason too: the intrepid spirit of the AACM pioneers, who had a particular kind of grit.

"The first-generation AACM founders were all children of the first wave of migrants to venture north," wrote Lewis in "A Power Stronger Than Itself."

Which meant that "all of these people that we are talking about came from very, very struggling environments," Jarman said in Lewis' book.

"Every one of them started out at the bottom—maybe not the flat bottom, but pretty close."

These musicians, who started with so little, simply willed the AACM—and its philosophies and musical practices—into existence.

And the organization survived, "in part, because support of one's own career wasn't the highest value," Lewis told me when his book "A Power Stronger Than Itself" was published in 2008. "People were invested in supporting each other and are [still] invested in supporting each other."

Indeed, a communal spirit has defined the AACM since the beginning and, in fact, has served as a model for the unusually collegial Chicago jazz scene in general.

That's not to say that the AACM didn't have internal battles to be expected in any human endeavor.

"We've had hard times, families have broken up, love affairs have fallen apart," Chicago multi-instrumentalist Mwata Bowden told me in 1995, during the AACM's 30th anniversary celebrations. "But we have persevered, we have continued to look forward, we have moved the music all the way around the world."

Moreover, it's critical to understand that the AACM did not signify a particular sound, style, idiom or aesthetic.

Each AACM band—from Cohran's soulful Artistic Heritage Ensemble to Braxton's hyper-cerebral experiments—was distinct from the others.

The AACM simply gave these far-flung musical explorers a common spiritual home.

The connective tissue among the bands and musicians of the AACM, past and present, lies not in the sound of music that cannot be categorized, but in a philosophy of experimentation informed by African antiquity and innovative instrumental technique.

Thus the AACM's motto: "Great Black Music, Ancient to the Future."

The past five decades have produced recordings of vast expressive and stylistic range, as well as lasting influence on other jazz demographics.

Would the innovations of Chicago saxophonist Ken Vandermark (another MacArthur Fellowship winner) and the North Side experimental scene he helped build have been possible without the AACM?

Would the cross-cultural innovations of Asian and Asian-American musicians such as Tatsu Aoki, Jeff Chan, Jon Jang and Francis Wong have flowered without the model and inspiration of the AACM? Seems doubtful.

Many of the early generation AACM players have left Chicago, with Threadgill spending a great deal of time in India, Abrams and Lewis based in New York, Nicole Mitchell in California.

Others have passed away, among them indelible figures such as trumpeter Lester Bowie, saxophonists Kalaparusha Maurice McIntyre and Vandy Harris, bassist Charles Clark and violinist Leroy Jenkins.

But the music still thrives in the gifts of new generations of Chicago players such as trumpeter Corey Wilkes, singer Saalik Ziyad and performance poet Khari B, now chairman of the AACM.

Times change, but the AACM continues, surely fueled by what William Russo once told me was the “spiritual and moral underpinnings to their art.”

Is that what Cohran, an AACM co-founder, hears in this music?

“It’s there,” Cohran says. “That’s all the AACM played. When you play somebody else’s music, you never will get that.

“To me, the greatest goal is to find a reservoir that provides you with this spirit.”

The AACM was that reservoir, and 50 years later, it remains so.

CHAPTER 1

Jelly Roll Morton

The following article launched the Tribune series "Jelly Roll Blues," which inspired the 2003 book "Jelly's Blues: The Life, Music and Redemption of Jelly Roll Morton." The book, which I wrote with Pulitzer Prize–winning investigative reporter William Gaines, documented previously unknown facets of Morton's much-mythologized life, including details on how he was systematically robbed by the music industry, as he always alleged but never was in a position to prove. That massive theft destroyed his career and hastened his demise, in 1941.

Jelly Roll Blues, Part 1

With William Gaines; Dec. 12, 1999

For nearly three decades, the yellowing musical scores gathered dust in cardboard boxes stacked to the ceiling in a cramped French Quarter apartment.

They contain the last music by the first composer of jazz, Jelly Roll Morton.

On a spring evening more than a year ago, copies of the manuscripts were placed on music stands in New Orleans' Le Petit Theatre. Fittingly, the long-lost scores were heard for the first time just blocks

Fig. 1 Jelly Roll Morton: Though Jelly Roll Morton came of age in his native New Orleans, he achieved the pinnacle of his art and influence in Chicago in the 1920s. Morton's work with His Red Hot Peppers established a new template for ensemble composition, performance and recording. Photo courtesy of The William Russell Jazz Collection at the Historic New Orleans Collection, acquisition made possible by the Clarisse Claiborne Grima Fund, 92-48-L.49.

from the notorious brothels and gutbucket saloons where Morton conceived the original masterworks of jazz at the dawn of the century.

The music—strange, exotic and mystical yet breezy enough to dance to—did not simply shatter long-cherished assumptions about Morton's art and legacy. It proved more advanced than any jazz music of its time, the late 1930s, when Morton wrote these scores as a destitute musician discarded by the industry he had helped create.

Remarkably, Ferdinand "Jelly Roll" Morton never could get this music performed.

At the end of his life, Morton no longer had a band to play his music, a record company to document it or an audience to listen to it. The gaudy showman who owned two luxury cars and more than 100 suits in Roaring '20s Chicago was reduced to hocking his clothes for food in 1930s New York.

Like his final scores, his final lament—that the music industry robbed him of millions—fell on deaf ears. As a musician of color, a Creole from Louisiana, he was easily dismissed by the white music executives who controlled his income and grew rich off of his art.

But an analysis by the Tribune shows he was right. That, in fact, Jelly Roll Morton was the victim of the first great swindle in American recorded music.

In a historical investigation that alters fundamental understandings of the seminal composer of the Jazz Century, the Tribune has done what Morton couldn't: pinpoint exactly how Morton was bled dry by an emerging music industry, his business associates and even those closest to him.

Morton's side of the story is outlined in hundreds of letters discovered in the same New Orleans apartment that yielded the old musical manuscripts. The Tribune has stitched together the complete picture of Morton's tragic decline through an examination of court and copyright records, personal letters, archival material and financial documents from New York to Los Angeles and Chicago to New Orleans.

Specifically, the Tribune found, Morton's Chicago music publisher was picking Morton's pockets at the very moment the musician believed he had hit the jackpot. And the very organization that collected performance royalties for Morton's popular music denied him his money, as it did other Black musicians writing what was considered insignificant "race music."

Morton, from his freewheeling days in New Orleans and Chicago to his lonely death in Los Angeles, not only ushered in a new American art form—setting the stage for Duke Ellington, Benny Goodman and every jazz great thereafter—but also served as a prototype for the exploitation of its greatest creators.

: : :

With a cowboy hat perched precariously on his head and a bandana tied rakishly around his neck, Jelly Roll Morton walked into the Melrose Brothers Music store at 6320 S. Cottage Grove Ave. in the spring of 1923. Even without such regalia, Morton cut a striking figure, his scant 140 pounds sleekly distributed on a 5-foot-9-inch frame, his black eyes set off from golden skin, a mole dotting the side of his neck.

Even his name proclaimed his individuality. Morton's sobriquet likely derived from a bawdy reference to sexual anatomy, or perhaps from a racy quip he made in a vaudeville show.

Morton was lured to Chicago because he wanted proper credit for his hit "Wolverine Blues," which the Melrose brothers had published a few months earlier. The success of the tune, with its joyously optimistic spirit, was a sure sign that Chicago was ready for Morton's brand of New Orleans jazz.

"I am Jelly Roll Morton," he announced as he entered the Melrose store, and he held the floor thereafter.

"He talked constantly for two hours, and we didn't get a word in edgewise," Lester Melrose recalled in Down Beat magazine years later. "All of the monologue concerned how good he was and damned if he didn't prove it."

All Morton had to do to back up his boasts that day was sit down at a piano and unspool the music he had been refining for fully two decades.

Playing piano as a teenager in the brothels of New Orleans, Morton learned how to seduce an audience with blues-laced melodies and coyly syncopated rhythms—the building blocks of early jazz.

Unlike many first-generation jazz musicians, Morton learned how to read and write music—an opportunity often accorded to Creoles in class-conscious, turn-of-the-century New Orleans but rarely to dark-skinned Blacks. Armed with this precious information, Morton immersed himself in the culture of New Orleans' Storyville, the red-light district where piano players competed ferociously for gigs and the flashiest man always won.

Though recent scholarship maintains that Morton was born in 1890, that is contradicted by Morton's letters and other documents, which support the composer's claim that he was born in 1885. Whatever the birth date, the timing for Morton's emergence in Storyville in the first decade of the century hardly could have been more opportune, for all kinds of music were blossoming in one of America's most cosmopolitan cities. French opera, Italian melodies, Western European symphonies, Negro spirituals, Black parade music—all that and more were in the air.

More than anyone, Jelly Roll Morton epitomized the new sound of American music. Here were populist tunes that sounded positively raucous compared with the refined European classics of another era. Yet jazz, even in its embryonic forms, also was more technically demanding and complex than anything American music had yet produced—and Morton helped make it so.

New Orleans' unique amalgam of genres permeated Morton's art, enabling him to develop a repertoire of startlingly original material.

Whether Morton was evoking the sounds of the jungle in "Animule Dance" or articulating hot rhythms in "Kansas City Stomps," he beguiled audiences in saloons across the Gulf Coast, along the Mississippi River, up the West Coast, down in Tijuana, Mexico, and up in Vancouver, Canada. Though details of Morton's early travels had been difficult to determine until now, they are laid plain in Morton's newly unearthed scrapbook, examined by the Tribune in California.

Morton's arrival brought a shot of energy into the Melrose store, and the place needed all the help it could get. Walter and Lester Melrose, two of four brothers born in southeastern Illinois, near a speck on the map called Sumner, were not exactly destined for success in big-time music publishing.

Walter Melrose, who focused on the publishing end of the business while Lester minded the store, was Morton's opposite number in every way. His short, stocky build, conservative dress and soft-spoken manner rendered him nearly undetectable when standing in the same room as the loquacious, dressed-to-the-hilt composer.

Walter loved music but never studied it, recalls his daughter, Mary Melrose, who today lives in Tucson, Ariz. Though Walter noodled at the piano, "he was not very good," she says, adding that he never was heard to sing a note. Lester Melrose possessed even less musical talent, she adds.

She recalls a family gathering where Lester and Walter sat at the piano, Walter playing and Lester singing, "She'll Be Comin' Round the Mountain" until everyone begged them to stop.

After serving in the Army in WWI, the duo opened a music shop in rented space at 6311 S. Cottage Grove Ave. By 1923, the year of Morton's entree into their lives, the Melrose Brothers Music store had moved across the street, where two large display windows invited passersby to peer inside. They saw a showroom crowded with Steger & Sons pianos, Conn band instruments, recordings from Gennett, Columbia and Vocalion, as well as an array of piano rolls, phonographs and sheet music. All this was set in indirect lighting and surrounded by light blue walls.

Walter also was a songwriter, penning and copyrighting words and music for such maudlin and obscure tunes as "Since I Lost You" and "My Old Home of Yesterday."

The music store never fared well, though it sat at the foot of the elevated train platform south of the University of Chicago and close to the Tivoli Theater, a Balaban & Katz movie palace that also featured stage shows. Like most independent shops, Melrose Brothers Music couldn't compete with chain stores that bought sheet music in large quantities and sold it cheap. Giant operations such as Woolworth, which in 1923 ran at least three stores within a mile of 63rd and Cottage Grove, had no trouble undercutting small fries like the Melrose brothers.

Everything changed for Walter and Lester Melrose, however, the day that Jelly Roll Morton paraded in.

Though Morton was a walking encyclopedia of jazz tunes, he never sold them as sheet music because—like most of the old-time piano professors—he was terrified of publication. Morton came of age when hot piano players from New Orleans to Chicago made their money dazzling listeners with the originality of their riffs and the novelty of their keyboard tricks. Morton, for instance, could make the piano roar like a lion by rolling his left forearm across the low end of the keyboard, as he did in "Tiger Rag."

To colorful piano men like Morton, these keyboard stunts—as well as the unusually piquant chords and complicated rhythms that went with them—represented hard-won techniques to be protected, not shared.

By the 1910s and '20s, however, sheet music was becoming the hot commodity in America. Upwardly mobile families aspired to have a piano in the living room or parlor, and sheet music was an essential accessory, with popular ditties selling millions of copies.

The moment clearly had come for Morton to publish an already deep reservoir of music. Because fellow New Orleans musicians such as cornetists Joe "King" Oliver and Louis Armstrong were taking over Chicago nightlife, Morton would have no trouble finding champions of his music. Morton's style hardly could have been a better fit for these musicians or the rowdy, colorful joints they played. And with the Great Migration of Southern Blacks to Chicago already under way, the composer would not lack for listeners attuned to music evoking the spirit of home.

Though jazz fans and musicians still primarily were Black, that was changing rapidly as white America began to discover the music. And an expanding audience meant there would be more money from jazz hits—both for publishers and composers alike.

: : :

Though Morton spent brief stints in Chicago as early as 1910 and '17, this time he stayed, transforming himself from showman-entertainer to composer-bandleader, from itinerant piano player to codifier of a new art form. The Melrose brothers arranged the business deals that no Black composer in 1923 had the connections or resources to consummate.

Once Morton joined Melrose, which in 1923 ran trade-paper advertisements trumpeting him as "staff writer," the firm wasted no time in publishing the composer's tunes and arranging for him to record them.

Though the Melrose brothers drew Morton's ire by retitling "The Wolverines" as "Wolverine Blues"—this stomping piece is anything but blues—they otherwise made nary a misstep in publishing, recording and promoting Morton in the '20s. In 1923 alone, they brought to the world such instant Morton classics as the ebullient "Grandpa's Spells," the rhythmically unpredictable "London Blues" and the melodically beguiling "The Pearls."

These tunes, and others, sold so briskly that by the close of 1923 Walter Melrose moved the music publishing business downtown to 119 N. Clark St. (on a block later leveled to build the Daley Center), while Lester continued to operate the South Side music store with a new partner. The location for the publishing business was enviable, in the old Hamlin's Grand Opera House, a magnet for vaudeville agents and music publishers, including Irving Berlin's Chicago office.

While music legend holds that the duo ran the music publishing empire through the late 1930s, in fact Lester quit the music store and Walter closed it, buying out his brother's interest in the music-publishing business on April 23, 1925, according to court records. The two parted ways commercially and artistically, with Lester becoming the foremost blues record producer in Chicago within a decade.

In the mid-1920s Morton's tunes rapidly turned Melrose Brothers publishing into a musical powerhouse. The company was acquiring a growing inventory of blues and Dixieland songs, but Morton's masterpieces were the firm's central asset and primary claim to fame: From 1924 to '26 alone, Melrose brought out Morton's "King Porter Stomp," the composer's single most enduring work; "New Orleans Blues," which he wrote more than two decades earlier; "Wild Man Blues," to which they inaccurately gave co-composer credit to Louis Armstrong (perhaps thinking Satchmo's name would help sell copies); and many more.

In addition to his role as hitmaker for Melrose, Morton played a significant role behind the scenes in Melrose's growing empire.

"With my general assistance by 1924 [Melrose] was considered a first line publisher," Morton complained to the U.S. Department of Justice in a 1940 letter. "Melrose knew nothing about music. Through my advice lots of successful things were done," added Morton, citing Melrose's acquisition of songs by W.C. Handy and Louis Armstrong.

This expansion propelled the Melrose publishing house in 1926 to prime real estate at 177 N. State St., adjacent to the Chicago Theatre, the heart of Chicago's Loop entertainment district.

Morton never had it so good. The success of his newly published music and his recordings for Gennett and then Victor—in sessions arranged by Walter Melrose—made Morton a bona fide star, awash in more cash than he ever had seen. With Morton's sound in great demand, money flowed in from live performances, recording dates and sheet music sales.

The listening public—primarily Southern Blacks, packed into substandard apartments in a newly emerging South Side ghetto—danced to this music in nightclubs, relaxed to it at rent parties in neighborhood flats and savored it on the new "race records" marketed specifically to urban Blacks.

Morton's popular Victor recordings of tunes such as "Black Bottom Stomp," "Milenberg Joys," "Mr. Jelly Lord" and "Sidewalk Blues" gave the record industry the most sublime documents of New Orleans jazz ever made, then or since.

On the road across the Midwest in the '20s, Morton and His Red Hot Peppers (a changing lineup of half a dozen musicians) averaged a then-staggering $1,500 a night. The band traveled in high style in the Morton tour bus, the leader in his own roomy Lincoln.

The success showed on every inch of Morton. He gilded himself with diamonds literally from head to toe. They glimmered on his fingers, tie-pin, watch, belt buckle, sock supporters and even on a front tooth, the unlikely setting for a half-carat rock.

His music was everywhere in Chicago. You could hear it across the South Side, particularly along The Stroll, the all-night strip of State Street jazz clubs, Black theaters and after-hours spots running from 31st to 35th Streets. In clubs such as the Dreamland Ballroom and Joe's Paradise, the air was thick with smoke, the stages filled with chorus girls and the tiny dance floors packed to capacity.

The South Side practically had a monopoly on jazz and its best musicians. New Orleans' music scene had imploded since the closing of Storyville in 1917, and New York still was more enamored by society quadrilles than stomps and blues.

Chicago in the '20s was a wide-open city where visitors to the Pleasures Inn could ogle, in near disbelief, a man in drag who called himself Gloria Swanson and hit notes higher than Mary Garden ever did at the Chicago Opera. Or they could wander to boxer Jack Johnson's Cabaret D'Champion, where the spittoons were famously made of gold.

In these hedonistic places, Jelly Roll Morton's music was perfectly at home.

: : :

What Morton didn't realize, amid the sensual attractions of Chicago nightlife in the '20s, was that the man who was helping him make money also was skimming off the top. Walter Melrose was coolly double- and triple-dipping on money due the composer, records show.

Documents in the Library of Congress reveal that after Melrose properly submitted copyright claims on four of Morton's biggest tunes—correctly listing Morton as composer and Melrose as publisher—he did something more. Within months of filing the original copyrights on "Milenberg Joys," "Sidewalk Blues," "Sweetheart O' Mine" and "Dixie Knows," Melrose listed himself as lyricist.

As Morton's publisher, Melrose had the responsibility of filing copyrights, and he liberally took advantage of it by becoming a collaborator on works of music he had no hand in creating. In this way, he could receive both publisher and composer royalties for sales of sheet music and recordings.

Melrose's ruse worked brilliantly, yielding Melrose extra money from Morton tunes that remained popular in swing-band arrangements long after the public had forgotten Morton's name. Melrose's lyrics were not exactly inspired, as in this verse from "Sidewalk Blues": "My baby's gone and I got the blues/It sure is awful to be lonesome like me/Worried, weary, up in a tree."

The practice of attaching lyrics to already completed musical works was not unheard of among 1920s music publishers, who operated in a virtually unregulated business. For instance, music store owners who knew Morton in California, the Spikes brothers, added lyrics to "The Wolverines" before Melrose published it.

But Morton did not approve of Melrose's additions to his work and said so explicitly in a letter obtained by the Tribune from the U.S. Department of Justice. The letter, dated June 10, 1940, and addressed to Assistant Atty. Gen. Thurmond W. Arnold of the Justice Department's antitrust division, contains a revelatory phrase buried on page 4: "Walter Melrose, never wrote a hit in his life. Melrose is my publisher, he [Melrose] inserted words to some of my hit tunes without my knowledge or permission & is receiving [royalties]."

This was a particularly egregious act in the case of Morton's music, because his 1920s scores were conceived and endure as instrumental music. Adding lyrics to Morton's scores would be akin to adding words to a Brahms Symphony. Morton, in fact, was one of the few jazz bandleaders in America during the 1920s and '30s who never employed a staff vocalist in live performance or on recordings.

To this day, Melrose's lyrics to Morton's tunes remain invisible. Yet Melrose's strategy enabled him to collect twice on the same Morton composition, a total of 75 percent of royalties—whether or not lyrics are used in any recording or performance.

And Morton was not the only composer Melrose hustled in this way.

The publisher similarly added lyrics to the music of Earl Hines ("Midnight in New Orleans" and "Lazy Mornin' "), Charlie Davis ("Copenhagen"), the New Orleans Rhythm Kings ("Tin Roof Blues," later reworked as the 1954 Jo Stafford hit "Make Love to Me") and Louis Armstrong, Benny Goodman and Frank Trumbauer ("High Society"), according to an examination of copyright records.

: : :

By 1927, toward the end of Morton's residence in Chicago, his life began to change. He was smitten by a stage dancer, Mabel Bertrand, whom he met at the Plantation Cafe, on East 35th Street, on The Stroll. Like Morton, she grew up in New Orleans, a physician's daughter who as a teenager worked her way across Europe in a song-and-dance duo. Within a year of their meeting, the two were living together.

Their courtship flowered as the music industry was maturing and its corporate presence in New York was expanding. Increasingly, Chicago's big musicians were heading to Manhattan, where Duke Ellington was making a name for himself at the Cotton Club, and where

Armstrong, Cab Calloway, Sidney Bechet and others would head before the decade was over.

The city belatedly was beginning to catch on to the new music, and it was only natural that Morton would head to the next hot spot.

But this time, Morton did something he never had done before: He brought a woman, Bertrand, with him. Though Morton developed a notorious reputation for seducing women in every city he visited, he always left them behind. In Los Angeles, for years he romanced a woman named Anita Gonzalez, an old New Orleans flame, but they split up before he came to Chicago.

With Bertrand at his side in 1928, Morton was ready to take Manhattan. Unfortunately, from the instant Morton arrived in New York he saw the value of his name plummet faster than the stock market would a year later. Ellington, Calloway, Fletcher Henderson and other young jazz bandleaders—whom Morton rightly regarded as beneficiaries of his ideas and innovations—had the town sewn up. The only job Morton could get in Manhattan was leading the house band at the Rose Danceland, at 125th Street and 7th Avenue, where women dirty-danced with paying customers, 10 cents a turn.

In 1930, RCA bought Victor Records and promptly canceled its contract with Morton. Rejection notices began piling up in his mailbox in the following years.

"Dear Mr. Martan," began one note from an Omaha booking agency, insulting him from the outset by mangling his name. And Gennett, the minuscule label in Richmond, Ind., that was the first to record Morton, in 1923, wasted few words: "We doubt . . . if your plan would be of interest to us."

Incredibly, Morton saved each of these letters, meticulously taping them into his personal scrapbook.

He fell so low on funds that in 1935 he fled Manhattan to become a fight promoter in Washington, D.C. His undistinguished roster of would-be pugilists got him nowhere, and soon he was playing piano in a saloon that changed its name every few months, from Blue Moon Cafe to Jungle Inn to Music Inn.

He worked three years in this squalid room, where one night a patron stabbed him in a brawl. Morton, depressed by his surroundings and his sinking stature, believed he had hit bottom. He was wrong.

The Gospel According to Jelly Roll

Sept. 25, 2005

Jelly Roll Morton was flat broke.

Playing piano in a dive in Washington, D.C., the first composer of jazz—the New Orleans genius who was writing hits when Louis Armstrong still was learning how to talk—considered it a great night when he pulled down $10.

But in that desperate year of 1938, three years before his tragic death at age 55, Morton sat at the keys in Coolidge Auditorium at the Library of Congress and rhapsodized on the story of his life, the birth of jazz and the ways in which Blacks and whites and Creoles like him lived and died in old New Orleans.

All the while, a pair of crude, battery-operated disc-recording machines captured his precious reminiscences on several dozen acetate plates, his gravelly voice singing tunes that the rest of the world had long since forgotten, his still-dexterous fingers re-creating the piano styles of earlier New Orleans pianists who had faded into oblivion.

In unsparing detail, he recounted the way the music unfolded in brothels and on street corners in Storyville, New Orleans' fabled vice district, the way it erupted in rambunctious parades that often turned into bloodbaths.

As Morton sang and talked and laughed and lamented, he not only mapped out precisely how and why a new American art form had appeared in the city of his birth, he also demonstrated his role as one of its two principal architects (the other being Armstrong). For if Armstrong, who was about 15 years younger, was the first great solo improviser in jazz, Morton was its groundbreaking composer, the first man to publish a jazz tune ("Jelly Roll Blues" in 1915), the first artist who cracked the code of putting to paper this seemingly unruly music.

Until now, the only way to hear those recordings in full was to travel to the Library of Congress in Washington, don a set of headphones and listen to nine hours of Morton's half-sung, half-spoken soliloquies. Though some of this material had been produced as a series of LPs in the late 1940s and again in the '50s, it was severely edited, omitting the often racy song lyrics that Morton recalled from his early days in New Orleans.

On Tuesday, when Rounder Records releases "Jelly Roll Morton: The Complete Library of Congress Recordings by Alan Lomax" (an eight-CD boxed set that lists for $127.98), an international public will begin to discover what some experts have known for years: That the composer-pianist not only penned such jazz masterpieces as "King Porter Stomp" and "Jungle Blues" but, equally important, that he built the intellectual framework for understanding jazz through his Library of Congress recordings.

Specifically, by explaining how the music emerged and detailing its central techniques and practices, Morton in these sessions effectively shaped the way listeners thereafter have perceived the art form.

The very notion, in fact, that jazz—a music that dared to draw inspiration from both the church and the whorehouse—could be considered an art form owed a great deal to Morton's breakthroughs as composer in the early part of the 20th Century and his explication of them several decades later, on these recordings.

"What you have in the Library of Congress recordings is the first musician-intellect of jazz addressing himself to the music he knew and helped create," says Richard Wang, professor emeritus of music at the University of Illinois at Chicago and lecturer in jazz at the University of Chicago.

"This is the first great oral history of this music.

"From Jelly Roll, we get a sense of history and analysis that we don't get from Armstrong, because Armstrong didn't comment with such critical insight and evaluation on this music and the way it was shaped and formed.

"Jelly Roll did."

Indeed, as Morton spoke to Lomax—a young folklorist whose questions revealed a lack of familiarity with the art form—Morton illuminated the meaning of "riffs" and "breaks," the jazz rituals of the classic New Orleans funeral, the backdrop of French Opera and Spanish dances and carnal songs that formed the pre-history of jazz. With unmistakable authority and knowledge, he explained why certain tempos are used in particular song forms, how melodies are to be embellished in the course of an improvisation and other rudiments of making bona fide jazz.

Yet none of this material—which in this remastered set sounds better than it ever has—becomes pedantic or dull. On the contrary, Morton emerges as the quintessential New Orleans entertainer, punctuating even the most intricate musical discussion with vivid anecdotes, typically accompanying them with a gently rolling piano accompaniment, his foot tapping audibly all the while.

Even his speech sounds like song, his Louisiana cadences undiluted by his years in Chicago, when he recorded triumphantly in the mid-1920s, or his period of defeat in New York and Washington, throughout the 1930s.

"I don't intend to say anything unless it's real facts," Morton drawls to Lomax during the first session, on May 23, 1938, as a kind of preamble for the great discourse yet to come.

Then Morton proceeds to speak—sometimes seriously, sometimes whimsically—about his early years in New Orleans, his ascent as one of its most sought-after piano professors and everything else under the Southern sun.

"I myself was inspired by going to the French Opera House once," he says, recalling his initiation into music.

"Because the fact of it was I liked to play piano, and the piano was known at that time to be an instrument for a lady.

"So I had it in my mind that if I played piano," he adds mischievously, "I would be misunderstood."

When Lomax asks if a solo "break" and "swinging" are the same thing, Morton chides his interlocutor: "No, no, that's not what swinging is. Swing don't mean that. Swing means something like this," he says, illustrating the distinctly swaying approach to rhythm on the piano.

During the course of these sessions, which ran through June 12, plus a final set on Dec. 14, Morton pours out his heart, remembering the vast amounts of cash that fell his way in the houses of New Orleans, confessing the tough times he was facing now in Washington. With relish, he retraces his journeys playing the vice districts across the Gulf Coast in the first decade of the 20th Century, the fortunes he made and lost in California and elsewhere from 1917 to 1923, the sense of freedom and possibility that he and others of color felt in Chicago, in the anything-goes Roaring '20s.

But New Orleans remains at the center of Morton's identity, the composer returning to it like a refrain, marveling at the merging of cultures that distinguished it from any other spot on Earth and made possible the hybrid art of jazz.

"Of course, it was a free and easy place," he says. "Everybody got along just the same. . . . There wasn't no certain neighborhood for nobody to live in, only with the St. Charles Avenue district, which is considered the millionaire district. . . .

"Why, everybody just went anyplace they wanted. Many times you would see some of those St. Charles Avenue bunch right in one of those honky-tonks. They was around—they called theirselves slumming, I guess, but they was there, just the same. Nudging elbows with all the big bums."

Musically, on these recordings Morton becomes a chameleon, his pitch-perfect aural memory enabling him to re-create at the keyboard the piano styles of long-lost New Orleans musicians and to conjure up a seemingly bottomless repertoire of songs. He unleashes glittering cascades of sound to impersonate the pianism of Sammy Davis (no relation to the famous entertainer of later vintage); he knocks off age-old blues and ribald sex songs and narrative ballads like a human jukebox; he describes the work of other early New Orleans musicians such as cornetist Buddy Bolden, bandleader Joe "King" Oliver, trumpeters Freddie Keppard and Manuel Perez and Bunk Johnson with the unimpeachable credibility of someone who knew them and heard them.

The exercise carries authenticity not only because of the persuasiveness of the performances and the breadth and depth of the information conveyed but also simply because of who is speaking—Jelly Roll Morton, born Ferdinand Joseph Lamothe, a founding father of jazz who in these sessions also becomes the first great analyst-journalist-critic of the music.

But Morton, it turns out, was both blessed and cursed by these sessions, Lomax giving him a kind of immortality but also at times demeaning him in the landmark book based on the recordings, "Mister Jelly Roll: The Fortunes of Jelly Roll Morton, New Orleans Creole and 'Inventor of Jazz'" (Pantheon Books, 1950, also included in this boxed set).

Were it not for these recordings, Morton—today nearly forgotten by the general public despite the stature of his compositions—might be underappreciated by the jazz public, as well. For although it's universally agreed that the recordings Morton made with his Red Hot

Peppers in Chicago in the mid-1920s represent the finest recordings of early New Orleans jazz ever made, his profile as raconteur, jazz champion and history maker owe largely to the Library of Congress recordings and Lomax's poetically written, often magical book.

Unfortunately, Lomax in the text of "Mister Jelly Roll" also portrayed Morton as a liar, writing that Morton pushed his birth date back to 1885, because this was "a date that puts in him Storyville earlier than most other jazzmen and gave him plenty of historical elbow room."

In addition, Lomax charged Morton with being ashamed of his race, claiming that "Jelly Roll's whole life was constructed around his denial of his Negro status" and referring to his "race prejudice," though without evidence.

These two assertions—that Morton was a liar and a racist—eventually rippled out into the culture, embellished in subsequent books and celebrated in the Broadway musical "Jelly's Last Jam" (of 1992).

Subsequent research has shown both claims to be dubious, at best. No birth certificate has been found to disprove Morton's claim of his birth year, while the chronology Morton presents in the Library of Congress recordings—as well as other documentation—support the 1885 date. To its great credit, John Szwed's liner notes to the new boxed set reaffirms the 1885 date, while acknowledging some dissent.

As for Morton's alleged racism, the Library of Congress recordings and other sources show Morton showering his most lavish critical praise on musicians such as pianist Tony Jackson (who wrote "Pretty Baby"), trumpeter King Oliver and ragtime genius Scott Joplin, all men "black as coal," as Morton once noted.

Considering the low regard in which Lomax held Morton's character, one wonders why he wanted to make the Library of Congress recordings in the first place.

"He didn't want to," says Szwed, observing that Lomax was more interested in folk traditions than in jazz at the time.

"He was pushed by the people he was hanging with to make the recordings. He admits that he started negatively. He thought this was a guy who was not going to tell him anything."

But even Lomax was seduced by Morton's way with words.

"I realized that Jelly was telling me the history of jazz, because jazz was a neighborhood project," Lomax once said.

"There was as yet no serious jazz criticism or jazz history. Jelly Roll was attempting to find a basis for such criticism and history."

Morton, however, did not reciprocate admiration for Lomax, who at the time worked as Assistant in Charge of the Archive of Folk Song at the Library of Congress.

Virtually penniless in the last three years of his life, Morton begrudged the amount of time he was asked to spend on the recordings for no pay.

"I wonder how Lomax think that I don't need money to live just the same as anyone else," Morton wrote in a letter to his friend Roy Carew in 1940. "I worked for months doing the [archives] & it meant nothing to me financially."

On balance, however, the recordings gave Morton a forum in which to be heard, not simply as composer but as intellectual, as personality, as flesh-and-blood human being.

Thanks to the release of the boxed set—more than half a century later—listeners can hear him speak for himself, without interpretation from Lomax (who died in 2002 at age 87) or anyone else.

He never has sounded more impressive.

CHAPTER 2

Louis Armstrong

Satchmo in Chicago

April 9, 1995

Late one night in August of 1922, a young and obscure New Orleans musician stepped off an Illinois Central train as it pulled into the La Salle Street Station, hopped a cab to one of the hottest joints on the South Side, the Lincoln Gardens, and proceeded to change forever the history of music in America and beyond.

Louis Armstrong didn't play his cornet that night—he was too scared and too awed by the big-city setting for that—but within days he would be blowing his horn, without inhibition, in the Gardens, at 31st Street and Cottage Grove Avenue. In so doing, the 21-year-old cornetist would launch the first and greatest period of his career, a decade that would establish him as the foremost jazz soloist who ever lived (before or since), the man who gave jazz a face, a sound and a personality that the world could embrace.

That much is apparent not only from history books and recordings but also from "Louis Armstrong: A Cultural Legacy," the expansive exhibition opening Saturday at the Terra Museum of American Art, at 664 N. Michigan Ave. Curated and first presented by the Queens Museum of Art in New York, the exhibition pays proper homage to Armstrong's roots in Southern and Midwestern musical culture.

Fig. 2 Louis Armstrong: Like Jelly Roll Morton, Louis Armstrong brought his New Orleans roots and sensibilities to Chicago. In the Roaring '20s, Armstrong established an artistic high point with his impeccably crafted solo improvisations in the Hot Five and Hot Seven recordings.

Indeed, through the inclusion of writings by and about Armstrong, and through recordings and memorabilia from the whole span of the great musician's life and career, the exhibition portrays Armstrong as precisely the New Orleans/Chicago creation he was.

In other words, though Armstrong's music was steeped in the traditions and the history of pre-jazz New Orleans, that comparatively small city could not launch Armstrong into the big-time nor ready him for the world stage.

Had Armstrong never left New Orleans, where his circle of friends affectionately called him "Gatemouth" and "Satchmo" (for his larger-than-life "satchel mouth"), had Armstrong headed for the East Coast or the West Coast or anywhere in the Deep South, he might have lingered in obscurity for years. What's more, the music that only a few years earlier had acquired the sobriquet "jazz" might never have achieved the sweeping popularity that Armstrong's rise in Chicago made possible.

But Armstrong didn't remain in New Orleans. He came instead to Chicago, just as hundreds of thousands of Blacks from the South had done before him and after, hoping to find better pay, better treatment and a better life in a sprawling, wide-open Northern city.

The call to come to Chicago came from Joe "King" Oliver, the formidable bandleader-cornetist who had left New Orleans for Chicago four years earlier. Oliver was a kind of surrogate for the father Armstrong never had, arranging for a teenage Satchmo to inherit Oliver's old job in Kid Ory's New Orleans band when Oliver headed north.

Now Oliver was inviting Satchmo to come up to Chicago and join his Creole Jazz Band, the most authentic New Orleans outfit in town, though the invitation was not exactly elegantly phrased.

"One night I sat backstage with King Oliver, Louis Armstrong and myself," the late Chicago jazz pianist Art Hodes once told this writer, "and King is telling Louis: 'You remember when I wrote to you and told you that you could come up and put your stinking feet in my bed?'

"That's the way they talked to one another. Of course, Louis lucked out with King, because King was his sponsor, King brought him here. Without King, where would he be?"

Certainly Armstrong wasn't exactly brimming with confidence as his train pulled into Chicago.

"Anybody watching me closely could have easily seen that I was a country boy," wrote Armstrong in his second volume of memoirs, "Satchmo: My Life in New Orleans" (Da Capo).

"I had a million thoughts as I looked at all those people waiting for taxi cabs. It was 11:30 at night. All the colored people . . . who had come up from New Orleans were getting into their cabs or relatives' cars. As they left they said goodbye and wished me good luck on my stay in Chicago. As I waved goodbye I thought to myself: 'Huh. I don't think I am going to like this old town.'"

Eventually, Armstrong caught a taxi of his own, and "as I opened the door to go into the Lincoln Gardens I could hear Joe's band swinging out on one of those good old Dixieland tunes," wrote Armstrong in "Satchmo."

"Believe me, I was really thrilled by the way they were playing. It was worth the price of my trip. But I was a little shaky about going inside. For a moment I wondered if I should. Then, too, I started wondering if I could hold my own with such a fine band."

Soon enough, Armstrong would discover that he could hold his own, and then some.

By March of 1923, Oliver, Armstrong and the Creole Jazz Band had begun making records for the Gennett label, in Richmond, Ind., and these would ignite the still emerging world of jazz. The rounded, golden tone that Armstrong brought to "Chimes Blues" (his first recorded solo), the two-cornet tours de force that Oliver and Armstrong showed off in "Snake Rag" and the virtuoso licks that Satchmo played in "Tears" announced the arrival of a young cornetist already more proficient, more inventive and more distinctive than his boss, "King" Oliver.

What record buyers didn't know was that the recording engineers had to go to great lengths simply to contain Armstrong's gargantuan sound.

"When they recorded Louis," Hodes recalled, "they had to put the mike five feet away from him so he wouldn't blow it out of business."

Indeed, as Armstrong noted in the first volume of his memoirs, "Swing That Music" (Da Capo), "I think it was then that I realized for the first time how strong my blowing had become with all those years of practicing and playing. The Gennett people found they had to put me 20 feet back of the other players because my high-register notes were so strong they would not record clearly any closer."

But Armstrong, who by now had divorced his first wife and in 1924 had married Lil Hardin, Oliver's pianist, ultimately was not content in Oliver's band. Furthermore, Hardin, a college-educated musician who encouraged and championed Satchmo at every turn, felt that Oliver had hired the young phenom essentially to keep him out of the spotlight that Oliver coveted for himself.

"She was certain that Oliver had hired her man to keep him under wraps as a potential rival to his crown," writes Dan Morgenstern in his notes to "Louis Armstrong: Portrait of the Artist as a Young Man, 1923–1934," a boxed set of recordings on Columbia/Legacy.

"She was aware how far superior Louis' playing was to Oliver's, something the modest young man would not admit without constant hectoring. Eventually she succeeded in cutting Armstrong loose from his mentor, not least, perhaps, because the King was caught holding out money from his men—the bane of many bands in the history of the music.

"In a charming recorded memoir, 'Satchmo and Me,' Lil describes how, after she left the band, she would hear her husband whistling on his way home, inventing the most beautiful music. One night she asked him why he didn't play like that, since he could whistle it. Reluctant at first, he eventually came around, of course."

So Armstrong packed up his instrument and headed to New York City for a 14-month stay that turned out to be disappointing.

For starters, the Fletcher Henderson band didn't approach the instrumental virtuosity, ensemble precision or hot-swing style of Oliver's Chicago band. Indeed, Henderson's somewhat dated outfit reflected the state of jazz in New York, where stodgy society dance forms and stilted Broadway songs were all the rage.

Worse, Henderson had been "embarrassed" by Armstrong's revolutionary scat singing, which the bandleader considered too "down-home" and unsophisticated.

Perhaps it was inevitable, then, that Armstrong would leave New York.

As he wrote in "Swing That Music," the East Coast experience had left him "very homesick for Chicago and [I] wanted to see Lil again. So when we finally came in from [a] tour, I told Fletcher I wanted to go back to Chicago."

Now, in 1925—three years after he first set out to make a name for himself outside New Orleans—Armstrong finally hit his stride.

Outside the Dreamland Cafe, another fabled South Side joint, a sign had gone up proclaiming the arrival of "The World's Greatest Trumpet Player," and the slogan did not refer to Oliver but to his more brilliant protege.

"I first heard Louis just when he came back to Chicago from New York," remembers 89-year-old trumpeter Doc Cheatham, "and I swear I hadn't heard anything like that music.

"Actually, it was his wife, Lillian, who had advised him to come back to Chicago. And when he came back, I have never seen so much publicity in all my life. Trucks and loudspeakers announcing 'Armstrong this' and 'Armstrong that.'

"When he went to play the Vendome Theatre [a Black entertainment palace on the South Side], you couldn't even get standing room in that place when Armstrong was there."

Even Armstrong, who was ever modest about his achievements (though he knew his worth), acknowledged that he was making quite an impact.

"It was at the Sunset [Cabaret], for the first time, that my name went up in lights," wrote Armstrong in "Swing That Music," referring to another popular South Side club.

"I will never forget the kick I got when I first saw that big bright sign reading: 'Louis Armstrong, World's Greatest Trumpet Player.' I couldn't help thinking I had traveled pretty far since I'd left the Waif's Home [in New Orleans], a little more than 10 years before. Mr. Joe Glaser was proprietor of the Sunset at that time. He was the first to give me a real big play."

What was it about Armstrong in Chicago in 1925 that caused the town to quake? To judge from the recordings he began to make with his first Hot Five and Hot Seven bands (some of which resound through the Terra Museum exhibition), Satchmo hit his audiences with the kind of musical arsenal that never had been heard before. The ripeness of his tone on "Gut Bucket Blues," the stunning minor-key solo on "King of the Zulus," the ebulliently scatted and historic vocals on "Heebie Jeebies" (all from Hot Five sessions) pushed forward the art of jazz improvisation with as much daring as showmanship.

But that was just the beginning. In the next two years, Armstrong would forge a musical vocabulary upon which an entire art form would develop. The sublime lyricism he expressed in "West End Blues," the stunning duet passages between Armstrong and Chicago pianist Earl Hines in "Weather Bird," the joyously melodic spirit in "Struttin' With Some Barbecue" would establish the new art of jazz, once and for all, as a timeless and important one.

Only in Chicago—its night life driven by such brilliant players as Oliver, Hines, clarinetist Johnny Dodds, drummer Baby Dodds, banjoist Johnny St. Cyr, singer Chippie Hill and trombonist Kid Ory—could Armstrong find so rich a setting in which to flourish. Only in Chicago—its rambunctious, freewheeling, anything-goes clubs run by mobsters (such as Al Capone) who loved both jazz and Satchmo—would the atmosphere be ripe for such musical experimentation. And only in Chicago—with its numerous publishing houses, record labels, national radio broadcasts and so on—could Armstrong launch his revolution nationwide.

Not that everyone in Chicago applauded Armstrong's second coming.

"Louis tore up Chicago, he tore it up," recalls Cheatham, "but at first, all the rest of the trumpet players didn't like the idea.

"Louis had too much publicity, too much attention from trucks with big loudspeakers going up and down the boulevard playing his records, and the trumpet players resented it in the beginning.

"One day, in fact, they planned a jam session in this little hall in Chicago, and they invited Louis to come. They had six trumpet players there, and they figured they would cut him [or 'defeat' him onstage with their own technical prowess].

"So Louis arrived, but before he went in, he listened outside to these guys jamming.

"And then he went in there—and, remember, in those days playing a high C was a big deal—and he let loose about 100 high C's in a row, and those trumpet players went out of there real fast.

"From that day on, the trumpeters had the greatest respect for Louis."

So did the critics, who did not try to restrain their enthusiasm.

"Louis Armstrong was featured at the Vendome Theatre last Sunday night," read one of many reviews featured in the Terra Museum exhibition and dating from circa 1928. "He played 'Sugar Foot Stomp.' In it, he fluttered, he cried, he raved and the band raved with him. Looking all around me, the audience was raving and swaying, too."

And another: "Louis Armstrong, the greatest jazz cornet player in the country, is drawing many Ofay [white] musicians to Dreamland nightly to hear him blast out those weird jazz figures. This boy is in a class by himself."

And another: "Louis is in demand in the Windy City, and there is a reason—he toots a wicked trumpet."

Armstrong would stay in Chicago until 1929, when he pushed on to New York, California, Europe and beyond.

Yet no matter how far he ventured, Chicago remained integral to his art and his success.

When he returned to the city for a long stay in 1931, for instance, he formed here a big band that he later termed "the happiest" ensemble he ever led. When he came to sweet home Chicago again in 1935, after a tumultuous and somewhat troubled second tour of Europe, he formed yet another big band in Chicago and engaged the manager who would be his closest confidant to the end of his life, the aforementioned owner of the Sunset Cabaret, Joe Glaser.

Eventually, Armstrong's achievements in film, on stage and on TV would make him an international celebrity, even as that celebrity would be used against him, with skeptics alleging that Armstrong had become "old-fashioned," "corny," "out-of-date," "an Uncle Tom" and worse.

Only in recent years has the general public begun to appreciate anew the significance of Armstrong's achievements, thanks largely to the concerted efforts of another great New Orleans trumpeter, Wynton Marsalis, through CD reissues of Armstrong's work and through the new exhibition.

Only now is the general public discovering once again that Armstrong, who died quietly in his sleep in 1971, at age 69, became a great musician in Chicago, a town he often went out of his way to thank.

Recalling that first opening night at the Lincoln Gardens, he wrote in "Satchmo: My Life in New Orleans," "When we cracked down on the first note that night at the Lincoln Gardens I knew that things would go well for me. When Papa Joe [Oliver] began to blow that horn of his, it felt right like old times. . . .

"After the floor show was over, we went into some dance tunes, and the crowd yelled, 'Let the youngster blow!' That meant me. Joe was wonderful and he gladly let me play my rendition of the blues. That was heaven. . . .

"The boys from downtown stayed until the last note was played and they came backstage and talked to us while we packed our instruments. They congratulated Joe on his music and for sending to New Orleans to get me. I was so happy I did not know what to do.

"I had hit the big time. I was up North with the greats. I was playing with my idol, the King, Joe Oliver. My boyhood dream had come true at last."

What If Armstrong Succumbed to Pandemic?

May 24, 2020

As we continue to confront the coronavirus pandemic, it's worth remembering that roughly a century ago an influenza pandemic similarly wreaked havoc around the world and swept through the city that invented jazz: New Orleans.

Between Sept. 8, 1918, and March 15, 1919, the Crescent City suffered 3,362 influenza-related deaths—almost 1% of New Orleans' population and twice the national rate, according to the Historic New Orleans Collection, a repository of data and primary-source documentation. Another analysis, from the University of Michigan, tabulates that "between October 1918 and April 1919, the city experienced a staggering 54,089 cases of influenza. Of these, 3,489 died—a case fatality rate of 6.5 percent and an excess death rate of 734 per 100,000. Only Pittsburgh (806) and Philadelphia (748)—the two cities with the worst epidemics in the nation—had higher death rates."

From a cultural standpoint, it's a little terrifying to realize that one New Orleanian who would go on to do more than anyone to personify and popularize the fledgling art form—Louis Armstrong—was in the cross hairs of this disease. Which could lead any jazz aficionado to wonder: What would have happened to the course of music history if a teenage Louis Armstrong, who remains the face of jazz, had succumbed?

"With everybody suffering from the flu, I had to work and play the doctor to everyone in my family, as well as all my friends in the neighborhood," Armstrong wrote in "Satchmo: My Life in New Orleans." "If I do say so, I did a good job curing them."

So Armstrong, who was 17 at the time and years away from the jazz breakthroughs he would achieve in Chicago in the mid-1920s, wasn't just present during the pandemic—he was exposed to its victims at close range night and day. Had he been afflicted, the nascent art form he would help define might never have conquered the world as quickly as it did—or in the way that it did—thanks largely to him.

True, "New Orleans music"—as locals described their indigenous sound before the term "jazz" came into vogue in the 20th century's second decade—had other progenitors before Armstrong. Cornetist Buddy Bolden, who was born in New Orleans in 1877 and died in obscurity in 1931 (after more than two decades in a mental institution), conquered the city with what was described as an unrivaled and thrilling clarion sound. When Bolden played what's believed to have been blues-inflected, ragtime-influenced solos at the Mississippi River's banks, it was said that people could hear him clear to the other side. Because no recording of Bolden's work is known to have survived, his contributions are preserved only in words, not sound.

Jelly Roll Morton, Armstrong's senior by many years, was the first to prove that the elusive, improvised, seemingly chaotic music played in New Orleans' bordellos, saloons and street parades could be articulated on paper. His "Jelly Roll Blues," copyrighted in 1915, forever stamped jazz as a music that was suited to Western musical notation for other musicians to read, perform and improvise on. Morton's recordings with His Red Hot Peppers, cut in Chicago, New York and New Jersey from 1926 to 1930, brought jazz's harmonic and structural sophistication to unprecedented heights. And his Library of Congress interviews with Alan Lomax, recorded in 1938, not only provided detailed accounts of the birth of jazz (complete with musical examples that Morton sang and played on the piano) but gave the world an intellectual framework with which to recognize jazz as a bona fide art form—one equal in complexity and sophistication to its European classical counterpart.

But it was Armstrong who in 1920s Chicago accomplished the triple feat of becoming the biggest jazz star of the era; the most brilliant trumpeter the art form had yet known; and the architect of solos so profound and ingeniously constructed that they're studied, analyzed and absorbed to this day. The recordings Armstrong made with his Hot Five and Hot Seven ensembles in the Roaring '20s became sensations because of his brilliant tone, comprehensive virtuosity and stratospheric high notes, helping establish Chicago as a jazz nexus and launching Armstrong into unending fame.

Armstrong may never have topped his musical achievements of the 1920s, but he went on to attain a degree of pop-culture stardom no jazz instrumentalist-vocalist ever has matched. Appearances in Hollywood films such as "High Society" (1956), "Paris Blues" (1961), "Hello, Dolly!" (1969) and in uncounted TV shows made him that rarest brand of celebrity, one universally known by a single name: Satchmo (short for "satchel mouth"). That he continued to perform around the world until his death in 1971, at age 69, brought jazz to millions of listeners and made him the embodiment of the music forevermore.

So what would have happened if Armstrong had not survived the pandemic of 1918–19? Which musician could have offered mass audiences a comparable combination of charismatic personality, unparalleled technique, singular sound and well-documented improvisational genius? Which trumpeter could have recorded solos of equal innovation, thereby pointing the way for acolytes such as Roy Eldridge, Dizzy Gillespie, Miles Davis and generations more? Who else could have given jazz such an indelible brand, yet one that was both welcoming to the uninitiated and satisfying to the cognoscenti?

The answer, of course, is no one. Without Armstrong, jazz would have lost the figure who set an exalted standard for all who came after and propelled an entire art form into global recognition.

Which makes you wonder: Amid all the death now surrounding us, how many visionaries and geniuses are we losing, and how will that loss echo for all time?

CHAPTER 3

Art Hodes

Born to the Purple

March 3, 1991

He was there when jazz was the hot new sound in Chicago.

He knew Louis, Bix, the King (Oliver) and just about everyone else who mattered at the dawn of the Jazz Age, 70-odd years ago.

Today, at 85, piano legend Art Hodes stands as one of the last survivors of Roaring '20s jazz in Chicago. Listen to him play—his sound lean, his tone deep, his style steeped in the blues—and you will hear a straight-ahead, unabashedly vintage kind of pianism that has all but vanished.

Younger pianists may play faster, louder and more ostentatiously, but no one evokes the origins of jazz piano as vividly as Hodes.

"I was lucky—I grew up among the royalty of jazz," says Hodes today in his south suburban townhouse, its tiny living room overwhelmed by a huge, ebony grand, its walls lined with yellowed photos of Hodes at the keyboard.

"There I was, a kid, a teenager, hanging out in Chicago with Louis Armstrong, talking to [bandleader] King Oliver, jamming with [cornetist] Bix Beiderbecke. It was almost like being born to the purple."

When Hodes steps to the piano Saturday night at the Green Mill Jazz Club on North Broadway, he will bring with him the sounds and styles of that rambunctious era. Though he insists he has changed with the times—"After you've heard people like Duke Ellington and Horace Silver, you're never the same," says Hodes—the essence of his style was cast well before he reached 20.

On the surface, it's a simple style: basic block chords; tremolo octaves and trumpeted melodies in the right hand; a bouncing, stride-tinged left hand.

The art is in the very economy of the notes Hodes chooses to play, and in the depth of his expression. Like a great blues vocalist who knows how to stretch a phrase past the breaking point or a brilliant trumpeter who can make a tune cry out even at a whisper, Hodes makes his instrument sing.

It's a style profoundly influenced by the popular music Hodes heard as a kid newly arrived in Chicago. His family fled Nikoliev, Russia, when he was an infant and landed in New York, eventually moving to Chicago's West Roosevelt Road. It wasn't long before Hodes was smitten by the rowdy American dance music of the day.

"I don't remember how I got it, but I had this crystal radio set that I kept by my bed when I went to sleep at night, and I couldn't believe the sounds that came out of it," recalls Hodes.

"I couldn't believe Bix and Louis and Bessie [Smith]—it shook me to hear what they were doing. I heard [pianist] Earl Hines, and I wanted to take my hands and dump them, because I couldn't believe anybody could do what he was doing.

"By the time I got to high school, I started ditching classes so I could sneak into theaters like the State and Lake, where I could get real close to this incredible music."

Picking up the essentials of piano playing at Jane Addams' Hull House—where Hodes first jammed with another gifted child of poor immigrants, Benny Goodman—Hodes soon immersed himself in the jazz life. Though still a teenager, he was befriended by Louis Armstrong, then a rising young star who had come to Chicago from New Orleans under the guidance of King Oliver.

"I hung out with Louis every day for years on the South Side," says Hodes, "and he opened all the doors for me. When he found out how I felt about the blues, he started showing me where to go to hear the real blues.

"He taught me a lot—like his incredible joy in playing, and his humor, and, I hope, his humility, because he carried himself very easily. He didn't act like he was a king or anything. His attitude was: 'Hey, you're one of the guys, come on in and partake.'"

After Armstrong, the musician who influenced Hodes the most had to be Beiderbecke, the groundbreaking cornetist whose instrument produced melting lyric phrases.

"He sounded quite different in person than he does on records," says Hodes. "On records, he sounds really loud and strong, but in person his playing was very gentle and lyrical and soft.

"But what impressed me most about Bix was when he sat down to play the piano. The thoughts coming out of that man's head were amazing. His sound was symphonic in a way, his phrases were so deeply musical, and his harmonies were really modern."

Beiderbecke and Hodes were among the white exceptions in a world of Black jazz and blues music. Did skin color ever get in the way during those times?

"That was the least troublesome part of being a jazz musician," says Hodes. "I could walk into the Michigan Theater at 55th Street, where Bessie Smith would be singing, and I would be the only white guy in the place, and nobody would bother me.

"Once I and the gal I was running around with went to some Black backroom, and the music was so fascinating that we just spontaneously got up to dance. And in those days, they danced on a dime and gave you a nickel change—I mean, it was very close, the dance floor was puny. So you didn't really dance or move around; you just sort of felt the rhythm.

"But nobody bothered us. It was obvious we were there just to hear the music.

"You could go hear a fantastic group like the King Oliver Band, and you were hearing real, genuine New Orleans–style jazz. You didn't hear a fellow play a chorus and cut out—it was all brilliant ensemble playing. Even in the solos, the ensemble was constantly backing up the soloist.

"Believe me, the whole thing was an experience you couldn't buy today, you couldn't relive. You had to be there the one time it came around."

By the late '30s, Hodes—now a professional, jobbing musician—left Chicago for New York. The work here, he felt, had dried up, and the burgeoning club scene in New York was thriving.

Though he made a strong foothold in Manhattan, by the early- to mid-'40s the music was changing. Beboppers such as Charlie Parker, Dizzy Gillespie and Bud Powell were rewriting the rules of rhythm, harmony and melody, and traditionalists such as Hodes were no longer welcome.

"At first, guys like me got along with the beboppers very good," says Hodes, "but then the writers and critics ruined it.

"At first, we musicians jammed together, lived together, drank together, ate together—we all were friends. But then the critics started rapping us. These writers decided that our music should go out with high-button shoes, and that included Louis Armstrong, too, and it caused a big rift.

"That was their right and their privilege, but at the time it was very painful. It hurt me, but I'm a survivor. A lot of other guys had to get out of the business."

By 1950, Hodes was back in Chicago, taking one-nighters where he could find them. And though he never was completely out of work, it wasn't until the late '60s and '70s that he began to take on the status of a legend. With the passage of time, listeners began to realize there was a musical treasure in their midst.

These days, Hodes (who remarried a few years ago, after the death of his wife) remains busy, even for "an old firehorse," as he calls himself. After his Green Mill date, he heads off for a European tour, returning to sweet home Chicago by spring.

And though he never enjoyed the immense fame of his old friend Benny Goodman ("who was good, but not as great as Pee Wee Russell," says Hodes), he's not complaining.

"Look—it's only the music that means something, and that takes the place of all the money and the prestige and the fact that you never made Johnny Carson's show," says the great pianist.

"Not all of us are going to be Sinatras. It's not written that way.

"It's like the sign that used to be at the Hull House, which I read every day as a kid: 'Act well your part, there all honor lies.'

"It may be a corny philosophy, but it works for me."

The Blues, Brother

Oct. 25, 1992

For a kid with a good set of ears and a taste for swing, Chicago in the '20s must have been heaven.

Louis Armstrong, Bix Beiderbecke, King Oliver—virtually everyone defining the music that was beginning to be called jazz was playing the dance halls, barbecue houses and gin joints around town.

Today, that freewheeling era exists mostly in history books and on vintage recordings, but one of the last surviving musicians of that period still recalls it in remarkable detail. In conversation and in his new autobiography, "Hot Man: The Life of Art Hodes" (with Chadwick Hansen, University of Illinois Press, $22.50), Hodes stands as one of our last direct links to music of that day.

"Coming to Chicago [in 1910] was a lucky break for me," says Hodes, whose family had emigrated from Nikolaev, Russia, landing first in New York, then heading to Chicago a few years later.

"See, the neighborhood we lived in was right between the Blacks and the whites. So I could go to a theater and hear the greatest jazz and blues musicians alive. If they didn't live here, they passed through.

"It was an era. New Orleans players were coming up the river, everyone was here. Bix, Louis, [drummer] Baby Dodds, [reed player] Jimmie Noone, Chicago was the place. It probably happened because of economics.

"The musicians found out that there was a good chance to make a livelihood out of your music, and it was true.

"Nobody made a fortune, but there were plenty of laughs."

For Hodes, who guesses he turns 88 on Nov. 14 (records did not survive his family's journey to the U.S.), the opportunities in Chicago were nearly overwhelming. At Jane Addams' Hull House, he could take music lessons cheap and jam alongside another aspiring jazz man, Benny Goodman.

And on stages and in clubs across the city, the legends of the day were within earshot.

"I remember the day I was fortunate enough to hear singer Bessie Smith," says Hodes, who began cutting classes at Crane High School to hear performances.

"There were 2,000 or so listeners in the theater. I had ducked inside because it was raining cats and dogs—I didn't even know who was playing.

"I doubt if there were any other whites in the audience.

"So Bessie takes the stage, without a microphone, and she's holding everyone in the palm of her hand. You didn't hear a whisper.

"She had such a powerful voice, and she had a story to tell. In other words, the blues were the story of her life.

"She'd sing: 'My man done left me . . . the 219 will bring him back some day.' And everybody knew then that the 219 was the train that came out of New Orleans.

"Now there were many other singers at the time, and they could sing the words. They could go over the song, but with much less meaning.

"We had imitators in those days, too. But when Bessie came to town, the lesser lights were in the audience."

If Smith inspired Hodes with the blues-drenched spirit of her singing, Louis Armstrong opened up to him the world of South Side jazz and blues. In the '20s, Armstrong was Chicago's reigning musical star, his sensational high notes, irrepressible swing and ebullient personality helping jazz take root here.

"If there were no Armstrong, there would be no Hodes," says the great pianist.

"When he found out that I loved the blues, he took me to the barbecue place at 47th and State. Don't look there now—it's a high rise.

"And he let me find my way into this world.

"Many nights I spent listening to Louis. He talked about [bandleader] King Oliver sending for him [from New Orleans]. He said King wrote him a letter saying: 'You can always come sleep in my bed with your stinking feet.'

"So Oliver took Louis into his band, and in no time he became the man to listen to.

"I remember Louis once told me, 'I've got some of Bix's records.' But Louis and Bix were like night and day.

"When they recorded Louis, they had to put the mike five feet away from him so he wouldn't blow it out of business. With Bix, they put the mike right in front of him, because Bix had a much softer, quieter sound.

"The important thing was that each of them sounded like nobody else."

There were other influences, as well. Earl Hines played piano with such virtuosity, says Hodes, "that he made me want to throw my hands in the river. But I learned from that kind of playing, too, how hard you had to work."

And a long-forgotten pianist who went only by the name Jackson proved to Hodes that "there was more to this music than just playing a lot of notes. Jackson was not a good pianist, but he knew enough to play. He had very few clothes, he looked skimpy, but the depth of feeling in the music really knocked you out.

"In fact, once I remember I went to the barbecue place, and he was really dressed up, but he wasn't playing blues.

"So I asked him: 'What happened?'

"And he said: 'See the new clothes I got and the girl I'm with? I ain't got the blues.'

"And that's when it struck me that the blues had a deeper meaning than just 12 bars of notes.

"The blues was a music that you felt. I can only describe it by saying it was a happening, a distress call. It's the depth of the sounds that makes the blues."

Even to Hodes, though, it must have seemed remarkable that Chicago's Black culture was giving entre to a white teenager. For some reason, the world of Black clubs and nightlife welcomed him.

"It never was a problem, and I wasn't the only one, though I was one of a rare few," says Hodes. "There were [trumpeter] Wingy Manone and [cornetist] Muggsy Spanier, too."

By the late '30s, Hodes was married and moving to New York. The big bands were pushing out the smaller ensembles that were his specialty, and he hoped to find more work on the East Coast.

Times were tough there, too, though. Be-bop was coming in during the '40s, making Hodes' brand of blues-tinged swing seem out of date to some New Yorkers.

By 1950 Hodes was back home in Chicago, trying to make a living playing music that evoked the grand old days of the '20s. Since then, his reputation as a living example of a critical chapter in jazz history has grown steadily with each season, each decade.

And though he has not played publicly in recent months, due to a variety of medical problems, his spirit seems undiminished. He teaches from the ebony grand piano that dominates his living room, he speaks of his new autobiography with fire, noting "the fullness" of the life it describes.

Of America's reawakened interest in jazz today, he says, "There's no question we're having a renaissance, but the flowering of Chicago jazz in the '20s is gone. The only thing that was even close to it was New York's 52d Street in the '50s.

"Chicago in the '20s was an age that was here and gone. I'm lucky I heard it."

CHAPTER 4

Anita O'Day

A Bright New O'Day

April 22, 1990

If you don't believe in miracles, consider the extraordinary case of Anita O'Day, the brilliant, 70-year-old jazz singer who has brushed up against death more times than she probably can remember.

A survivor of two backroom abortions, one rape, a botched tonsillectomy that nearly mangled her throat, two volatile marriages, 15 years of heroin addiction and roughly a year in prison, O'Day literally was deemed dead of an overdose in 1966.

By coincidence, an intern at UCLA Hospital in California happened to have an electric-shock device (then still experimental) and jolted life back into O'Day's body.

The miracle, however, is not simply that O'Day is still breathing, but that she apparently is singing exquisitely, while enjoying an utterly unexpected comeback. Last year, just as O'Day was turning 70, the singer who gave Gene Krupa and Stan Kenton (among others) their first big hits received her first Grammy nomination (for "In a Mellow Tone" on DRG).

And in recent months, O'Day—who lives alone with her dog, Emily, in a three-room trailer parked deep in the Hollywood hills—has hardly been able to keep up with requests for her services. She'll return to her hometown, Chicago, May 4–6 for a rare, local engagement at the Jazz Showcase in the Blackstone Hotel.

By all accounts, she's singing as adroitly as in her youth, if not more so.

"I'm fine, I really feel terrific these days," says O'Day, who began weaning herself off drugs after the overdose and sounds strong of voice and spirit.

"The important question is—how's the weather in Chicago?

"The first thing I'm going to do when I get to town is nostalgia myself," adds O'Day, who phrases a sentence as uniquely as she does a melody.

"I'm going to take a ride in a car with somebody and go on up to Uptown, where I grew up. I hear there's a college there now [Truman College]. Not bad, considering it used to be a slum."

It was on the mean streets of Uptown that O'Day set the tone for the triumphs and tragedies ahead.

Or perhaps she was simply the victim of her terrible childhood.

"When Dad came home, [Mom] had the door bolted from the inside," writes O'Day in her searing autobiography, "High Times, Hard Times" (written with George Eells and recently issued in paperback by Limelight Editions, $12.95).

"They had terrible fights, screaming at one another through the door, blaming each other, while I cowered in one of the back rooms, praying, as my grandmother had taught me to do, that they wouldn't hurt one another. And my prayers were answered, because Dad would always eventually disappear."

Even so, "Dad might be gone, but that didn't mean I didn't hear a lot about him," writes O'Day. "Every time I did something that rubbed Mom wrong, she struck up the same refrain: 'You're just like your father! You're no good! You'll grow up just like him.' Have that dinned into you long enough, and it's bound to happen."

Indeed, by the time O'Day was a teen, she had cut out of school to toil briefly in a burlesque show. From there she graduated to the grueling Walkathons, in which Depression-era kids would dance for days, weeks and months on end, the last one to collapse winning the cash prize.

"At the time, it seemed very tough," says O'Day, as if to imply it was nothing compared to the horrors she was later to experience. In one

Walkathon, she lasted 97 days, logging 4,656 miles in 2,328 hours—and finished second.

But O'Day had been blessed with an ear for music and a voice that could sweetly reproduce it. She made extra change singing and dancing at the Walkathons (where she rubbed elbows with fellow Walkathoners Red Skelton and Frankie Laine) and spent most every spare moment hanging around Chicago's great old jazz clubs.

"I used to go to the South Side to all these big jazz joints and hear my dues," says O'Day (meaning that's where she learned to pay her dues).

"And then I'd come back on the North Side and sing the dues I learned on the South Side, and everybody thought I was great."

The feat was all the more remarkable because O'Day had suffered a tonsillectomy in which the doctor cut off her uvula (the bell-shaped gland in the back of the mouth that helps a singer control tone and color). To this day, she can only create a vibrato by gently shaking her head.

Nevertheless, O'Day developed a light, silvery sound that can skip along a phrase like a pebble across water. And her ability to play with a rhythm without distorting it epitomizes pure swing style.

At first, O'Day didn't make much money, which is why she changed her birth name, Anita Belle Colton, to O'Day—it's Pig Latin for "dough," which she wanted to make. Still, she was learning the art with pioneer jazz players such as trumpeter Jimmy McPartland, pianist Jay McShann and fiddler Stuff Smith.

And then there was a wild-man drummer named Gene Krupa.

"I'll never forget the sight and sound of him as sweat popped from his forehead, ran down his face, dripped off the tip of his nose, moistened his flying hair and came through his shirt as his arms flailed in 20 directions to produce different musical sounds," writes O'Day, who joined Krupa's band in 1941 as "canary," the less-than-liberated nickname for female band singers of the day.

The Krupa years made O'Day a star, particularly when she and the band released "Let Me Off Uptown," Krupa's first big hit (in 1941); it remains esteemed for the way it partners O'Day's light soprano with the late Roy Eldridge's buoyant trumpet solos.

As a mere canary, however, O'Day "received my customary $7.50 per side, and Gene earned enough to buy a house in Yonkers," she writes.

Even when O'Day was in the money, ranking as one of jazz's biggest song stylists in the late '40s and '50s, she frittered most of her fortune away on drugs, booze and husbands. Today, she estimates she shot $400,000 through her veins.

Even the prison time (for a drug conviction) wasn't entirely grim, compared to the drug life.

"Those were the only times anyone saw to it I ate properly," writes O'Day. "I also spent a lot of time exercising and sleeping. I looked on serving my sentence as a kind of vacation. When I'd slept myself out and didn't feel like working out, I'd lie there thinking about songs.

"I wasn't worried about my career. A couple prisoners who were fans told me I'd probably earn more bread when I got out just because I'd been in. So I emerged thinking it was no big deal. Rehabilitated? Hardly. Rested? Definitely."

Yet, even considering O'Day's stormy childhood, why would one of the country's successful jazz singers self-destruct in drugged excess?

O'Day—whose high-life habits long ago earned her the nickname "The Jezebel of Jazz"—will only say that, "whenever I get too happy, I'm eating too well, I got a nice place to stay, I get a little bored.

"But that's the past. I hardly even get out anymore, up where I live. I go to bed at four in the afternoon; of course, I get up at three in the morning. But for me, it's a chance to see how the other part lives."

If there is a spot of sunshine in O'Day's ordeals, it's that they probably have deepened her art. In her book, she writes of Billie Holiday's heroin addiction: "Only somebody who'd gone through the things she did and had survived could sing from the soul the way she did."

Maybe the same is true for O'Day.

"I guess that's sort of the case," says O'Day. "I hit the bottom of the barrel, man, out there in the streets, waiting for the connection.

"When you've survived all that, and the music still comes out—that's heaven. That's what makes you do what you do."

Yet if she had it to do all over again today, she probably wouldn't.

"I don't think I'd even stay in singing today," says O'Day, who finds that most of her fans these days are "moms and pops."

"The big bands [of Woody Herman, Benny Goodman and the like] gave me my downbeat, but that just ain't around now.

"There's no way to learn to be a jazz singer these days," says O'Day, who—along with Ella Fitzgerald, Lena Horne, Rosemary Clooney and a handful of others—represents a vanishing species.

"For now, the trick is to just keep yourself on top of the wave—know what I mean?"

O'Day Is Back in Town

May 6, 1990

One of the most seductive voices in jazz belongs to a 70-year-old woman who rarely sings much above a whisper and, even with microphone in hand, barely projects beyond a purr.

Yet Anita O'Day's voice ranks among the most enticing of instruments, for whatever she lacks in decibels and vocal luster she generously repays with the sheer cunning of her improvisations.

O'Day, who returned home to Chicago Friday evening for a three-day stint at the Jazz Showcase at the Blackstone Hotel, doesn't merely embellish a song; she rewrites it, turning melodies upside down, stretching phrases long past the breaking point, tossing in nonsense words and scat sound-effects that confound expectations. It's a safe bet that O'Day is incapable of singing a song the same way twice, nor would she care to.

For O'Day—from her early years as a local lounge singer right through the glory days as "canary" with bands of Gene Krupa, Stan Kenton and others—epitomizes the jazz singer as creative artist.

Other vocalists may have been blessed with a bigger sound (Carmen McRae), a more magnificent range (the late Sarah Vaughan) or a closer bond to the songwriter's intent (Ella Fitzgerald).

But O'Day epitomizes swing style of a fiercely personal sort.

Her voice is genuinely another instrument in the band, bending pitches and toying with rhythms as only the best instrumental virtuosos can.

The marvel is that after all of O'Day's personal tragedies—including drug addiction, prison terms, alcoholism and other forms of woe—her voice sounds as light, buoyant and, in its way, sweet as her oldest recordings suggest.

She approached every phrase of Cole Porter's "You'd Be So Nice to Come Home To" with a different spin, constantly changing colors, sounds, attacks and intonations. This performance crammed a lifetime of experimentation into a five-minute tour de force.

There's a calmer, more reflective side to O'Day's art, as well, which was evident from the long, sinuous phrases she spun in Lewis and Young's "(On the) Street of Dreams." Anyone can hit a blue note, but the way O'Day leans on one suggests ineffable heartache.

O'Day's opening set offered the obligatory nostalgic section, including her first big hit, "Let Me Off Uptown," which made her a star with Krupa's band. Even aside from historical reference points, however, this was song-styling at its most adept.

Though O'Day endured a ragged backup band and a somnambulent opening act (with Johnny Frigo's saccharine "jazz" violin), such distractions ultimately seemed unimportant.

The fact that O'Day is back in town, through Sunday, is what counts.

CHAPTER 5

Dorothy Donegan

Dorothy in Dreamland

Sept. 19, 1993

Seven months shy of her 72nd birthday, Dorothy Donegan has made the big time.

Not that Donegan hasn't long been admired by jazz aficionados for her startling keyboard virtuosity and her frenetic sit-down comedy. Imagine an aesthetic mixture of Chico Marx, Art Tatum and Vladimir Horowitz, and you have the basics of Donegan's rather uninhibited act.

It's just that the world at large has been slow to recognize her decidedly idiosyncratic gifts. So long as Ella Fitzgerald, Sarah Vaughan and Carmen McRae had the spotlight, Donegan was just another working musician, albeit an inspired one.

Lately, however, all that has changed, and not simply because Donegan's better-known peers have left the scene.

Just last Sunday, for instance, a national television audience saw Donegan all but setting the piano afire during "In Performance at the White House," an all-star jazz concert that had been taped earlier this summer.

And less than two years ago, the National Endowment for the Arts gave Donegan a $20,000 award, acknowledging the Chicago-born artist's lifelong contribution to jazz.

Come Tuesday, Donegan, who now lives on the West Coast, will come home for a two-week engagement at the Jazz Showcase, which rarely features even celebrated performers for more than a five-day stint.

Clearly, Donegan's time has come.

"Let me tell you—when I found out about that NEA grant, I almost turned white," says Donegan, an African-American artist and born raconteur who never turns her back on a punch line.

"This woman called me up and said, 'I've been looking for you for 10 weeks.'

"So I said, 'Do I owe you money?'

"And she said, 'No, the NEA wants to give you $20,000.'

"I didn't believe her at first. But then I started to cry, like I was in church or something. I'm actually a big softie."

Even more surprising to Donegan, however, was the invitation to play the White House, a first for her.

"When I got invited to that," says Donegan, "I thought to myself, 'Well, from the outhouse to the White House—not too bad.'

"I loved going to the White House. Mr. Clinton is charming, his wife is charming, and they can get you to work for free.

"Actually, they pay you a few dollars, they put you up, they send for you, and they give you some bean salad and chicken.

"Well, when I walked in there, the other pianists, like Herbie Hancock, their lips dropped when they saw me. I think they figured they needed me like Custer needed more Indians."

Donegan does not exaggerate—or not too much, anyway—for she is the kind of pianist who genuinely can put fear into the hearts of peers. With a technique that won't quit, extensive classical training and a stage manner that would make Al Jolson seem introspective, Donegan yields to no one.

And yet that makes her years of relative obscurity seem all the more puzzling. How could anyone with a talent and a personality as large as Donegan's possibly have been stopped?

"Because that's the way it's set up," says Donegan. "The whole attitude in show business was divide and conquer. The idea was there was only room for one Black at a time. So for a time it would be Hazel Scott, or it would be Mary Lou Williams [both noted jazz pianists].

"Now it's a little better, because the other two died. We were all jealous of each other, although I think they were more jealous of me.

"But music is a sexist industry where the men don't like to acknowledge the women, especially if they're as good or better than the men.

"So that made the women fight it out among themselves. A couple pianists once complained about me to the [musicians'] union. They actually complained that I wasn't only playing the piano but I was wiggling my hips, and that was unfair, so they said a special entertainers' tax ought to be put on me.

"Well, I told them—I deal from the hips, not the lips. It's called showbiz."

Show business, above all else, is what separates Donegan from her colleagues.

In a typical Donegan set—if there is such a thing—she will draw torrents of sound from the piano, hit its frame with the palm of her hand to emphasize a downbeat, plunge into a few bars of the Grieg Concerto, swing out into a boogie-woogie passage, leap up from the bench in mid-phrase to tell a joke or to comment on the loud tie somebody in the front row is wearing.

It's a funny and vastly entertaining act, but it's also a bit removed from her original goal—to be a concert pianist.

"I started taking lessons on the South Side of Chicago when I was 8, and it was classical all the way," she recalls.

"But there were [racial and gender] barriers back then, you know? I mean, I wasn't going to make any money at classical, and you have to eat.

"Plus there was a lot of competition. Back then you had Vladimir Horowitz and Arthur Rubinstein, so there was no hope."

Thus, at 15, Donegan turned to jazz, studying from two proteges of her hero, pianist Art Tatum.

"Tatum was the alpha and the omega and the genesis and the living end, as far as I was concerned," says Donegan, referring to a jazz keyboardist whose work has not been matched to this date. "He was the Horowitz of jazz.

"So I figured if I couldn't study with Tatum himself, I'd study with two guys who had gone around with him and drunk with him and could play pretty much like him. Rozelle Gayle and Raymond Walters had lots of technique and lots of feeling."

They weren't Donegan's only teachers. As a student at DuSable High School, already a legendary training ground for young jazz artists, Donegan studied with Capt. Walter Dyett, teacher of Nat Cole, Gene Ammons, Von Freeman and dozens more.

"Capt. Dyett used to cuss us out," recalls Donegan.

"He was a great teacher, and he would give the young musicians scholarships, and he would get people out of trouble and out of jail. He was there for us.

"Of course, if you made a mistake, he would begin screaming. That man could hear anything. He could hear a mosquito urinating on a bale of cotton."

Apparently, Dyett and Donegan's other teachers had done well by her, for by age 19, she was making her Orchestra Hall debut in a "Jazz Meets the Classics" program. Even then, she was daring to be different, mixing two idioms that remain apart even to this day.

"Yeah, I did the first half classical, the second half I dragged through the swamp," quips Donegan. "The audience ate it up."

From that Orchestra Hall gig, though, it was downhill all the way, with Donegan working tough, low-paying jobs in joints such as the Garrick Stage Bar and the Latin Quarter, both in the Loop. It wasn't glamorous, but it proved educational.

"It was at the Latin Quarter that I learned larceny—in other words, my show business," says Donegan. "I mean, in a nightclub, it's not just playing Bach all night. You've got to learn tricks, like the gestures, how to walk out onstage, how to play to the audiences, how to keep the derrieres in the seats, how to make the audience a part of you.

"I had to work with everyone, comedians, singers, jugglers. I worked with the Duncan Sisters, who played in blackface. They'd put burnt cork on their white faces. And I'd say to them, 'What are you going to do if that stuff don't come off? Then you've got problems.'

"But they taught me, too. Everyone did. I'd play in clubs where they used to tell me, 'Get hot or go home.'"

Donegan chose to get hot. By the time she was 21, she was hot enough to impress Tatum himself.

"Rozelle Gayle brought him over to the house, I played for Art and he decided to take me under his wing. I was the only woman he ever taught.

"It was incredible to hang out with him. He played so fast it was like a blur. So I would just gorilla the things he did. You hear it, you catch it, you go with it.

"He took me around to all the places in Chicago, and then he would take me to all the sewers in New York. I call them sewers because they were dumps—you know. . . . You'd have a whole cross-section of an audience—hustlers, pimps and prostitutes."

Donegan has been toiling ever since, her life on the road yielding three marriages ("too many," she says), three divorces, two children and a loyal, growing audience.

"It's been hard for about 60 years now," says Donegan. "When they gave me the NEA award, the lady said it was long overdue.

"Maybe she's right. Maybe I should have gotten it when I was young and pretty.

"But people like to wait till you get real old, with one foot on the grave and the other on a banana peel.

"People used to say 'Dorothy who?' Now they say, 'Oh, we saw you at the White House.'

"Praise the Lord."

Piano Madness

Sept. 22, 1993

It's a good bet that Dorothy Donegan covered more tunes Tuesday night at the Jazz Showcase than most pianists do in a week's engagement. Considering that Donegan will be at the Showcase for a fortnight, she just might run through most of the standard repertoire before it's all over.

That's because Donegan can't get very far into a number without digressing—musically—into at least two others. Somehow, the perpetually evolving themes, musical allusions, sight gags, one-liners and loopy facial expressions make perfect sense when Donegan is at the keyboard. In a musical world cluttered with imitators, rip-off artists and clones, Donegan stands out as an original.

Of course, those who have been following her since her early days in Chicago, in the '40s, know all that. Yet even the many loyal fans who turned out for her opening night set seemed startled anew by the sheer rush of her show, the energy of her presentation, the seemingly anarchic nature of her musical comedy.

Who else, after all, would spice up George Shearing's "Lullaby of Birdland" with snippets of Bach's Prelude and Fugue in C Minor (except, perhaps, Shearing himself)? Who else would juxtapose "Lover" with "Night and Day," then surreptitiously segue into "Green Dolphin Street," with "Can't Help Lovin' Dat Man" as a counterpoint? And who else would dare fracture the sublime lyrics of "As Time Goes By," rendering nearly every line a naughty double-entendre?

Not since the heyday of Chico Marx have so many musical motifs collided to such gloriously comic effect.

Yet at the center of this seeming mayhem is an artist who can make a piano do precisely what she wants it to. Sweeping arpeggios, crystalline scales, huge block chords, blues riffs in the right hand, rumbling bass notes in the left—Donegan has spent a lifetime building this arsenal, and she dispatches it at will.

Considering the breadth of Donegan's talent, she ultimately never really received her due, if only because, in the old days, a woman who was Black and played jazz had three strikes against her. Perhaps it's not much different today. Yet for those who have savored Donegan's deliciously unconventional act, that always has been beside the point. For anyone savvy enough to have sought her out, the musical pleasures have been ample, the comedy memorable.

Now in her 70s, Donegan still plays with plenty of fire and fury. Backed during this engagement by drummer Joel Spencer and bassist Larry Gray, she remains a galvanic force.

CHAPTER 6

Ahmad Jamal

Still Inventing

Oct. 8, 2014

Without the piano innovations of Ahmad Jamal, would the breakthroughs of contemporary keyboard lions such as Jason Moran, Vijay Iyer, Matthew Shipp and others be possible?

True, none of those artists sounds quite like Jamal, but no one really does—his music is too mercurial and startlingly unpredictable for anyone to imitate persuasively. But the freedom that Jamal declared at the piano more than half a century ago surely opened up new possibilities in sound for any jazz pianist who touched the instrument after hearing him.

No longer would pianists feel tethered to comfortable backbeats, conventional song structures, ornate bebop syntax and the like. Instead, Jamal offered up jagged shards of melody, striking chord clusters, abrupt silences, open spaces and an emphasis on gesture, color and mood. A palpable tension has coursed through Jamal's recordings and live performances, making his music as gripping as it's been innovative.

Remarkably, Jamal at 84 still sounds fresh and perpetually modern at the piano, as his recent performances and recordings have affirmed. So where does his knack for perpetual surprise come from?

"Music and life in my opinion are about discovery," says Jamal, who

Fig. 3 Ahmad Jamal: The Pittsburgh native found his voice and his audience in Chicago. Jamal's pianism introduced radical new ideas on the use of rhythm, meter, space, texture and gesture. These concepts remain influential to this day.

will open Symphony Center's jazz season Friday night in Orchestra Hall leading his quartet. "You have to discover things. I don't care if you're a journalist or a musician or a doctor or an Indian chief.

"You don't create anything. You can't create a fly or a raindrop. How do you do that? You try and be in tune with life and all the wonderful things it has to offer, so you can discover. I try to discover things every day, musically."

Maybe that's it. Maybe when Jamal is at the piano, he's taking us on a freewheeling exploration into sound, the pianist darting restlessly from one idea to the next, from one discovery to another. One moment, he tosses off a technically brilliant passage worthy of Franz Liszt. The next, he produces an impressionistic series of chords evoking Claude Debussy. Then he swings hard for a few bars before stopping and proceeding to something entirely different.

It's a stylistically far-reaching brand of pianism that draws on Jamal's wide-open ears but not necessarily one that would seem to have been destined for wide popularity. Yet in 1958 Jamal released a recording that clung to the Billboard charts for more than two years, positioned him as a bona fide jazz star and forever linked him to the city where it was recorded: Chicago.

"Ahmad Jamal at the Pershing: But Not for Me" documented his ephemeral pianism and ran counter to what most everyone else was playing in the late 1950s, from classic bebop to hard-bop to cool-jazz idioms. Yet "Pershing" tracks such as "Poinciana" and "But Not for Me" became radio hits and have long since been enshrined as jazz classics, underscoring the paradoxical nature of Jamal's art: a hyper-sophisticated musical language that reached the masses. How did it happen?

"What influenced me is the fortunate thing that we don't have often: I became an artist-in-residence at a place called the Pershing," says Jamal, referring to the lounge in the long-gone Pershing Hotel on the South Side. "When you're working every night, five, six nights a week in the same ensemble, magic happens. Magical things happen. Wonderful things happen.

"So that and support by some of the finest musicians in the world," adds Jamal, referring to bassist Israel Crosby and drummer Vernel Fournier, his trio partners at the Pershing. "Certain things happen when you can stay and play every night, but that doesn't happen [anymore]. You don't have many rooms where you can sit and stay there."

Did Jamal have any sense that "Pershing" would emerge as the pop hit and jazz landmark it became?

"I wanted to record at the Pershing [because] I knew we had something," says Jamal. "I didn't know we'd get that many, but I knew I'd get one or two people who would like what we were doing. . . . I spent eight or nine days mastering, editing and programming. I spent a lot of time picking eight tracks out of 43. What I did was diametrically opposed to [radio] airplay. Nobody was playing 7:45-minute recordings. We weren't going to get any airplay, according to the rule of thumb. But what happened?"

"Poinciana," "But Not For Me" and other tracks saturated the airwaves and still turn up with regularity on terrestrial and satellite radio alike. Perhaps there's no definitive explanation for why this music seduced so many people and continues to do so, but Jamal has come to his own conclusions.

"Pershing" enticed listeners, he says, "because it was a record composed [of]—made up of a lot of interesting textures. Lot of textures. . . . The lines that Israel [Crosby] played, for example, people are still trying to emulate. . . . It was the textures, it was the things that we were doing. . . . Improvisation is an acquired skill. It's not an accident."

Jamal's mastery of that art was hard won. Born and raised in Pittsburgh, he was drawn to the piano at age 3, received classical training and was out playing on the road as a teenager. He first came to Chicago in 1948, he says, when "they still had jitneys on South Park—it's probably not even called South Park anymore." Indeed, it's King Drive.

The scene was rich.

"63rd Street was alive and well," remembers Jamal. "You could see [saxophonist] Lester Young walking up and down the street with his porkpie hat. You had the great saxophonists—Von Freeman. I worked with Von when I first went there. All of us were struggling."

Jamal believes the essence of his radical approach to the piano was in place, though not fully formed, when he came to Chicago. "Maybe in a timid fashion," he says. "Naturally, you don't have as much confidence, but that's everybody. Evolution: You crawl, you walk and you run."

Even before the success of "Pershing," Jamal had attracted attention from cognoscenti, most notably Miles Davis, who long cited the pianist as a key influence.

"I had gone to hear [Jamal] once I was out that way [in Chicago], and he knocked me out with his concept of space, his lightness of touch, his understatement and the way he phrased notes and chords and passages," Davis famously observed in "Miles Davis: The Autobiography" (with Quincy Troupe). "I loved his lyricism on piano, the way he played and the spacing he used in the ensemble voicing of his groups."

After the success of "Pershing," Jamal briefly opened his own club in Chicago, the Alhambra, an experience he looks upon today as "a nightmare. That's why I closed it."

By the early 1960s he'd moved to New York to pursue a lifelong dream of studying at the Juilliard School but found himself in too much demand as a performer to do so. Perhaps that was for the best. Jamal's music bristles with the kind of inventiveness that cannot be taught. It continues to this day, his novel ideas and ferocious spontaneity distinguishing his two most recent albums, "Blue Moon" (2012) and "Saturday Morning" (2013).

What has Chicago meant to him?

"That's where my career was launched," he says. "Chicago is my second home, absolutely, always will be. And not only that—it was a melting pot for a tremendous amount of talent.

"If you can make it in Chicago, you can make it anywhere in the world—you can make it in New York," says Jamal, paraphrasing a song about that other great American metropolis. "We didn't stand back for New York. We joined New York, and they joined us. We weren't afraid of New York at all."

Or anything else.

88 Years Young

Oct. 13, 2018

Sixty years ago, a young pianist in Chicago startled the jazz world—and listeners far beyond—with a recording that remains a classic: "Ahmad Jamal at the Pershing: But Not for Me."

On Friday evening, an 88-year-old Jamal returned to the city, reminding everyone why the album—recorded at the long-gone Pershing Hotel on the South Side—made him a star. Based on Jamal's performance in Orchestra Hall at Symphony Center, it's safe to say that if Jamal were a young man launching his career today, he'd once again galvanize a new generation of listeners.

For even now, there's simply no one who sounds quite like Jamal. Others may imitate his stop-start rhythms, unexpected silences, bursts of keyboard color and other mercurial signatures. But the utter unpredictability of Jamal's keyboard musings and the man's singular way of shaping and developing a phrase can be mimicked but not rekindled by anyone else. There's simply no telling what Jamal will do at any single moment, his restless improvisational style catching even his band members off guard, as often was the case on Friday night.

Not surprisingly, an overflow crowd came to its feet as Jamal took the stage, launching the 25th season of Symphony Center's jazz series. Though born and raised in culturally vibrant Pittsburgh, the pianist lived in Chicago from 1948 to 1960 and has been embraced by the city ever since (long after he moved to New York).

No sooner did Jamal seat himself at the keyboard than his fingers began flitting across its full range, an impressionistic swirl of sound leaving everyone—including the rest of his quartet—to guess when a theme would emerge. It eventually did with Jamal's "Autumn Rain," its insinuating primary riff punctuated by keyboard clusters, dramatic pauses, glittering runs and other bits of musical pointillism.

As its title suggests, Jamal's "My Latin" conveyed an Afro-Caribbean lilt. But the pianist, for whom subtlety apparently remains the highest ideal, steered clear of obvious dance rhythms and glib phrase-making. Instead, he produced still more stream-of-consciousness keyboard utterances, albeit with an implied Latin rhythmic undercurrent. Meanwhile, Jamal rode a seductive, syncopated backbeat from drummer Herlin Riley, bassist James Cammack (another former Chicagoan) and percussionist Manolo Badrena.

It took a while until the melodic profile of the standard "Blue Moon" rose up from Jamal's sprawling chords, right-hand octaves, delicate arpeggios and other keyboard gestures. Even when it did, the pianist compressed, expanded and otherwise reshaped the famous melody so that it became something personal.

Everyone knew that, sooner or later, Jamal would have to play "Poinciana," perhaps the most beloved song from the "Pershing" album. When he did, the audience seemed to exhale all at once, a sweet sign of recognition that linked everyone in the house to a storied moment in Chicago jazz history. But Jamal did not choose to retread his past, putting down notes at unlikely junctures and leaving ample room for his colleagues to step in. If there's a space-time continuum, as the science-fiction writers insist, Jamal clearly knows how to bend it to his will.

Through it all, one was struck again by the silvery quality of Jamal's keyboard touch. Though jazz pianists tend toward a percussive keyboard attack, Jamal always has produced a glowing tone of a sort we associate with their most sensitive classical counterparts. Combine this with the sustained elegance of Jamal's pianism, and David Raksin's "Laura" became a beguiling jazz nocturne. The hushed intimacy Jamal expressed in the Gershwins' "But Not for Me" left a similar impression, and the coda that Jamal and colleagues produced was a testament to the spontaneity of his music-making and the responsiveness of theirs.

Toward the end of the evening, Jamal told the audience that "This is the Life," from the Broadway musical "Golden Boy," stands as one of his favorites, and it became a canvas for the pianist's free-flowing experiments in sound. Moments of turbulence alternated with passages of tenderness; the piano itself became a kind of orchestra, Jamal drawing from its 88 keys an astonishing range of timbre and texture.

Even at this late date, the instrument clearly inspires in Jamal a sense of wonder. As always, we the listeners were the beneficiaries.

CHAPTER 7

Sun Ra

Out of This World

Feb. 24, 1991

Onstage, the band is blowing up a storm, its members, most in turbans and capes, blasting incredible waves of sound.

Offstage, a cadre of caped dancers is running, dancing and somersaulting through the crowd, banging on hand-held percussion instruments and chanting in high-decibel yowls. And in the house, a sea of young faces is laughing, singing, shouting, cheering and begging the performers for more.

This scene is not a rock or rap concert, nor a blues fest gone amok. It's another night in the life of a nearly 80-year-old bandleader and unrepentant revolutionary, the inimitable Sun Ra.

That Ra recently suffered a stroke seems immaterial, for he's still taking his exuberant stage show around the world, his next stop being the Cubby Bear Lounge (1059 W. Addison St.) at 7:30 and 10 p.m. March 8.

"I'm feeling much better now, so why not keep doing it?" asks Ra, whose speaking voice sounds as strong as ever. "I've still got my mission, you know."

Indeed, Ra is in the eighth decade of that mission, which, in retrospect, has amounted to nothing less than a rewriting of the rules of jazz performance and musical structure.

Fig. 4 Sun Ra: In Chicago, Herman "Sonny" Blount—a jobbing musician from Birmingham, Ala.—became the mystic Sun Ra. His otherworldly music liberated the art of improvisation via electronic sounds, non-chordal harmonies and stream-of-consciousness music-making.

Long before anyone had heard the terms "performance art" or "multimedia shows," Ra was virtually inventing the genres. Daringly chromatic music, African dance, misty lighting, glittering costumes, heady poetry readings—all have long been inseparable elements of Ra's work with his band, the Arkestra.

For Ra, the revolution began in Chicago in the late '30s, when he was a jobbing pianist from Birmingham, Ala., and known around the South Side as Herman "Sonny" Blount.

"I already had a lot of my ideas back then, but I had to keep a low profile to keep from being thought ridiculous," recalls Ra.

"Even when I was playing the Club DeLisa [a legendary, long-gone jazz den on South State Street] in the '40s, I had to be careful, because I was dealing with something that was really ahead of its time.

"When I was playing for Fletcher Henderson [who virtually invented the big jazz band] at Club DeLisa, I had a lot of trouble. The band members kept saying I was too 'different.'

"And when I went to play the Club Morocco in Canada [in the late '50s], I got fired because the man said I was playing God's music. He asked me to change my style, which I refused to do, so they paid me off and told me to get out."

For the most part, that's how Ra's innovations have been received around the world. Yet, over time, his breakthroughs have redefined the sound of modern music.

He was using the first, primitive electronic keyboards as early as the '40s, because "I felt we were moving into a different age—a 'space age,' and I used that term years before people started reading it in the newspapers.

"So I realized I needed something besides just a piano. My arrangements were always colorful, almost symphonic, so that's why I turned to electronic keyboards."

And years before avant-gardists such as Ornette Coleman and Cecil Taylor pushed modern jazz into freer forms, Ra was laying the groundwork. In the '50s in Chicago and the '60s in New York, his music expanded into vast, seemingly free improvisations, with band members exploring non-chordal harmonies, high-register harmonics and stream-of-consciousness forms.

Taking the name Sun Ra and anointing his band the Arkestra ("because that's how I pronounced the word 'orchestra,'" says Ra), he plunged whole-heartedly into mysticism. Both his shows and his music suggested a kind of inter-galactic, new-age philosophy; yet his music remained infinitely more gritty and substantial than the term "new age" means today.

Ultimately, his radical ideas pointed the way for the exhilarating experiments of Chicago's pioneering collective, the Association for the Advancement of Creative Musicians.

"I remember one time when Muhal Richard Abrams [a founding father of the collective] visited me in New York during the World's Fair there," says Ra.

"I said to him, 'Let's go the fair,' and he said, 'No, I just came here to talk to you.'

"And then he said, 'I wanted you to know that when you were in Chicago, I was one of the people who tended to make fun of what you were doing. Now I find out we have to do those same things.'"

Yet even if Ra accrued a degree of notoriety for his experiments over the years, his appeal is far from universal. Even today, many listeners and colleagues scorn him.

"When I was in England four months ago, I worked with an Indian drummer who was magnificent," says Ra.

"But when he told his fellow musicians that he was playing with the Arkestra, they asked, 'Why would you want to play with a band like that? Why not work for a real one?' So that's how many musicians feel. They still don't get it."

But today's young audiences do. The visual splendor of Ra's shows, the way he unabashedly combines world musics with swing and avant-garde styles draws large, young crowds every time.

"The kids hear the beautiful percussion we have been using in the Arkestra for years, and they recognize it from the rock and rap music that came later," says Ra.

"But more important, my music is the language of youth," adds Ra, who declines to give his age, though he is thought to be in his late 70s. (His spiritual beliefs once led him to tell an interviewer that he was "5,000 years old.")

"Unfortunately, the old people don't understand what the kids and I do," says Ra. "I guess you could say it's a generation gap."

Cosmic Tunes

May 3, 1992

Night after night, in city after city, Sun Ra still wages the battle.

Never mind that he's approaching age 80, that he recently suffered a stroke, that he has been inciting musical revolutions as far back as the late 1930s. Now, in his eighth decade on the front lines of the avant-garde, he refuses to relinquish the stage.

"I still face a lot of opposition, I've still got a lot of work to do," says Ra, on the eve of returning to the city where his tumultuous musical journey began more than half a century ago.

"You know, physically, I actually feel pretty good," adds Ra, who will bring his Arkestra to the Oak Theatre, 2000 N. Western Ave., Friday. "But [emotionally] I'm not feeling too well, because I've still got a lot of opposition.

"See, the public still comes around to see me, but it's the musicians—they can't own to the ideas I have."

Indeed, the jazz musical establishment has been resisting Ra nearly since the beginning, often dismissing him as crackpot, fraud, lowbrow comic and worse. But Ra, a man who was born to swim upstream, in a way relished the resistance. The more he was spurned, the more far-out his ideas became.

Born in Birmingham, Ala., the innately gifted musician came to Chicago in the late '30s (on the invitation of bandleader Fess Whatley), where he was known as Herman "Sonny" Blount. His gifts as pianist and arranger quickly established him as a force to be reckoned with, and by the early '40s he had become part of the first great swing band of them all, led by Fletcher Henderson at the long-gone Club de Lisa.

"Fletcher was a splendid musician with a splendid band," recalls Ra, who wasted no time in shaking things up. "You might say I arranged for the crazy side of Club de Lisa."

Having learned a few things playing the burlesque houses of Calumet City, he began sprucing up the Club de Lisa stage shows with flashy costumes, free-flowing choreography and other uninhibited expressions. But that was just the beginning.

"The whole thing really all started in Chicago, because that's where I had my first outer space experiences," says Ra, who had changed his name to reflect his new, cosmic orientation.

"When the first electronic piano came out [in the early '40s], I got one right away," and, for Ra, at least, the space age had begun.

While other jazz musicians were trying to master the complexities of '40s bebop or, later, the "cool" school of Miles Davis and the post-bop dissonance of John Coltrane, Ra was practically on another planet with his newly coined "space music."

Donning glittering turban and gowns, forging a music that careened between classic swing and seemingly free-form improvisation, Ra was inventing a new and original musical language.

More than that, he was creating a vocabulary for art forms that had yet to be conceived, including performance art and multimedia shows. The free-wheeling improvisations of Ornette Coleman, the percussion experiments of Chicago's avant-garde of the '60s (and beyond), even the pre-bop revival of today all owe a debt to Ra.

To his group of instrumentalists, singers, dancers, baton-twirlers and the like he gave the name Arkestra, "because that's how I pronounced the word 'orchestra,"' says Ra, who was not exactly welcomed by less daring elements.

"Even when I was playing for Fletcher Henderson, I had a lot of trouble," says Ra. "The band members kept saying I was too 'different.'"

Yet Ra persevered, venturing to such far-off places as "Saturn" and "Magic City," two of his early recordings, long before anyone had so much as set foot on the moon.

To those who actually listened to the music before putting it down, there was no question that Ra was not some musical counterfeiter but the real thing.

"I used to go to some of the rehearsals of his band," recalls veteran Chicago jazz impresario Joe Segal, "and it was clear that Sonny had hit on something. He was a real musician who could really swing, and he found a new way to do it, and I respected him for it."

Aided by such virtuosos as alto saxophonist Marshall Allen and tenorist John Gilmore, Ra took his act to New York, Europe and anyplace else with an open ear. Eventually, in the '60s and '70s, Ra and his Arkestra became at least a cult success, and it's easy to understand why.

The sheer exuberance of the music—with its odd mixture of vintage tunes and other-worldly sounds—was bound to surprise the ear. Throw in gyrating dancers and the like, and you have a show that, if nothing else, stood out for its sheer novelty.

Why did Ra stick to his guns?

"Because I knew it's a historical thing where people, or at least musicians, always have rejected new ideas," he says.

"But I knew I was having at least a little better time of it in Europe, where people were more friendly to me."

More remarkable still, Ra has lived long enough to see signs of mainstream acceptance even in the States (for the record, the history books say he was born in 1915, though Ra once told an interviewer that he was "born on Saturn 5,000 years ago").

The Evidence label recently released a series of compact discs documenting rare Ra recordings of the '50s and '60s (the CD titles are "Sound Sun Pleasure," "Holiday for Soul Dance," "Jazz in Silhouettes," "Monorails and Satellites" and "Supersonic Jazz). And no less than the New England Conservatory of music recently honored the great inventor by establishing a "Sun Ra Day" during a recent visit.

Is Ra delighted with these unmistakable signs of acceptance?

Of course not—what revolutionary worthy of the name would be?

"Sure, I was amazed about that 'Sun Ra Day' thing," he says, "and I'm glad about the CDs. But this fight isn't over, because I'm doing a lot of other things now that aren't on record yet. I'm still talking about the avant-garde, I'm still talking about outer space, and I'm still facing opposition from musicians," adds Ra, returning to a favorite theme.

"The musicians, the ones who are academic, they still want to hold onto the past, they want to hold onto the one thing they know how to do. But people want something fresh and new.

"And all I'm saying is that the space age is here to stay—and nobody can really run away from it."

CHAPTER 8

Oscar Brown Jr.

An Appreciation

June 5, 2005

Oscar Brown Jr. knew he should have been rich and a lot more famous.

Having penned the lyrics for such civil-rights era classics as "Signifyin' Monkey" and "Work Song," having reached a national TV audience with his groundbreaking show "Jazz Scene U.S.A.," having created iconoclastic stage musicals such as "Kicks & Co." and "The Great Nitty Gritty," he was experimenting in multiple media long before anyone breathed the word "synergy."

But in the days leading up to Brown's death May 29 at age 78 in Chicago, of complications from a blood infection, jazz devotees were conceiving fundraisers to help defray expenses for a man who had minimal funds, few engagements and an afterglow of fame that radiated mostly among longtime fans.

Brown often pondered the severe disconnect between his artistic achievement and his personal fortunes, sometimes accepting his fate, other times lashing out at it.

"In a way, I don't mind that I've been broke most of my career, because that has kept me creative," he told me in 2002. "I've had to keep creating to stay alive.

"If I had become rich, I would have spent more time collecting awards than creating material."

A few years earlier, however, he acknowledged the primary reason for his shortage of money and broad recognition: himself.

"I was always trying to be free—free of knuckling under to what somebody else told me to do," he said in 1995, two years after he had come home to Chicago, after decades of struggling on the road.

"And that costs you."

Indeed, the very forces that inspired so many of his indelible lyrics—his indignation at racism and injustice, his anger at inner-city poverty and crime, his sorrow at the decay of his beloved South Side—may have dimmed his commercial possibilities. For in Brown's most enduring creations, his words cried out sharply against a society that crushed generations of Black life.

The incendiary phrases and shattering music of his landmark "We Insist! Freedom Now Suite" (which Brown wrote with Max Roach in 1960), the devastating evocation of life on a chain gang in Brown's lyrics to Nat Adderley's "Work Song" (1962) and the unvarnished look at dope dealing, Black-on-Black crime and other urban pathologies in the musical "The Great Nitty Gritty" (1983) were the work of a man who never held back.

Long before it became fashionable to sing about the terrors of big-city slums, decades before hip-hop songs turned ghetto poetry into gold, Brown was rhyming and riffing on life in the streets. Singing about pushers and pimps, cops and coke, ranging from despair to hope and back again, he did not flinch in portraying the world around him.

"I can only assume that his social consciousness rubbed certain tastemakers and power brokers the wrong way," said Kurt Elling, a noted Chicago singer-songwriter whose work builds on Brown's innovations, in contemplating the disappointments of Brown's career.

"And maybe the public wasn't ready for the full extent of his message."

But a segment of the public—African-Americans who identified with Brown's art and others inclined to tune in—revered Brown's work. They heard in it something authentic, original and unexpected.

"Oscar was writing right down at street level, where the music came from," said Chicago singer-impresario Geraldine De Haas, who often presented Brown at the South Side concerts she organized.

"What he wrote came from the soul of the people—the everyday people."

Moreover, when Brown reconceived the age-old Black folk tale "Signifying Monkey" as a buoyant swing tune, transforming it into a cunning metaphor for battles among the races, he showed that ancient art could convey contemporary truths. The piece epitomized the visionary quality of his 1962 recording debut, "Sin & Soul . . . and Then Some" (on Columbia/Legacy), which also recounted a harrowing slave auction in "Bid 'Em In" and recalled neighborhood street cries in "Watermelon Man" and "Rags and Old Iron."

These works, and others, "opened our eyes to Black folk culture in a way that we may not have done without him," said Samuel Floyd, founder and former director of the Center for Black Music Research at Columbia College Chicago.

"The content of 'Signifyin' Monkey,' and so many others that Brown sang, just grabbed your attention. We never heard anything like it before."

No one had. The shock of Brown's works propelled him into the '60s radical elite, and he consistently refused to dial down the intensity of his music to cross over into a wider audience. Tunes such as "Forty Acres and a Mule" (on the brilliant live CD "Mr. Oscar Brown, Jr. Goes to Washington," of 1965) and "Feel the Fire" and "Gang Bang" (on "Movin' On" in 1972) were more than songs. They were manifestos, though made palatable by the salty exuberance of Brown's delivery, as well as by somewhat more upbeat fare, such as the disarming "Dat Dere," about a child's relationship with his father, and "Hazel's Hips," still one of the sexiest tunes ever written.

For all the notoriety and critical acclaim that Brown accrued, however, he seemed destined to just barely scrape by.

"Several years ago, I first became aware of what a mess my father's publishing situation was, " his daughter Maggie Brown, also a gifted singer-songwriter, told me in 1995.

"And it was because of the kinds of contracts he signed in the '50s and '60s, which were typical of the kinds of contracts that Black men all over signed at the time.

"Basically, they sold their rights away."

Yet Brown's passion for his work never waned. In a career stretching back to the 1940s, when Brown read the day's headlines on "Negro

Newsfront," a community-TV operation on the South Side, he penned hundreds of songs.

The tragic death of his musician son Oscar Brown III, in a car accident at age 38 in 1996, visibly aged Brown but did not stop him.

Just three years ago, he unveiled a major new work at the Chicago Humanities Festival, his "Sweet Langston Suite" bringing arching melodies and seductive rhythms to excerpts of Langston Hughes' epic poem "Montage of a Dream Deferred." Even at that late date, with so many of his own dreams deferred, Brown found the creative wherewithal to capture the late-night languor of Hughes' "Boogie: 1 a.m." and an unnerving sense of doom in Hughes' "Dead in There."

Last summer, in yet another failed attempt to revive "Great Nitty Gritty" as a commercial entity, Brown enlisted a cast of students—plus a few professionals—to stage a makeshift production at Kennedy-King College, on South Wentworth Avenue. The set was crude, the staging rudimentary, the music more powerful than ever.

More than 20 years after I attended the premiere of "Great Nitty Gritty," at the long-shuttered Playhouse in McCormick Place, I was struck anew by the timelessness of "The Children of Children," a lament on teenage pregnancy; the tragicomic currents of "I'll Drink to That," a withering dissection of alcoholism; and the intellectual clarity of "We Never Reference Our Ethnicity," a lacerating satire on racial identity.

For all his frustrations, Brown never tired of speaking his peace.

"I'm given to be driven," he said to me, a couple of years earlier.

"I don't know how not to create."

Behind the Music

Oct. 14, 2005

When the jazz genius Oscar Brown Jr. died in Chicago last May, at age 78, he was broke, under-employed and nearly forgotten.

The man who penned the lyrics to such classic tunes as "Work Song" and "Afro Blue," the creator of groundbreaking urban musicals such as "Kicks & Co." and "The Great Nitty Gritty" had been scraping by for years—decades, really.

Though his songs and larger works became anthems for the civil rights era, though jazz musicians around the world riffed on Brown masterpieces such as "Dat Dere" and "Hazel's Hips," money and fame commensurate with his enormous talent always eluded him.

But an unflinching new documentary, "Music is My Life, Politics My Mistress: The Story of Oscar Brown Jr.," sets the record straight, eloquently summing up Brown's enormous achievements while capturing the man's wizardry as performer, songwriter and undaunted social activist.

"I've always thought of Oscar as one of those people who is a grand contributor to the music but is never really recognized because of the content of what he does," the writer Amiri Baraka says early in the film, pinpointing one of the primary reasons behind Brown's struggles.

For Brown spoke his mind—in poetry and song and conversation—decrying the blatant racism of the Chicago he grew up in, bemoaning a nation that throughout its history regarded Blacks as unequal.

"I always wondered as a kid how would it be to [live] in a country where you really could love the country, and feel that the country was your country," he says in the film, which overflows with illuminating footage of the man in conversation and in performance.

"Because I always had this feeling that I was in a hostile situation here."

Brown transformed his rage into some of the most searing song lyrics and soaring melody lines ever penned in the jazz tradition. The slave trader callously peddling human flesh in "Bid 'Em In," the street vendor hawking "Rags and Old Iron," the griot spinning the ancient tale of the "Signifyin' Monkey" revealed the meaning of race in America, all set to a swing beat and a deep blues undertow.

Exquisitely edited, "Music is My Life" links key moments in Brown's biography with corresponding passages in his work, showing how inseparable the two were. Only a man incensed at the tragedies visited on generations of African-Americans could have railed so passionately in "Forty Acres and a Mule"; only an artist who embraced his community would have been able to enlist members of the Blackstone Rangers to perform his inner-city musical "Opportunity Please Knock," in the mid-1960s.

To the credit of director donnie l. betts, it's all there in the film: the artistic triumphs and the colossal commercial defeats, the stylistic innovations and the feuds with other musicians, the generosity of spirit and the inevitable personal shortcomings. The director even plunges headlong into the greatest tragedy of Brown's life, the death of his comparably gifted son, Oscar Brown III—whom everyone called "Bobo"—at age 38, in 1996, at the hands of a drunk driver.

If some moments of this film inevitably produce tears, others inspire optimism, for it's impossible not to be elevated by the rhythms of Brown's music and the sight and sound of him performing it.

CHAPTER 9

Johnny Hartman

Back into the Spotlight

June 4, 1995

> *Once in every life, someone comes along. And you came to me, it was almost like a song.*
> —From "It Was Almost Like a Song," by Hal David and Archie Jordan

Sung softly, tenderly and with considerable ardor, the tune sounds as if it were written specifically for the scene, in which two characters savor the final moments of a brief and bittersweet love affair.

In truth, however, this haunting music, performed by Chicago jazz singer Johnny Hartman, was recorded and released 15 years before Clint Eastwood and Meryl Streep caressed to it in the film "The Bridges of Madison County."

No doubt Hartman's heartbreaking way with a ballad—his ability to sing more slowly, more softly, yet with more plushness of voice than virtually anyone else—helps establish the melancholy tone of the film. To behold Eastwood, as photographer Robert Kincaid, and Streep, as farm wife Francesca Johnson, falling in love while Hartman's nocturnes play on the radio is to appreciate anew the soft, warm glow of the man's music.

What's more, Hartman, who received minimal recognition while he was alive, seems poised now to be discovered by a wide audience—12 years after his death at age 60.

The CD soundtrack of "The Bridges of Madison County," which has just arrived in record stores, includes the four ballads that Hartman is heard singing in the film: "Easy Living," "I See Your Face Before Me," "For All We Know" and the aforementioned "It Was Almost Like a Song."

Eastwood, a jazz devotee who has featured the music in many of his films, launches his new Malpaso Records label with the soundtrack. In addition, he has purchased the rights, from Bee Hive, to reissue Hartman's "Once in Every Life" album on a Malpaso CD. The penultimate and possibly best recording of Hartman's career, "Once in Every Life" carries all of the songs in the film, as well as Hartman's hushed readings of "Wave," "Nobody Home" and "I Could Write a Book."

It's the kind of massive promotional push not typically accorded jazz artists.

"I believe that if Johnny were alive today, this movie and the soundtrack would have totally resurrected his career," says Susan Neumann, whose Evanston-based Bee Hive Records recorded "Once in Every Life" in 1980 and released it the following year.

"Not that people didn't appreciate Johnny when he was alive. Jazz lovers knew how great he was. But the rest of the world really didn't."

Indeed, Hartman's career, for all its formidable musical accomplishments, never approached mass-market dimensions. Unlike Billy Eckstine, whose regal bass-baritone clearly was Hartman's model, and Frank Sinatra, whose long-lined ballad singing also proved an important inspiration, Hartman never fully made the transformation from jazz virtuoso to show-business celebrity.

Perhaps because Eckstine, Sinatra and others of their generation came of age when big bands dominated America's musical landscape, they were launched into the popular consciousness in a way that Hartman, roughly a decade younger, never was. Or perhaps the understated and sublimely sophisticated nature of Hartman's work simply was not destined to reach a mass audience.

Regardless, Hartman brought to his music an emotional profundity that only Sinatra and Tony Bennett, among male jazz singers, has equaled or topped.

Born July 3, 1923, in Chicago, Hartman was trained in the same hothouse that produced Nat "King" Cole, Gene Ammons, Von Freeman, Johnny Griffin and other jazz legends: DuSable High School, on the South Side.

No less than singer-pianist Dinah Washington, another fabled Chicagoan whose recordings are featured in "The Bridges of Madison County," accompanied Hartman at the keyboard in a South Side Baptist church; and pianist Earl Hines, whose big band kept Chicago dancing through the Depression, put Hartman on the map by featuring him in 1947.

By the time Hartman slowly had begun to accrue a national and international reputation among jazz fans, in the '50s and early '60s, however, "the Beatles had invaded the United States, and the major record labels were losing interest in jazz musicians," says Bee Hive owner Neumann. "Great jazz musicians, like Johnny Griffin and Dexter Gordon, were moving to Europe. The scene in the States was drying up."

Nevertheless, Hartman turned in his share of gems on smaller, independent labels, most notably "John Coltrane and Johnny Hartman," "The Voice That Is!" and "All of Me," all reissued on Impulse CDs.

Among them, Hartman considered "Once in Every Life" his finest achievement, and the critics concurred.

"Johnny Hartman is a master of intimate balladry," wrote Nat Hentoff in Cosmopolitan in July of 1981. "Although he has recorded with several jazz giants, Hartman has not had an album that fully realized his mesmeric romanticism until 'Once in Every Life.'"

The recording won Hartman his only Grammy nomination (as best male jazz vocalist) in 1981, but he lost to singer Al Jarreau.

By the summer of '83, Hartman, then living in New York, was diagnosed with lung and throat cancer, and by September he was dead. Since then, he has been all but forgotten, his name overlooked even in jazz dictionaries, his old LPs difficult to find even in the best resale shops.

"In fact, it was precisely because Clint Eastwood couldn't find 'Once in Every Life' in the record stores that his office first contacted me last year," says Bee Hive owner Neumann.

"He had heard one of the cuts on the radio and wanted to consider it for 'Bridges.' So I sent him the LP by overnight delivery, because I just knew that if he heard the whole album, he would want to use more of it in the film."

Neumann was correct in noting Eastwood's long-running passion for jazz and his tendency to use the music generously in his films. The Erroll Garner classic that gave a name and a mood to Eastwood's "Play Misty for Me" (1971), the revolutionary and hard-charging music that defined "Bird" (1988) and the ethereal Miles Davis tracks that formed a wistful leitmotif in "In the Line of Fire" (1993) have established Eastwood as one of the few advocates for jazz in Hollywood.

With "The Bridges of Madison County," Eastwood effectively raised the stakes, by selecting the music first, then building whole scenes around it.

"When the couple is dancing together on the second night, Clint knew which music they would be dancing to and how he would build the scene to play out with the whole song," says Bruce Ricker, Eastwood's musical consultant on the film, referring to "I See Your Face Before Me."

"You'll rarely see a movie in which whole songs are played all the way through, but that's exactly what happens here. So the movie almost plays in real time, which adds to its power" and, one might add, the prominence of the score.

Though Robert James Waller's best-selling novella "The Bridges of Madison County" carries numerous musical references, none point specifically to Hartman, whose inclusion owes entirely "to Clint Eastwood's personal tastes," adds Ricker. "He's the one who picked all the songs and how they would play."

By giving Hartman so vital a role in "Bridges," Eastwood may have done more than enrich the texture of his film.

In effect, he may have revived the name and the work of a singer whose moment in the sun is well overdue.

A Singular Voice

June 12, 2024

Think of the male voices to come out of Chicago, and a few instantly stand out.

Jazz would not be the same without Louis Armstrong's gravelly tones and wordless melodic flights, which in the 1920s gave birth to the art of scat singing. Mel Tormé put a high sheen on that method, crafting instrumental-like vocal lines and a crushed-velvet tone that could hold their own alongside the greatest female jazz vocalist of them all, Ella Fitzgerald.

Nat "King" Cole's plush timbre and easy swing, Oscar Brown Jr.'s raspy incantations, Frank D'Rone's silken phrases and Kurt Elling's early-period virtuosity all enriched the male vocal tradition in Chicago and beyond.

Yet among them all, one Chicagoan had an instrument with no real rival: Johnny Hartman. The man could have been singing the phone book, and it would have sounded compelling simply on the strength of those incomparably resonant low notes, that creamy mid-register and high notes that couldn't have caressed the ear more tenderly.

Anyone familiar with the singer's discography will cite "John Coltrane and Johnny Hartman" as the treasure among his releases, for good reason. The pairing of these singular artists—enriched by McCoy Tyner's piano, Jimmy Garrison's bass and Elvin Jones' drums—represents a high point in the art of intimate music-making.

But another, less celebrated Hartman album—"I Just Dropped By to Say Hello"—deserves similar attention.

For starters, in these October 1963 sessions (recorded seven months after the Hartman-Coltrane classic), the singer found himself in similarly superb company, thanks to the contributions of pianist Hank Jones, bassist Milt Hinton, drummer Elvin Jones and guests Illinois Jacquet on tenor saxophone and Kenny Burrell and Jim Hall playing guitar on various tracks. Hartman did not always get to record with musicians of this stature, and, as on the album with Coltrane, the instrumentalists brought out the best in him.

You can hear it from the opening track, "Charade," the Henry Mancini–Johnny Mercer movie music to which lesser musicians often condescend. Hartman instead gives the tune the ample respect it deserves, taking it slow and easy, the better to linger on every turn of phrase. Even in his upper voice, Hartman provides the kind of tonal cushion that eluded most of his contemporaries in any register.

It took a certain degree of gumption for a male balladeer to take on "In the Wee Small Hours of the Morning," after Frank Sinatra made this jazz nocturne his personal property with his 1955 recording. But Hartman prevails here, the extraordinary tenderness and vulnerability of his delivery a striking counterpoint to Sinatra's heated sense of yearning.

The vocal pleasures keep coming, especially with Hartman's signature, rumbling low notes on "If I'm Lucky" and some full-throated tone and breezy swing on "Don't Call It Love."

Better still, hearing Hartman interact with the instrumentalists reminds you that he wasn't only about that remarkable voice—he also showed a deep-seated musical intelligence.

Listen to how adroitly Hartman maneuvers alongside Hinton's walking bass lines on the opening of "Sleepin' Bee." Or how the singer contrasts his straight reading of the melody line with Jacquet's arabesques on tenor in "Don't You Know I Care." Or how dexterously Hartman duets with the pianist on the album's title track, two master musicians toying with rhythm, pitch and tone, yet without disturbing the song's steady flow.

By the end of the album, all the musicians turn up the emotional dial, Hartman producing his most generous vibrato on "How Sweet It Is to Be in Love," a nearly operatic performance—complete with various melodic ornaments and unexpected turns of phrase. That the band offers a rhythmic backdrop that palpably evokes tango makes this the most vivid of the album's tracks—an exclamation point to all that has come before.

Hartman never enjoyed anything near the celebrity that was lavished upon Sinatra, Cole and Tormé, though a moment of posthumous fame came his way with Clint Eastwood's 1995 film "The Bridges of Madison County." That treacly version of the pop novel used the high romance of Hartman's album "Once in Every Life" as a de facto substitute for the artificial kind onscreen.

Even here, though, the urgent expressiveness of Hartman's singing could not be denied, the music overshadowing the film rather than the other way around.

CHAPTER 10

Johnny Griffin

A Jazzman's Return

April 18, 1993

As he prepares to celebrate his 65th birthday in his hometown, Chicago, tenor saxophone giant Johnny Griffin is making no plans for retirement.

On the contrary, he has managed to scale new artistic heights.

His most recent album, "Dance of Passion" (Antilles), is winning considerable praise and visibility. More important, the recording bristles with Griffin's characteristically intense bebop solos as well as melodically accessible passages that are reaching a wider audience than Griffin ever has enjoyed.

Add to that his high-intensity touring schedule, which brings him to the Jazz Showcase Tuesday through April 25, and it's clear that Griffin has plenty to celebrate.

"Actually, I didn't really expect that 'Dance of Passion' was going to be a big deal," says Griffin of an album with a most unusual origin.

"I mean, the title, 'Dance of Passion,' and the [title] piece itself, actually came from a dream I was having. That happens to me sometimes. Then I get out of bed and go to the piano and try out whatever I was hearing, write it down or put it on tape.

"In the case of 'Dance of Passion,' it was almost like I was waking up in a mist, and I was in the midst of all these belly dancers. It was really strange.

"So then I went to the piano and wrote down just those few notes, and then, later, started developing it."

As its title suggests, "Dance of Passion" is a mesmerizing piece in which an insinuating motif is repeated constantly, as in Maurice Ravel's similarly entrancing "Bolero." Because "Dance" is built on an exotic melodic scale and because its harmonies are decidedly non-Western, it suggests music of Middle Eastern antiquity—as in the belly dancers of Griffin's dream.

But it takes more than a catchy tune to make a substantial piece of music, as Griffin's recording establishes. The ingenuity lies in the way that Griffin transforms the musical material of this piece and others on the CD.

Obviously, it has taken Griffin a lifetime to learn to spin such alluring sounds, but he considers the source of his art the training he received on the South Side of Chicago.

"People don't realize how important it is having a foundation like the one I got there," says Griffin, referring to Du Sable High School, where the fabled Capt. Walter Dyett trained several of the world's most revered jazz artists. Nat Cole, Von Freeman, Gene Ammons and Griffin, among others, were introduced to the rigors of jazz by Dyett.

"He was one hell of a musician," adds Griffin. "He knew all the instruments, but he also was a strong man, a disciplinarian, a father figure. He would take no nonsense at all, he'd short-shrift anything disturbing in class.

"But that was good for the kids, because it gave them something, it gave them some support. Dyett taught dignity and honesty and, on top of that, music.

"So when I graduated from high school at 17, three or four days later I had a gig playing with Lionel Hampton's band and was able to do it with no problem whatsoever."

At that time, the mid-'40s, Chicago teenagers with talent and training could find themselves catapulted abruptly into the big time. With a war on, many of the best players in jazz had given up their seats in the big bands of the day. And because Chicago's South Side was teeming with jazz clubs, a young player such as Griffin could sit in with Hampton's band one day, win a full-time gig the next.

"And that's when I really started to learn things," says Griffin of his years on the bandstand with Hampton. "From Hamp, of course, I learned a lot about show business, because Hamp was—and still is—one of the best showmen.

"But I also just learned so much from the old pros in the band, because they threw me out there [in the solo spot] challenging [tenor virtuoso] Arnett Cobb playing 'Flying Home,'" the Hampton band signature piece that originally made a star of another young tenorist, Illinois Jacquet.

With the age of bebop already under way by the '40s, Griffin knew he had to learn the tough, harmonically complex language. So he headed to New York—briefly in the late '40s, and again, after an Army stint, in the '50s—where 52nd Street was alive with the sounds of bop.

To this day, Griffin remains at once awestruck and grateful that the first generation of boppers personally showed him what the volatile new music was all about. Trumpeter Dizzy Gillespie, pianists Thelonious Monk, Bud Powell and Elmo Hope, and others took the fledgling Chicago tenor into their sphere.

"Elmo, Bud and Thelonious really were like three brothers to me," recalls Griffin, "and whenever I wasn't working, I'd just hang with them in New York, listening, studying.

"That was my university training, staying around those three musicians. Because I didn't want to sound like any other musician on tenor saxophone, so I spent my time around those guys and around Dizzy, who adopted me, and [trumpeters] Kenny Dorham and Fats Navarro and later on Clifford Brown.

"They were the ones who gave me a chance to peep at them and ask questions. That music was so tough that sometimes it would take me four or five months to understand something they were telling me about. And then it suddenly would hit me: 'Oh, that's how those changes work.'

"Because I hadn't done that much formal study as far as theory and harmony goes, so I got it straight from these guys, right from the source.

"The thing is," adds Griffin, "it was just like hanging out with friends and having fun, you know? Everybody was treated as equals. They didn't treat me like a kid or anything, although I was a few years younger than they were, but I was just having a good time, and I don't really know why they adopted me.

"But it happened even with the older generation. Ben Webster heard that he had been one of my first influences, so he adopted me. And the same with Coleman Hawkins and Prez [Lester Young], all my idols really made me welcome on the New York jazz scene."

Nevertheless, Griffin went to Europe in the early '60s and never moved back. Facing "problems with the IRS" and a split with his wife, he apparently found a kind of peace on the other side of the Atlantic.

There were more than just personal problems, however, that kept him away from the States.

"I also had problems with the so-called 'jazz critics' who were propagating avant-garde music," recalls Griffin. "And I thought that music was a bad hoax, or a bad joke on the people listening to it.

"Although, actually, I went to Europe without any idea that I'd never move back. It's just that the way they received jazz musicians in Europe was quite different from what they do in the States, and it's still like that even today.

"Jazz has a high profile in Europe. And people just seem to have more leisure time to enjoy the things of esthetic value than they seem to have over here.

"Plus the people in Europe just know more about music and about jazz history than the average American, by far."

So Griffin, who still lives in a rustic area outside Paris, built a new life for himself overseas.

"Even now, whenever I'm in Paris," he says, "just going out to sit on the Champs Elysses, I feel like I belong, not even knowing the language. There's something about the atmosphere in France, it gives you a feeling of well-being. And all the people passing around in the rainbow of colors, people from Africa and everywhere else, you just feel right."

Still, each year at this time, just as sure as showers are going to rain down on Chicago, Griffin comes back home to celebrate his April 24 birthday in the city where it all began.

"Oh yeah, that'll never change," says Griffin, whose homecoming long ago became a rite of spring at Jazz Showcase.

"In fact, I hear jazz is going pretty good in Chicago.

"That's beautiful, man. That means I'm going to be having a real good time back home this year."

"Little Giant" at 62

April 29, 1990

When Johnny Griffin picks up his tenor saxophone Sunday afternoon at the Jazz Showcase, it will be easy to guess what he's going to play.

"I suppose it'll have to be 'Happy Birthday,"' said the Chicago born-and-bred saxman, already tuning up for his annual birthday jam at the Showcase.

Though Griffin turned 62 Tuesday, he postponed the official celebration by a few days partly out of reverence for tradition. For years, Griffin, who has lived in Paris since the early 1960s, has capped his annual, month-long U.S. tour with a weekend birthday bash in sweet home Chicago.

"So why should this year be any different?" said Griffin, who plays the Showcase through Sunday (the 4 p.m. set will serve as the major birthday celebration, with subsequent shows at 8 and 10 p.m.).

"Every year at this time I come back home, stay at my mamma's house on the South Side of Chicago and celebrate a bit. That's just the way I do it."

At first, it might seem a bit odd to hear of such homey traditions from a man long considered one of bebop's most fiery revolutionaries.

Coming up on the heels of Lester Young, Coleman Hawkins, John Coltrane and the like, Griffin emerged in the late '40s and '50s as one of the most hard-driving of the young tenor saxophonists. To this day, his playing can be emotionally turbulent, high in decibels, and torrential in the sheer onslaught of sound.

No wonder Griffin, who stands about 5-feet 5-inches, long ago picked up the nickname "Little Giant."

But jazz has moved in other, perhaps less volatile directions since the post-war years of Griffin's heyday. And though his Thursday night set at the Showcase easily proved that Griffin remains at the top of his skills, he has no patience for much of contemporary jazz.

"Frankly, I don't think the music of the '40s and '50s has even been fully understood or completely investigated yet," Griffin said.

"And anyway, look at all this junk they call jazz nowadays; all this electronic noise and rock beat and all that stuff. What has that got to do with jazz?

"Or look at it this way: What has happened musically since bebop? I can tell you the answer, real simple: zero."

Whether or not one concurs, there's no doubt that Griffin, and others of his generation, gave jazz some of its most dynamic sounds. The harmonic, rhythmic and melodic complexities of bop and post-bop still thrill the ear and pique the intellect.

The best players of Griffin's youth individualized this music with their own sensibilities and eccentricities. As far as Griffin is concerened, none was bolder or more individual than Dexter Gordon, who died Wednesday in Philadelphia, at 67.

"Dexter's music was genuinely revolutionary, and it still is," said Griffin, who first met Gordon in the mid-40s, when Gordon was playing with the likes of tenor Gene Ammons and alto Charlie Parker in Billy Eckstine's fabled band.

"Dexter was absolutely his own man—you couldn't imitate him no matter how hard you tried," Griffin said.

"He was a big man, and he had an enormous sound. But he had this way of playing behind the beat that no one else could quite get.

"But what I remember best about Dexter's playing, as well as the man himself, was his incredible sense of humor.

"He'd be playing the most intense passage, then all of a sudden he'd throw in some kind of goofy musical quote—you know, a classical theme, or a country-western tune, or a nursery rhyme or something.

"And that's how he was in person too. Always acting, always cutting up, big gestures, always with a laugh.

"With all that he went through," Griffin said, referring to Gordon's prison time for narcotics possession and other bouts with drugs and alcohol, "I can hardly ever remember him being down or depressed. He just didn't seem capable of it.

"Now that he's gone, there just isn't anyone who sounds like him. It's gone, except on records."

But the fierce musical vocabulary of the era still speaks pungently, thanks to survivors such as Griffin. In his case, there's usually a warm, lyric message beneath the surface frenzy. In ballads, especially, Griffin's playing sometimes suggests the romantic warmth of the late Ben Webster's tenor. During Thursday night's late set at the Showcase, for instance, Griffin offered hushed melodic poetry in his own composition "Woe is Me."

"Maybe I'm historic," Griffin said, "but living in France, I learned long ago that folks in America are often obsessed with everything new, young, different.

"Well some of the old sounds have something to say too."

CHAPTER 11

Von Freeman

Freeman *Is* Chicago Jazz History

Sept. 20, 1992

Never mind that the man noodling on the yellowed keys of his piano doesn't exactly look like one of the world's reigning tenor saxophonists, at least on this particular morning.

Having gigged until the small hours the night before, tenor legend Von Freeman is just getting his day started, which invariably means heading directly to the Starck grand in his small house on the South Side of Chicago. Wearing a pair of faded jeans and a purple T-shirt—a get-up somewhat less swank than the fine suits, flashy ties and dark glasses he typically sports on the bandstand—Freeman is playing strange, dissonant, far-out chords.

His piano is laden with music, his records are strewn all over the place, his every other word concerns music.

"I've even got chord progressions posted up on the wall in the bathroom—I think about this stuff all the time," says Freeman, whose gifts finally are making him an international name—on the eve of his 70th birthday.

Earlier this year, Steeplechase Records ventured to Chicago to record Freeman for a double-CD set due out later this year. A few days ago, Jazz Midwest, a Minnesota-based organization, presented him

Fig. 5 Von Freeman: A Chicago-born virtuoso of the tenor saxophone, Freeman dared to sound unlike any of his peers. His idiosyncratic approach to tone, pitch and manner symbolized the fierce individuality of Chicago jazz—and showed the way for future iconoclasts. Photo © Lauren Deutsch.

with its prestigious Jazz Masters Award. And in a couple weeks, he'll be ensconced at the La Villa Lounge in Paris, a tres chic club that booked him nearly a year ago for a birthday stint.

No doubt about it, Von Freeman, who turns 70 on Oct. 3, is hot.

"I guess I'd have to say that I've been extremely lucky in the past couple of years," says Freeman, who has spent most of his life blowing tenor for "strip joints, taxi dances, vaudeville shows, comedians, jugglers, weddings, bar-mitzvahs, jazz clubs, dives, Polish dances, Jewish dances, every nationality.

"I don't know why all this stuff is happening to me right now, because I'm surely not getting any younger. Maybe it's because in the past couple years all these [Chicago] clubs have been pairing me with those hard-blowing kids, like Ed Petersen and Eric Schneider [both fire-breathing tenorists].

"And those guys can play. So instead of laying back and just resting, I had to really come on strong and study some more and eat some more Wheaties.

"See, when you pass 60, nine-tenths of this thing is stamina. Because you've got to be able to stand up and play, because nobody is going to have any mercy on you because of your age. They feel if you can't cut it, retire.

"So you've got to just lean in there."

The miracle is that Freeman has been doing precisely that for nearly all his life, long before much recognition or anything beyond subsistence pay was within reach. Somehow, says Freeman, who raised four children in the process, "I was able to eke out a living. Guess I was lucky."

That depends on how you define luck. Certainly Freeman was blessed as far as musical talent is concerned.

"Von was always a natural," says Freeman's younger brother, George, an exceptional guitarist.

"He always was able to catch on and hear things, he could pick up piano or horn or anything so fast, it was amazing."

And Von lucked out—as did George and their other brother, Bruz, an accomplished drummer—in that their father adored jazz.

"I got all this music by osmosis," says Von. "My daddy used to play trombone—not professionally, because he was a Chicago policeman. But he had records on all the time.

"And because he was detailed at the Grand Terrace Ballroom [a fabled club of the '30s], he'd bring them all over to the house. Louis Armstrong used to come by from the time I was about three years old, and he'd always say to me: 'Hi Pops.'

"Earl Hines came over, and Fats Waller played this piano of mine."

The reigning sound of the day was the tenor saxophone, with ground-breaking melodists such as Coleman Hawkins, Lester Young and Ben Webster creating a new vocabulary for the instrument. So at age 6, Freeman taught himself tenor.

"With this music, nobody else really can teach you or tell you that much," says Freeman. "You've got to perfect it yourself and find your own ideas of what you want to express.

"I did my first nightclub gig when I was 12—my mother had to write a note for me. She wrote: 'Don't let him drink, don't let him smoke, don't let him consort with those women, and make him stay in that dressing room.'

"It was a club out in Gary, and I played seven nights a week. The guy who hired me said, 'Put something on your lip so you look a little older,' so I drew a mustache on."

By the time he was a teenager, Freeman was jamming with his friends at Du Sable High School, where the legendary Capt. Walter Dyett was building one of the country's premier jazz programs.

"Everybody in Chicago who had an instrument and wanted to play music back then tried their best to get to Du Sable," says Freeman.

"Like 'Jug' [Gene Ammons, the great Chicago tenorist]. He always had a beautiful tenor sound even then. He used to play in concert band, and he would wipe out all of the double-reeds.

"I guess Jug and I were like the two hotshots around school with solos and what-not. And when Earl Hines left Chicago [in the late '30s], King Kolax took a band in there and asked Jug and me to go in his band and maybe tour with him. This was a big break, and Jug left school and of course never looked back, just zoomed to the top."

Freeman, though, wasn't interested in the touring life, so he signed on with the Horace Henderson band in 1940, before being drafted. Artistically, that was a blessing in disguise, for it was in the Navy band that Freeman found a kind of musical inspiration.

"I met this saxophone player named Dave Young, and, man, he had this sound that I had been looking for all my life," says Freeman.

"Because I loved Prez [Lester Young], but he didn't have that power. He had a relatively soft tone, though beautiful. And Coleman Hawkins had all this power, man, he could blow, you could hear him around the block, but he didn't have this floating thing of Prez's.

"But when I heard Dave Young, he had the power and the floating sound, like Lester, and that's what I wanted to try to get."

It must have rubbed off, for not long after Freeman left the Navy in 1946, he and his two brothers quickly cohered into one of the most hard-charging units in Chicago jazz. Booked as the house band in the famous Persian Lounge, they backed virtually all the legends of the era, from Charlie Parker on.

"Actually, I had found out about Bird from my daddy after I got out of the service," says Freeman. "He said, 'You think you're a hotshot? Listen to this.'

"And he put on a Charlie Parker record, and I was sold.

"Playing with Bird was really beautiful, one of the few geniuses I have ever met in music. He just played what he wanted to play, and in jazz music, that's what you really try to do.

"Through any key, any idea, any tempo, Bird would just play."

Perhaps Parker's only equal in the nascent be-bop language was trumpeter Dizzy Gillespie, "who was really identical to Bird in the things he could do on trumpet," says Freeman.

"I played with Roy [Eldridge] too, and he was the king of the trumpet, until Dizzy. He had this tone and this range, even though he was a little man, but just commanding."

By the '50s, Freeman was becoming something of a master himself. Thus Miles Davis tried to hire him as replacement for John Coltrane.

"Actually, my mother got the phone call, because I was in New York playing with a blues band," recalls Freeman. "And she said, 'Well, he has four kids, and he's got a wife,' so Miles said he understood.

"That probably would have been my big break, but I missed it."

Maybe, but Freeman simply went about concentrating on his art rather than his career.

"What I was trying to do was to play something that was a little more sophisticated than just what everybody else was playing," says Freeman. "I've always tried to do that, no matter what anybody said, and people did criticize me.

"They said I played out of tune, played a lot of wrong notes, a lot of weird ideas.

"But it didn't matter, because I didn't have to worry about the money—I wasn't making [hardly] any. I didn't have to worry about fame—I didn't have any. I was free.

"So I'd spend a lot of time in Calumet City, playing behind a curtain—you know, strip places. And I learned a lot of different music there.

"It didn't hardly pay anything, but it was better than just laying around saying how great you were.

"And I'd be playing a lot of Bird tunes, and almost every night somebody sitting out in the audience would sit up and notice and say, 'What is that guy doing back there?'"

The sweet irony is that the utter musical freedom of this life probably made possible Freeman's musical accomplishments of today. Not beholden to any one style or any single audience, he developed a language that somehow fuses ornate ballad playing of the '30s, hard-hitting bop of the '50s, and chromatically dissonant explorations of the avant garde. It's an incendiary, technically complex sound like no one else's.

In a way, Freeman's late-blooming fame comes at a perfect time, when his technique and his ability to improvise are at their peak.

"I'm not entirely happy with myself, but I'm kind of happy that my playing has improved in the last 20 years," says Freeman, who sometimes tours with his son, saxophonist Chico Freeman.

"And I hope my sound will improve some more.

"Basically, you've just got to pray and cry and suffer to try to find these ideas, because they're hidden. They're in the shadows, in the wind and in the breeze and in nature.

"And they're inside everyone. The art is bringing them out."

Freeman's Birth Year Is Wrong

Jan. 11, 2011

For generations, musicians from around the world have trekked to Chicago for a chance to play with the city's most revered living jazz artist—tenor saxophonist Von Freeman.

They gather Tuesday nights at the New Apartment Lounge, on East 75th Street, hoping the great Vonski (as everyone calls him) will invite them to the stage for a chorus or two.

But it turns out that all of Freeman's admirers around the globe—and all the reference books that detail his biography—have been wrong about a critical fact: Freeman's age. Moreover, Freeman himself has been mistaken about his true birth year, and even about the spelling of his name.

Check any musical reference work, and you'll see Freeman's birth date listed as Oct. 3, 1922, which would make him 88 years old. Some jazz dictionaries list his full name: Earl Lavon Freeman.

But the saxophonist's birth certificate, obtained by the Tribune, corrects the historical record, showing he was born Oct. 3, 1923, which means he's actually 87 years old. And the birth certificate shows that his first name is spelled "Earle," not "Earl."

None of this information in any way affects Freeman's position at the pinnacle of jazz in Chicago and around the globe. But because historical accuracy is essential to understanding an artist's life and work, every reference source on Freeman now will have to be fixed.

Why try to verify Freeman's age in the first place?

Because of something unexpected that happened New Year's Eve, at the Green Mill Jazz Club.

I had arrived early to cover the show Freeman was going to play with former Chicagoan Ed Petersen, another mighty tenor saxophonist. Just before the performance began, Freeman made a startling announcement. He told the folks sitting at the front of the room that he had discovered a note written by his late mother: It said he was a year older than he thought he was.

Immediately after the first set, I went up to the stage and asked Freeman to tell me more. He explained that the note said he was born in 1921, meaning he would turn 90 next October, a significant milestone not only for Freeman but for Chicago jazz. The new birth date, Freeman joked, would help explain why his legs were killing him—he was almost 90!

Later, in a phone conversation, he fleshed out the contents of the message from his mother: "It was just her writing a note to tell me about 'the way you and your brother's age is misplaced. You were [born] 1921 and he was 1919,'" added Freeman, referring to his elder sibling, the late drummer Eldridge "Bruz" Freeman.

But Von Freeman's birth certificate, on file at the Cook County Clerk's office, tells a different story: Freeman is actually a year younger than he thought, not a year older.

Why was Freeman's mother incorrect about his birth year?

"I never did get a chance to talk to her about this," Freeman said, noting that the document from his mother had recently disappeared amid piles of paper.

As for the spelling of his first name, Freeman says he always has used "Earl" and has no plans to change.

And though Freeman now knows he'll have to wait until 2013 to celebrate his 90th, he's not too perturbed about finding out his correct age.

"It really doesn't make any difference to me, one way or the other," Freeman said. "People have always classified me the wrong ways.

"People have me going to Wendell Phillips—that's the wrong high school," added Freeman, who indeed famously attended DuSable High School.

"I guess I'm infamously famous. . . . But it's wonderful, if you're alive and kicking."

Which Earle Lavon Freeman most definitely is—at age 87.

CHAPTER 12

Fred Anderson

The Velvet Lounge

Aug. 28, 1997

Admittedly, it's not a glamorous sight: a weather-beaten front door "protected" by badly rusted burglar bars.

There's a small barbecued chicken joint on one side, a tiny currency exchange on the other and—sandwiched between them at 2128 1/2 S. Indiana Ave.—a storefront bar that looks like something out of a particularly seedy Nelson Algren novel.

It's what happens inside the Velvet Lounge, on the Near South Side of Chicago, however, that draws music lovers from across the city and beyond.

Put your ear up to the bolted door, and you'll hear some of the most glorious music to come from the horn of a Chicago jazz musician. It's a huge, dark, rumbling sound rising up from the lowest reaches of the tenor saxophone, and it could belong to only one musician on Earth.

"I was just trying to get some practice in," says saxophonist-saloon owner Fred Anderson, admitting a visitor on a recent weekday afternoon.

"This is a never-ending process, you know," adds Anderson, who has been playing tenor for more than half a century. "The more I play,

Fig. 6 Fred Anderson: A native of Monroe, La., Chicago tenor saxophonist Anderson represented a bridge between the bebop music of his youth and the "free jazz" idioms of his followers. He also nurtured uncounted jazz artists at his indispensable and long-missed Velvet Lounge. Photo by Michael Jackson.

the more I realize that you've got to keep pushing ahead, finding new sounds, or you'll lose ground."

That has been Anderson's philosophy since the beginning, but perhaps not even he could have expected that, at this late stage of the game, his legend and his club both would be riding high.

Though Anderson never has been able to make enough money to work full time as a musician, though he never has had a manager, agent, record contract, publicist or any of the other trappings of success, he has become something of an icon to several generations of Chicago musicians.

More tangibly, the man who has been content to live his life well outside the margins of the music industry now has—incredibly—as least half a dozen independent records on the market, each a testament to his originality as tenor virtuoso and jazz improviser.

What's more, the Velvet Lounge, which used to present live music just twice a month, in recent years has emerged as an epicenter of musical experimentation on the South Side. From Thursday through Sunday evenings, some of the most accomplished virtuosos of the Chicago avant-garde converge there for rambunctious jam sessions.

And this year, after each night of the Chicago Jazz Festival in Grant Park, listeners will be heading to the Velvet Lounge for after-fest sessions.

"I don't know exactly why all this is happening right now," says Anderson, who surely never planned it. "I've been here all the time, but now I've got all these records out and all these people are listening to them.

"Maybe it's because people began to realize that I'm playing some basic stuff that they need to hear. I'm not trying to set the world on fire. I'm just trying to stay as close to the basics as possible and still try to be Fred Anderson."

That's saying quite a lot, considering that Anderson, who was born in Monroe, La., nearly 69 years ago, always has been one of the most individualistic of musicians.

"You know how Fred Anderson sounds today?" Chicago tenor saxophonist Von Freeman once said. "Well, that's how he always was playing, right from the beginning, right from the '60s.

"It's just taken 30-odd years for the rest of the world to catch up with him."

For Anderson, the journey has not been easy. Having come to Chicago with his mother at age 8 (his father had abandoned them in Louisiana), he picked up a tenor saxophone that belonged to a cousin and quickly found his life's calling.

A couple months of lessons and music theory was all the formal training he received, his real education coming from records by professors named Bird [Charlie Parker] and Prez [Lester Young].

"Hearing those recordings of Bird blew my mind," remembers Anderson, who first listened to the bebop god in '47.

"I knew I never could play that swift and precise way that he did, but I thought maybe at least I could learn to understand what he was doing. That's when I got serious."

Yet from the time he first heard those Parker recordings until the early '60s, Anderson played mostly for an audience of one: himself. Performing for adoring audiences and winning acclaim wasn't important to a musician who preferred to devote his energies to finding a musical voice, a harmonic language and an instrumental technique of his own.

By the time Anderson considered himself ready to appear in public, in the early '60s, the South Side of Chicago was rising again as a cauldron of musical innovation.

Neighborhood jazz clubs may have been folding in the wake of rock 'n' roll, but musicians such as Anderson, saxophonist Joseph Jarman, keyboardist Muhal Richard Abrams, reedist Roscoe Mitchell and others were forging new musical sounds and putting on concerts in churches, school auditoriums and anywhere else they could find.

Recordings from the period, such as Jarman's "Song For" (on Delmark), not only documented free-ranging improvisations by Jarman and Anderson but suggested the emergence of a new musical movement. By 1965, it would be consolidated as the Association for the Advancement of Creative Musicians (AACM), a collective of South Side performers, composers and ensembles who would show the world that there was more to playing jazz than reeling off endless variations of "I Got Rhythm."

The music of the AACM was harmonically audacious, rhythmically volatile and technically innovative, all the while bringing ancient rituals of African music into the mix. “Great Black Music, Ancient to Future” was the group’s motto, and Anderson found himself at the heart of the movement.

“Fred meant so much to me and the other guys going all the way back to the early AACM days,” recalls Jarman today.

“He would always be showing me things about the saxophone—how to get certain sounds, how to express certain ideas.

“His own music was very strange and beautiful, like nothing else, really. That’s why so many musicians hung around Fred. They wanted to figure out what it was he was doing and how they could learn from it.”

Listen to tapes of Anderson during this period, and you are hearing a thoroughly idiosyncratic approach to the tenor saxophone. Whether he was playing duets with Jarman or improvising in larger ensemble settings with trumpeter Billy Brimfield and drummer Steve McCall, Anderson was creating lines that leaped freely from one key to the next at a moment’s notice.

“Even in those days, everyone said I was playing far out, but I never could see it,” says Anderson.

“I was just trying to play some good, serious music, trying to have my own sound.

“I don’t just hear music in one key. I hear all these 12 tones together, they all relate, and you’ve got to deal with all their possibilities.

“And, anyway, no matter what they say about how far out the AACM music was, it was really all about blues, when you came down to it. It was playing blues in new ways.”

Though other AACM artists such as Anthony Braxton and the Art Ensemble of Chicago headed to Europe in the late ’60s and eventually returned as stars, Anderson didn’t get there until a decade later. But if his family obligations kept him hustling as a waiter by day and a musician by night, his art was maturing all the while.

That much is apparent from the recent reissue of recordings such as “The Missing Link” (Nessa) and “Fred Anderson and Steve McCall: Vintage Duets” (Okka Disk), which show a saxophonist delicately balancing tradition and innovation, euphony and dissonance.

“For me, Fred was the link between [traditional] saxophonists like Illinois Jacquet and a newer, more modern sound,” says Edward

Wilkerson Jr., a formidable Chicago tenorist who considers Anderson a major inspiration.

"His playing was also unusual because he was all over the instrument. Some players, you know, vary in sound from the top to the bottom of their horns, but Fred always was incredibly even in sound and tone everywhere on the instrument.

"And he always had this open attitude. He would allow young kids, like myself, to come up and play with him. He was a lot like Von [Freeman] in that way: The feeling was that music is for everyone, come and share in it."

In 1982, Anderson hung up his waiter's apron and bought the Velvet Lounge in what was then a down-and-out part of town. The South Side, after all, had fallen on hard times economically, and Anderson remembers his first decade of running the lounge as "weathering a storm."

But as the years passed, small record labels went out of their way to record Anderson's saxophone soliloquies. Records such as "Dark Day" (Message) and "Another Place" (Moers Music) point to the emergence of a tenor giant.

Anderson, an artistically restless soul, never stopped evolving musically. On recordings such as "Fred Anderson/DKV Trio" (Okka Disk) and "Fred" (Southport), the legendary musician can be heard pointing the way for younger avant-gardesmen such as reedist Ken Vandermark and bassist Kent Kessler.

Meanwhile, the Near South Side neighborhood in which Anderson set up shop 15 years ago also appears to be showing new signs of life. Lofts, banks, condos and the like are going up everywhere near the new McCormick Place South Building (a couple of blocks southeast of the Velvet Lounge).

The South Side as a whole, in fact, has been reawakening as a focal point for music, with audiences supporting performances at the refurbished Sutherland (47th Street and Drexel Boulevard), DuSable Museum of African-American History (on East 56th Place) and the South Shore Cultural Center (at 79th Street and the lakefront), among other venues.

"Things are definitely picking up, which is good for the bar," says Anderson, who still divides his time between playing music and running a neighborhood saloon.

"I'm glad I stayed in Chicago. That's where most of the great jazz musicians come from, anyway.

"The city's been good to me, and it looks like things are getting even better."

Straight, No Pretense

June 11, 1995

One by one, they stroll toward the back of the room, open their instrument cases, pick up their saxophones and trumpets and begin noodling scales, arpeggios, trills and whatnot.

Before you know it—before the crowd even has begun to move away from the bar and over to the impromptu performance area, just a few feet away—the show has started.

No introductions, no announcements, no spotlights, no emcees, no "sit back and relax" patter, no pretense whatsover. Just six musicians jamming, gloriously riffing on jazz themes as if no one were in the house at all, off in a dark corner of a cramped South Side bar.

Yet among those who cherish jazz improvisation at its most unadorned and authentic, the Sunday evening sessions at the Velvet Lounge, 2128 1/2 S. Indiana Ave., represent a cherished holdover from the days when jazz was more an art form than a business, when the music was more about communication than commerce.

In an era when jazz players are meticulously packaged and marketed by international record conglomerates, when major jazz shows routinely carry outsized signage for various corporate sponsors, the unpromoted and musically uncompromising sessions at the Velvet Lounge come as a breath of fresh air.

Perhaps that's why the Velvet Jam band has become one of the more talked-about ensembles in the city. Just last January, the band made a guest appearance at the annual Jazz Fair at the Blackstone Hotel, winning both critical accolades and noisy audience ovations.

Since then, Velvet Lounge owner and tenor saxophone virtuoso Fred Anderson has made the band's sessions into a weekly attraction, and the crowds have been growing steadily. What's more, this unlikely aggregation of neighborhood jazz musicians has been invited to play the 1995 Chicago Jazz Festival on Labor Day weekend, a coup for any jazz band, let alone one as unassuming and informal as this.

"I can tell you in two words why the Velvet Jam band is getting hot," says Billy Brimfield, the ensemble's veteran trumpet player.

"The two words are: Fred Anderson. What I know about music, I learned from Fred, and I bet the guys in the band feel the same."

Indeed, Anderson's freewheeling spirit and iconoclastic musical language inspire the house band and permeate the club, which is shoehorned into an ordinary block of buildings near the newly expanded McCormick Place. Just as the bar and its rambunctious ensemble thrive well outside Chicago's glittering downtown nightlife scene, so has Anderson built a formidable career almost totally outside the music industry.

Without benefit of a major-label recording contract, booking agent, personal manager, publicist or other handlers, Anderson has come to be regarded as one of the foremost avant-garde saxophonists in the Midwest, a name respected wherever innovative jazz is played around the world.

His remarkable journey began inauspiciously enough, 66 years ago in Monroe, La., "a smallish town a small ways outside New Orleans," he says, sitting on a slightly battered folding chair in the Velvet Lounge.

By age 6, explains Anderson, he had begun teaching himself boogie-woogie piano, "though I had no idea what I was doing."

A few years later, when his father had abandoned the family, his mother sent him to live with an aunt in Evanston, before she moved up to join him.

It wasn't until age 12, though, that Anderson picked up a tenor saxophone he found at his aunt's house. The instrument would fascinate him from that point forth.

"You know who taught me to play that saxophone?" asks Anderson, rhetorically. "Charlie Parker did. I used to hear his records on the radio, and he'd be playing 'Hootie's Blues' with Jay McShann's band.

"Then a friend played for me a record of Charlie Parker doing 'Now's the Time,' and that blew me away.

"I didn't know what Bird was doing, but I knew it was great. And I didn't care what stories they told about Charlie Parker, about drugs and all that. I wasn't interested in his lifestyle. It was the music that was so incredible."

By beginning his self-styled studies with the intricate music of Parker, the most revolutionary saxophonist of the '40s, Anderson clearly was placing himself at the cutting edge of jazz, a place he has remained ever since.

Yet it wasn't until the 1960s, after fully two decades of playing only for himself, that Anderson went public, offering his craggy, expansive, fiercely individualistic solos in tiny and forgotten Chicago clubs. Even at that early date, when Sun Ra and Joe Daley and Ornette Coleman were formulating a new, non-chordal musical language that eventually would be termed "free jazz," Anderson already was steeped in an innovative language of his own.

No doubt Anderson's solos—which leap unexpectedly from straight-ahead riffs to seemingly free-form improvisations, from hard-swing sections to utterly unmetered passages—could not have been easy for listeners to digest a generation ago.

Certainly the daring nature of Anderson's music was not going to draw large crowds for him; hence he supported his family by waiting tables, installing carpet, tending bar and otherwise earning a buck outside the music business.

As he once told Arlee Frantz and Yorke Corbin in a Cadence magazine interview, "I subsidized myself . . . I spent a lot of money . You had to be able to afford to play this music."

Oddly enough, however, the very hardships of the avant-garde musician's life—the spotty pay, the catch-as-catch-can gigs—may have been a saving grace for Anderson, at least so far as his music was concerned. For if Anderson wasn't able to support himself on music alone, neither would he have to compromise his ideas to meet the demands of record producers, music publishers, critics, publicists and the like.

If Anderson couldn't get many jobs playing his kind of music, he could help form an institution that would welcome and nurture new sounds. This he did with Muhal Richard Abrams, Steve McCall and several other Chicago avant-gardists, who 30 years ago banded together to establish the Association for the Advancement of Creative Musicians, an organization that gave jazz musicians new performance and recording opportunities precisely when the music was being cast aside by the commercial record industry.

Along the way, Anderson introduced to Chicago, and to the world of music, such estimable innovators as trombonist George Lewis, reed virtuoso Douglas Ewart, tenor saxophonist Chico Freeman, percussionist Hamid Drake, and many others who played with Anderson's bands in the '70s and '80s.

Over time, small but influential independent labels began to document Anderson's distinct tenor sound. On recordings such as "Dark Day" (Message), "Another Place" (Moers Music), "The Missing Link" (Nessa), and "Vintage Duets" (recently reissued on OkkaDisc), on compositions such as "Little Fox Run," "Ballad for Rita," "Bernice" and "The Birdhouse" (the latter named for a small, short-lived, North Side club that Anderson owned in the '70s), Anderson produced a sound and a musical language that were uniquely his.

Though there's no mistaking the larger-than-life, tough-tenor imprint of Chicago saxophone giant Gene Ammons, whom Anderson revered from his earliest days, there's a warmly melodic element to Anderson's playing, as well. Even in his most adventurous passages, Anderson's playing offers deeply expressive lyric lines, carefully considered phrases and an economy of means that instantly distinguish him from his colleagues.

Since he bought the Velvet Lounge in 1982, Anderson has been holding his jam sessions there and consistently attracting young musicians eager to sit in with him. The prestigious Jazz Masters Award he won in 1990 (sponsored by Arts Midwest, an arts advocacy group based in Minneapolis), only enhanced his reputation among up-and-coming players searching for a bit of guidance.

"I keep asking the young musicians, 'What do you want to play with me for?' but they just keep coming," says Anderson.

Adds Brimfield, "I'll tell you why they come. They know there's only so much you can learn in a music school. Jazz, you see, is not an academic art. It's a very creative art, a spiritual art and, as a wise man once said, you can't teach spirituality.

"So you've got to learn by playing with the big boys. That's how I learned—Fred Anderson was my conservatory. And for a lot of the young cats, that's what the Velvet Lounge is all about."

CHAPTER 13

Herbie Hancock

Herbie's Blues

March 21, 2004

After a grueling two months playing one-nighters around the world, Herbie Hancock ought to be exhausted, yet he can't wait to get his hands on a piano.

So he seats himself at the 9-foot concert grand that dominates the living room of his Los Angeles home, and his fingers immediately—almost instinctively—begin wandering the keys.

With his right hand slowly caressing the quiet notes up high and the left hand answering softly down below, he's not so much playing a tune as communing with himself, in harmony and rhythm. Lost in thought, he articulates no discernible melody or recognizable chord changes, yet the sound is pure Herbie: mysterious, lyrical, seductive.

For more than 40 years, Hancock, who has scheduled a week of Chicago performances next month at Orchestra Hall and other venues, has been beguiling audiences with precisely this disarming brand of piano jazz, a self-styled idiom that can veer from sublime sophistication to danceable accessibility at the drop of a sixteenth note. His knack for careering between complexity and simplicity, between art and entertainment, has won him nine Grammys, three gold and two

Fig. 7 Herbie Hancock: The protean pianist-composer-bandleader credits the sounds he heard growing up on the South Side of Chicago for planting the seeds of his earliest hit, "Watermelon Man," and a lifetime of genre-bending experimentation. Photo by Steve Jurvetson.

platinum records, one Oscar and enough plaques to cover several walls of his home, a short stroll from the Sunset Strip.

Yet on this typically golden California day—the midday sun is flooding in through his picture window and glinting off the top of his ebony piano—Hancock despairs for the very jazz world that catapulted a talented kid from a tough Chicago neighborhood to unanticipated stardom.

He realizes that practically every institution that enabled his talent to blossom—nightclubs, record labels, radio stations, concert halls, schools—has been diminished, at least so far as jazz is concerned, during the long arc of his triumph. Somewhere along the way, jazz, the music that made him famous at age 23 and revered around the world ever since, got shoved into the margins of American culture.

All that remains are the remnants of what once was the jazz industry in America, and Hancock grieves for the next talented youngster who won't transcend a rough-and-tumble childhood the way he did.

"It's all about money now, how the radio stations and the record companies and everyone else can make money putting out the hits as fast as they can," says Hancock, after stepping away from the piano and leading a visitor to his upstairs studio.

"When one company owns 65 percent of radio, when 'smooth jazz' is pushing out the core music, when musicians have to write tunes to fit the formats of the radio stations to get anyone to listen to them, that's backward, and that's dangerous. It's bad for the artists, it's bad for the listeners, it's bad for humanity."

Not the sentiments one might expect from an artist whose oft-joyous music—despite its famously kaleidoscopic changes in style and direction—always has been optimistic and life-affirming at its center.

But Hancock, who turns 64 next month, has not given up on jazz or even on its chances of surviving into its second century. He simply rages against the forces he sees as conspiring against the music that gave him everything and hopes that someone, somewhere, will hit upon a way to keep it alive in America.

Herbie Hancock does not need a bar graph to understand the way the music business in America is edging jazz into a kind of oblivion.

Outside of long-standing jazz capitals such as Chicago, New York, New Orleans and San Francisco, bona fide jazz clubs are scarce in the U.S., and musicians who can make a living playing this intricate but profoundly American music are an endangered species, at best.

Among the major record labels, only one—Blue Note—can be said to maintain a thriving roster of jazz recording artists. Even mighty Columbia Records, once the home of Miles Davis and Dave Brubeck, has decimated its roster of jazz musicians, with no less a figure than Wynton Marsalis recently ending a two-decade career there and switching to Blue Note. The vast majority of jazz musicians record for tiny independent labels that consider CD sales of 3,000 copies a hit and 6,000 copies a blockbuster.

Jazz record sales in America hover around 2 to 3 percent of total album sales, according to the Recording Industry Association of America, and the increasingly popular phenomenon of computer downloading stands to diminish even that.

The consolidation of radio-station ownership into a few conglomerates, with Clear Channel Radio dominating the market, has long favored easily digested, mass-appeal music, relegating jazz to the ghetto of public radio stations on FM and dreadful-sounding outlets on AM, both with slender audiences. Even in Chicago, revered around the world as a jazz nexus since at least the Roaring '20s, not a single radio station offers the music around the clock, though WBEZ 91.5 FM and WDCB 90.9 FM program jazz during parts of the broadcast day.

On purely artistic terms jazz remains remarkably robust, with gifted younger players such as reedist Ken Vandermark in Chicago, trumpeter Maurice Brown in New Orleans and pianist Matthew Shipp in New York brilliantly redefining the music on their own, fiercely personal terms. Yet the newcomers have succeeded in building audiences in spite of the crumbling jazz industry, not because of it.

"Some months, our business is half of what it used to be," says Bob Koester, owner of the Jazz Record Mart, billed as the largest such store in the world, and Delmark Records, one of the most respected and enduring independent labels in the country. "At Delmark, we're deleting titles we'd rather not, simply because people aren't buying them.

"In some record stores, they're giving jazz half the space they once did, which makes it harder to sell our recordings. And our sales on new product is terrible. Most of our recent releases sold between 656 and 2,148 copies."

To get by, many jazz musicians sell their discs from the bandstand, play gigs for comparatively low fees and painstakingly book their own tours. They can make a living in music but enjoy nothing close to the rewards and vast audience that Hancock accrued after just a few years in the business.

Born in Chicago on April 12, 1940, Herbert Jeffrey Hancock grew up in various apartments between 45th Street and 62nd Street on the

South Side, showing an interest in the piano at age 6 and receiving a $5 wreck of an instrument for his 7th birthday.

He began formal lessons a few months later, after his parents had saved up enough money to afford them, and his progress was so swift that by age 11 he had won a piano competition to play the first movement of a Mozart Piano Concerto in B-Flat Major with the Chicago Symphony Orchestra. When CSO managers informed him that they didn't want him to perform that concerto, the young pianist simply spent a few weeks mastering Mozart's "Coronation" Concerto in D Major, playing it in a pair of short pants in his Orchestra Hall debut.

For all of Hancock's talents, however, growing up in a South Side tenement was not easy. Though his father, who never finished high school, worked practically without pause, his income as owner of a small grocery store and later as a government meat inspector, was not sufficient to make ends meet without taking in roomers. So Hancock's parents, Wayman and Winnie, vied for space in a small apartment with their three kids—Wayman Jr., Herbie and Jean—and a recurrent population of boarders.

"It wasn't exactly the projects, but it was just barely a cut above that," recalls Hancock, who witnessed stabbings in his neighborhood and routinely saw gang members, drug pushers and numbers peddlers working the block. At age 6, he was robbed at gunpoint on his newspaper-delivery route.

But he found escape in music, announcing in an article in a neighborhood newspaper, at the time of his CSO debut, that he intended to become a concert pianist.

"He practiced piano so much I used to tell him, 'Please, Herbie, let the damn piano alone—go out and play with somebody,'" his father recalled in a 1997 Tribune interview (Wayman Hancock died in 2001, at age 90, and his widow, Winnie, lives in a Chicago-area nursing home).

With Count Basie, Duke Ellington and Fats Waller blasting on the record player at home, nightclubs such as the Checkerboard Lounge and Theresa's Lounge swinging along the 43d Street corridor nearby and jazz giants such as Miles Davis and John Coltrane playing the Regal Theatre down the block, Hancock discovered a music quite apart from Mozart's concertos. But to Hancock the new sounds proved as mysterious as they were alluring, for he could not understand how these jazz geniuses invented so much glorious art—on the spot—without a note of music in front of them.

For a youngster who had been trained in Bach, Beethoven and Brahms, the thought of improvising an entire performance seemed incomprehensible at best, unachievable at worst. Yet once Hancock heard kids his age playing jazz at Hyde Park High School, which counted among its musical alumni the legendary Mel Torme, he leapt right in. Doubly blessed with a keen ear and an ability to learn at phenomenal speed, Hancock began imitating the recordings of pianist George Shearing, which he played over and over on the phonograph at home until he knew the solos note for note.

"It didn't take long before he was known as the top musician in the school," recalls his older brother, Wayman Hancock Jr., a retired salesman of computer supplies who lives in the Chicago area (their younger sister, Jean, died in the 1985 crash of Delta Flight 191 in Dallas).

"Herbie wrote music, he played all these different instruments, he formed a doo-wop group," marvels Wayman, "and with all that, he still graduated school two years ahead of time."

By 16, the precocious teenager was majoring in electrical engineering at Grinnell College, a small liberal arts school in Iowa, but he couldn't kid himself much longer: He was no more going to be an electrical engineer than he was going to ride a spaceship to the moon.

"The straw that broke the camel's back was in 1957, my second year at Grinnell, when I decided to put together a big band," says Hancock, smiling at the memory. "Now this is at Grinnell, where I had these 16 musicians who didn't really know how to play jazz. So I had to rehearse all the sections of the band myself and teach them how to phrase. And that was after I had to listen to all these Count Basie records and copy the parts to write up the charts.

"It trained my ear like crazy, but I never went to classes, so I was getting a D in one class and everything else I was flunking—the handwriting was on the wall," he continues. "I saw what was driving me, what was pulling me like a magnet, where my real heart was, and as much as I liked science, jazz was the thing."

After graduating from Grinnell as a music major in 1960, Hancock returned to his old summer job at the Chicago Post Office but quickly launched one of the most stunning ascents in modern jazz history.

By October, he was hired to accompany the regal tenor saxophonist Coleman Hawkins, one of the pioneers of that instrument in jazz, in a Chicago nightclub. And that December, when the famed New York trumpeter Donald Byrd came to town and suddenly needed a sub for a pianist who had ducked out on him, Byrd decided to give Hancock an audition.

"I completely freaked out when I heard this kid," remembers Byrd, 71, speaking from his New Jersey home. "He was already trying to get into new things, new sounds, new chords. I was amazed by how precocious he was, how much intelligence he had, how much integrity.

"In fact, when my original pianist, Duke Pearson, finally showed up for the gig, I said to him, 'You left me, you abandoned the band—and I'm so happy that you did that I'm giving you a first-class airplane ticket back to New York. Now get the hell out of here.' So Pearson went to New York, and Herbie joined me on the road."

Byrd was so smitten with Hancock's talent that he invited the 20-year-old to live in his New York apartment, and by 1962 had set about getting Hancock a date to cut his own record on one of the most artistically dynamic labels in jazz, Blue Note.

Knowing that Blue Note would be reluctant to record an unknown artist, Byrd called Alfred Lion, the founder of the record label, and told him that Hancock had been drafted and wanted to make a record before going into the Army.

"That was the scheme," laughs Hancock now. "And Lion said OK."

Hancock's aptly named debut, "Takin' Off," made history, and not only because Lion allowed Hancock to build the entire recording on original tunes, a strategy virtually unheard of in a music business that typically tries to introduce young artists with well-worn hits. Equally important, the recording opened with Hancock's "Watermelon Man," which soon would become one of the biggest hits of the decade and an enduring jazz classic.

With its funk-tinged rhythms, coyly lilting melody and unpretentious, down-home sensibility, the tune ascended the charts in the summer of '62. The following year, when bandleader Mongo Santamaria recorded an Afro-Cuban version, "Watermelon Man" became nearly inescapable in urban America, cracking Billboard's Top 10. Eventually, more than 200 artists recorded it.

"I was walking down the street, and all I would hear coming out of people's windows was 'Watermelon Man,'" remembers Hancock. "What a feeling—I was 23 years old."

He says that when he wrote the song, he thought of his South Side neighborhood and a particular gentleman who would come by his building at 45th Street and South Park Way (now South King Drive).

"He'd sing, 'Wateh-meh-LONE, wateh-meh-LONE,'" Hancock says. "And the melody came from the women calling out from the porches: 'Hey, watermelon man,' and from the watermelon man's song.

"Now this is before James Brown sang, 'I'm Black and I'm proud,' before the whole pride thing. So watermelon was one of those things that we were ashamed of. I didn't know if I should call the tune 'Watermelon Man,' but I couldn't be that kind of a coward. So I just said to myself, 'There's nothing wrong with a watermelon man,' and I stood by it."

To a lesser artist, "Watermelon Man" might have afforded a quickly fleeting 15 minutes of fame, but to Hancock it was just the first step in what would be an extraordinary, decades-long artistic evolution. His potential rings out from every track of "Takin' Off," but specifically in the exquisite warmth of his tone, borne of years of classical training, the easy fluidity of his technique and the harmonic invention that drives his still youthful pianism.

Moreover, he was able to hold his own against the top-notch Blue Note artists who had agreed to join him for his debut as leader, including the veteran tenor saxophonist Dexter Gordon and the phenomenal young trumpeter Freddie Hubbard. With Billy Higgins playing drums and Butch Warren on bass, Hancock was forging a diverse range of musical talent into a genuinely cohesive unit, signaling his development from prodigy to artist.

Though conventional wisdom has given much of the credit for the freshness of Hancock's early playing to Chris Anderson, a pianist with whom Hancock briefly had studied in Chicago during the summer of 1961, Anderson knows better. "He already sounded like that when he came to me," says Anderson, 78, a visionary musician who played with Charlie Parker and long has lived in obscurity in New York.

"Herbie had his own style developing for a long time, before he even recorded for Blue Note. I heard him early in Chicago, and I don't think you can give anyone else credit for that.

"In fact, when he first came to me, I was surprised at how much alike we both sounded. And he had studied music a lot more than I had."

Like Anderson, Hancock had been developing an impressively sophisticated harmonic language that flowered at Blue Note. The ingenuity of his arrangements on "Inventions and Dimensions" (1963), the lyric beauty of tunes such as "Oliloqui Valley" and "Cantaloupe Island" on the masterpiece "Empyrean Isles" (1964) and the utter originality of compositions such as "The Eye of the Hurricane" and the title track on the great "Maiden Voyage" (1965) established Hancock as one of the most promising young pianist-composers of the era.

But for all the breakthroughs of Hancock's Blue Note albums, the greater revolution came with his work in Miles Davis' second great quintet. Davis, who throughout his career had shown an uncanny ability to hire players on the precipice of greatness, brought Hancock on board in 1963. With bassist Ron Carter and the prodigious drummer Tony Williams powering what would become the most honored rhythm section of the decade, and with the innovative reedist-composer Wayne Shorter joining Davis on the front line, the band opened up previously unimagined possibilities for jazz improvisation.

During their 5 1/2 years of recording and performing together, they also brought extraordinary vitality to a jazz world already reeling from the effects of emerging, teen-oriented rock 'n' roll. Though a music as sophisticated and rhythmically unpredictable as these Davis sets never was going to challenge the Beatles for record sales or celebrity, it proved that there was still plenty of invention and potential left in an art form born at the dawn of the 20th Century—eons ago, by the standards of perpetually changing American popular taste.

Nowhere is the explosive character of this band more palpable than in live sessions recorded at Chicago's pint-sized, long-deceased Plugged Nickel jazz club, at 1321 N. Wells St., on Dec. 22 and 23, 1965. A truncated recording of these fabled Plugged Nickel dates didn't come out until 1982, and the complete sessions were not released until 1995. But in retrospect this music shows Davis and friends torching the long-accepted rules for jazz improvisation.

No longer were the players observing 32-bar choruses or politely waiting for one another to solo, nor were they even observing the melodic contours and harmonic underpinnings of the standards they were performing. In fact, they were veering so far from the template of tunes such as "My Funny Valentine" and "If I Were a Bell" that the originals often were rendered unrecognizable, the sheer fluidity of the group improvisation and the freedom of the instrumental dialogues far upstaging the tunes themselves.

If this music stunned audiences, it forever changed Hancock, up-ending everything he thought he knew about jazz.

"What happened was that, by 1965, everyone in Miles' band got so comfortable playing together that we knew all the signals, we knew what to expect from each other, we knew that when a certain guy did this, he would follow it with that, and it became boring," says Hancock. "Well, not really boring, but almost boring. But at least we knew that we had to do something to break out of that."

He recalls that it was drummer Williams who came up with an idea. "He said, 'Look, on this next gig at the Plugged Nickel, I'm not going to play the things that you expect. I ain't going to do that.' And I said, 'I'm going to do the same thing. I'm not going to play anything that leads to what you expect it to lead to.' And we decided to call it 'anti-music.'

"Miles was cool with that, so we walk into the Plugged Nickel the first day, and what do we see? A bunch of tape recorders. And Tony looked at everyone and said, 'Oh, no, it's the worst time.' Because we knew that these people, this audience, were just going to be guinea pigs for a rebirth, a painful rebirth of this band. And they were going to have to suffer through that, for the good of all."

There was more pleasure than pain to be had, however, for the "Plugged Nickel" sessions not only opened up a new era in ensemble improvisation but proved to Hancock that he could adjust—on the spot—to practically any musical ideas swirling around him.

Davis, in particular, was in awe of Hancock's development during these years, noting in his memoirs: "A lot of times I would let Herbie play no chords at all, just solo in the middle register and [let] the bass anchor that . . . because Herbie knew he could do that. See, Herbie was the step after Bud Powell and Thelonious Monk, and I haven't heard anybody yet who has come after him."

The band thrived because "there was no jousting over who's got the power," says Shorter from his Florida home, taking a brief pause from a still intense schedule of international touring. "It was not that kind of competition going on.

"We never entertained any fear of risk. We didn't worry about whether we went a little too far. We felt we never went far enough."

By the time the group disbanded in 1968—because, according to Davis' memoirs, most of the players wanted to go in different musical directions—Hancock had been transformed.

"I used to have this kind of tunnel vision about jazz, but Miles totally opened me up," says Hancock. "When we'd be hanging, I'd notice that Miles would have all these albums strewn about the room and lying on his bed. He'd have James Brown and Jimi Hendrix and flamenco guitarists and the classical pianist Arturo Benedetti Michelangeli. So when I saw that Miles, who to me was the epitome of cool, was open to all that different music, I realized that it was cool for me to be open to it too."

The rush of new ideas inexorably led to Hancock's fundamental rethinking of his art, and when he released his breakthrough electric album "Head Hunters," in 1972, he instantly became one of the biggest pop stars of the day, his fame rivaling that of Davis himself. The LP took its place as the biggest-selling album by a jazz artist up to that date, and though it still makes some purists scoff, its nearly symphonic tapestry of electric keyboards and synthesizers, electric bass and arsenal of ancient and modern percussion instruments made it one of the defining funk releases of the '70s.

Though critics began blasting away at Hancock's "selling out" of the jazz tradition, he tuned out the din, anchored by his embrace of Buddhism and what he considers his constant need to search for new sounds.

"I was being open, when the critics were being closed," asserts Hancock. "I believed in what I was doing, I was still improvising, I was still challenging myself, and I was still learning. So that's their problem, not mine.

"I mean, if they didn't like what I was doing, that's one thing. But what I picked up most of the time was that they didn't like the fact that I was doing it. Now who are they to tell me what I was supposed to be doing? I'm the one who decides that, not [critic] Leonard Feather.

"Some articles would say, 'Well, he's doing it because he wants to sell records.' That wasn't why I was doing it. I was doing it because it was a part of me that I wanted to explore.

"Look—it's Black music, it's part of my background, give me a break. I'm Black. This is our stuff."

In truth, the tension between Hancock and the self-appointed guardians of jazz convention said more about the plight of the music during the fusion-driven 1970s than it did about Hancock's art or his journey. For although much, if not most, of the jazz-pop ventures of the period justly have been forgotten, Hancock's efforts generally were a cut above.

By this time, the business of jazz was in serious trouble. All around them, jazz devotees saw clubs folding, record labels dropping jazz artists and radio stations changing their formats to youth- oriented rock. The situation became so dire that jazz players across the country began presenting their music in churches, school auditoriums, lofts and anyplace else that would have them. They formed organizations such as the Association for the Advancement of Creative Musicians in Chicago and the Black Artists' Group in St. Louis, which attempted to pick up where the clubs and the record companies left off.

Still, the demise of such storied Chicago rooms as the Blue Note and the London House in the Loop, the Crown Propeller Lounge and Rhumboogie Club on the South Side and the Plugged Nickel and High Note on the North Side took its toll. As their world faded from the marketplace, jazz lovers found themselves powerless to do a great deal about it.

But Hancock continued to invent, bringing turntable-scratching and synthesized, techno-blast rhythms into the mix with his "Future Shock" album (1983) and its hit dance single, "Rockit"; combining electric keyboards with Foday Musa Suso's vocal chants and an Afro-Cuban rhythm section on "Jazz Africa" (1986); and returning to acoustic work with recordings such as his sublime—though decidedly unconventional—duets with Shorter on "1+1" (1997).

Along the way, there were disappointments as well, most notoriously the disco-driven "Feets, Don't Fail Me Now" (1979), with its relentlessly hammering backbeats and strangely lugubrious vocals.

But even Hancock's critics had to acknowledge that the man was willing to try anything once, and his small role playing a jazz pianist in

Bertrand Tavernier's 1986 film "'Round Midnight" won him not only another measure of visibility but an Oscar for his haunting, elegiac score.

Looking back on it, the critical and popular success of "'Round Midnight," arguably the greatest jazz feature film ever made, raised the curtain for what seemed a promising new era in acoustic jazz. It was in the mid-'80s, after all, that trumpeter Wynton Marsalis burst onto the scene, getting a running start by playing in Hancock's V.S.O.P. band.

Marsalis' massive success helped launch a bevy of similarly gifted artists, among them trumpeter Nicholas Payton, pianist Marcus Roberts, drummer Herlin Riley and saxophonist Wess Anderson.

But the jazz bubble of the '90s was to burst right along with the stock market. Although a new generation of players began attracting young people back to the music, most eventually lost their major-label recording contracts when the big record companies slashed their jazz departments to cut costs. If the new millennium has demonstrated anything about the business of music, it has been the lionization of increasingly bland, retro performers such as Norah Jones and Diana Krall, whose unadventurous warblings pull down huge profits, leaving the real jazz musicians virtually locked out of the cultural mainstream in America.

"To me, jazz, in order to be jazz, it must evolve," says Hancock. "It's part of its nature. And when you don't have the evolution of music, then it's not going to have the spirit of jazz anymore. Those people in the past played the music that they created. At best, we can only be second best at trying to emulate what they did. And I don't see young people being encouraged to find their own voice."

He says he's also disappointed in what has happened in radio: "[It's] not broadcasting anymore—it's narrow-casting. I see people getting their music from the Internet, which means that people can go directly to what they want to hear. So how do they get exposed to music they don't know they want to hear, the way you used to on radio?

"[It] keeps people confined within their own little worlds. It's like being in jail."

As night falls in Los Angeles, Hancock still is riffing on music in America, bemoaning the demise of a jazz culture that once enabled charismatic players such as Davis to reach a wide audience without necessarily diluting their art. Yet Hancock's own travels in music proceed apace, as the perpetually ringing phone attests.

The celebrated producer Phil Ramone is calling to see if Hancock can participate in a tribute concert to Sting; a TV producer wants to make an appointment to talk about a new TV animation program featuring Hancock's voiceovers; and all manner of agents, bookers and managers are pleading for a bit of his time.

Meanwhile, Hancock's longtime assistant, Melinda Murphy, and his daughter, Jessica Hancock, work the phones, while his wife of 35 years, Gigi, pops into his studio occasionally to remind him that guests will be arriving soon.

No matter how the business of jazz develops—or recedes—in coming years, there's no question that Hancock will be out there swinging.

"I don't think you're going to see Herbie becoming a victim of the status quo," says Shorter. "You won't see him dwelling on the past or being unable to let go of something from before."

Indeed, Hancock, who says he has been approached to write his memoirs, has declined because "I've got a few more pages to turn before I do that.

"You know, when I perform, I see all these young people in the audience," says Hancock, who exudes a sense of youthfulness not uncommon among the most enduring jazz musicians. "And I'm not talking about 20 percent of them that are young—I'm talking about half or more that are young people.

"So if they're coming to hear music from a 64-year-old guy, that tells me there's an audience out there, but they're clearly not being served by radio or the recording scene or the rest of it.

"After the old guys like me are gone, who's going to play for the kids next?"

Dark Days

Nov. 12, 2014

Herbie Hancock has lived many lives in music.

In 1952, at age 11, he made his bow with the Chicago Symphony Orchestra, playing a Mozart piano concerto in Orchestra Hall, cheered on by a hometown audience.

A decade later, his debut album—the well-named "Takin' Off"—instantly made him a force in jazz, its single "Watermelon Man" famously recorded by Mongo Santamaria and uncounted other artists.

Within a year, Hancock was playing in what would become Miles Davis' second great quintet, thereafter fronting his groundbreaking, Afro-centric Mwandishi band in the early 1970s before diving into funk music later in the decade with his popular Head Hunters ensemble. Then Hancock moved on to techno with his "Future Shock" album and its huge single, "Rockit," in the 1980s.

And if anyone wondered whether he was still around, in 2008 he took the Grammy Award for album of the year for "River: The Joni Letters," his tribute to the songwriting of Joni Mitchell.

Did we mention that he also won an Oscar for best original score for Bertrand Tavernier's "'Round Midnight," the greatest jazz film ever made?

Today, at 74, Hancock has decided to revisit those moments, and many more, in a lyrical, startlingly candid autobiography, "Possibilities" (written with Lisa Dickey), which frankly explains that his life has not been an endless run of artistic triumphs and awards ceremonies. Hancock describes those, of course, but he also proves quite frank in discussing what he considers his own shortcomings, setbacks and losses.

Two weeks ago, Hancock sat down with me at the Union League Club in the Loop to reminisce before an audience as part of its long-running Authors Group Program. Toward the end of our conversation, I asked Hancock why he had decided to be so open about his life, though I didn't specify the big, dark revelation of the book.

He did.

"One of the difficulties I had in writing stories for this book was the fact that at one time I had a substance-abuse problem—and it was with crack," said Hancock, who had begun smoking it in the mid-1990s. "And I never told anybody that. As a matter of fact, I tried to suppress that from my own memory, because I was so embarrassed and ashamed about it.

"This went on for about a couple years. . . . Because I was embarrassed, I tried to keep it from my family, I tried to keep it from the music, and so there were months between forays. But it started with me being just curious about cocaine in that form."

As in the book, Hancock acknowledged that he had been no stranger to cocaine before then, the drug ubiquitous in the freewheeling 1960s and thereafter.

"So I knew about cocaine," he continued. "But I was wondering, what is this about, smoking it, that everybody is kind of going nuts about?

"Well, I found out that sometimes curiosity kills the cat. And I realized at that first time [smoking crack] that I should have never done this."

Eventually, Hancock's family found out and confronted him as he came home after another binge. Hancock describes what happened in a riveting scene in the book.

"It all just came crashing down on me in that moment, and I burst into tears," he writes, recalling that his wife, Gigi, told him that she knew what was going on. "Gigi's eyes were red from crying. 'Herbie, I'm not going to watch you die,' she said. 'If you continue this way, you are going to have to move out.' I just looked at her, my heart aching. . . . This was an intervention, and I was so embarrassed, but there was another feeling creeping in, too: relief."

Hancock checked into rehab that night late in 1999, and since 2000 he has been free of drugs, alcohol and smoking, he said. But considering his status as one of the most universally beloved figures in jazz, as well as one of the most innovative, why did he choose to reveal this? Why not just move on with life, preserving a rather exalted reputation?

"With this book, I thought this was a great opportunity to turn poison into medicine—that's a phrase from Buddhism," said Hancock, who has been practicing that faith for more than four decades.

"And that is to take this circumstance" and draw something positive from it, added Hancock. "I mean, people don't believe, wouldn't believe, that I actually went to that [smoking crack cocaine]. Herbie's not that kind of guy, right? . . . There is no 'that kind of guy' that is immune to substance abuse.

"And there are different forms of that, too, of course. And it wasn't a relief from anything, something missing from my life. It was curiosity. But, anyway, I wrestled with that demon and I conquered it. . . . And I thought this book is going to be an opportunity perhaps to help someone else who may be struggling with some kind of addiction."

"Possibilities" surely is that, but it's much more, as well. The volume takes us inside Hancock's creative process, explaining how and why he constantly changed artistic directions, and how he tried to stay true to the inquisitiveness that is at the core of any great jazz musician's art. Above all, Hancock attributes his fearlessness in investigating musical genres unfamiliar to him to the influence of Davis, who emerges as Hancock's guiding spirit throughout the book.

"Miles was a great mentor that taught me a lot of lessons by not actually teaching me," Hancock said, somewhat paradoxically. Then he hastened to explain.

"You know where a lot of teachers just talk about hierarchal viewpoint, where the teacher presents him or herself as the person who knows, and the student doesn't know? Miles wasn't like that. Miles freely worked together with his musicians. As a matter of fact, he encouraged us to help shape the sound of the band. And he told us that he paid us not just to play perfect all the time, and not just to be in the background, but he paid us to work on stuff all the time and explore new territory.

"I mean, how many bosses tell you to explore new territory? It doesn't happen that often."

Once our conversation had turned to Davis, Hancock riffed freely, taking on criticisms that are still hurled at the trumpeter long after his death in 1991, at age 65.

Hancock cited Davis' "defiance in the way that he really wanted to always present the best show he could for an audience, even if it meant that he would have to—in order to have a musical dialogue along with the drummer—he would face the drummer, which would mean he would have his back to the audience, right? Well, critics . . . would say, 'You know Miles, he never respected people, he's a racist, and he's always turning his back to the audience,' and things like that.

"No. Every conductor in the world that I know, that conducts any orchestra, always turns his back to the audience, because he has to face the orchestra. That's what Miles was doing."

Perhaps because Hancock was just in his early 20s when he began working with Davis, the trumpeter's boldness shaped who Hancock became as a mature artist: a searcher. Hancock didn't always succeed: His rippy Mwandishi band, for instance, became too rarefied to reach much of audience: "We were requiring a tremendous amount of attention and patience from our listeners," writes Hancock in the book. "No wonder our audience was limited."

But more than many musicians, Hancock always has been willing to risk failure, then risk it again. So perhaps we shouldn't be surprised that he discloses so much about himself in "Possibilities." As always, he's out there on a limb, risking it all.

CHAPTER 14

Kelan Phil Cohran

Inspiring Generations

June 30, 2017

Chaka Khan and Earth, Wind & Fire's Maurice White studied with him.

The globally influential Association for the Advancement of Creative Musicians (AACM) was co-founded by him.

And generations of musicians drew inspiration from the pioneering work of Chicago composer and multi-instrumentalist Kelan Phil Cohran. He died Wednesday at the University of Chicago Medical Center at 90, said his son Tycho Cohran.

"He was a major contributor to the whole structure and the idea" of the AACM, said Muhal Richard Abrams, another co-founder of an organization that changed the course of music starting in 1965.

"I think he had a profound influence on many organized groups," added Abrams. "They more or less cut their teeth in Chicago, and their major influence was Phil Cohran."

Said Chicago percussionist-bandleader Kahil El'Zabar, who helped organize a 90th birthday tribute to Cohran on May 8 at St. Adalbert's Church on West 17th Street: "He was an innovative cultural institution unto himself."

That's not an exaggeration, considering that Cohran played and recorded with the groundbreaking Sun Ra Arkestra in the late 1950s;

invented an instrument he dubbed the Frankiphone—a version of an African kalimba or "thumb piano," which White brought to Earth, Wind & Fire; created the Affro-Arts Theater, which in the 1960s was a South Side epicenter of experimental arts; and founded the Artistic Heritage Ensemble, which influenced bands as far-flung as El'Zabar's avant-garde Ethnic Heritage Ensemble and Earth, Wind & Fire.

"He was definitely one of my mentors at an early age," said Roscoe Mitchell, a founder of the pioneering Art Ensemble of Chicago, one of the first AACM bands to attain international acclaim. "I had nothing but respect for him as a musician and a teacher."

Indeed, the two roles were inseparable to Cohran, whose long career in music essentially linked early jazz traditions to its most contemporary off-shoots.

Born May 8, 1927, in Oxford, Miss., Cohran moved with his family to St. Louis when he was about 10, immersing himself in the city's robust jazz scene and playing alongside trumpeter Clark Terry in the late 1940s. Pianist-bandleader Jay McShann, who had given a young Charlie Parker his first major job, hired trumpeter Cohran, and "that was where I really learned to swing," Cohran told DownBeat magazine in 1984. "The crowds would be so thick, people would be falling on top of you and drinking and everything; it got so bad you'd have to lean back and play."

Cohran was drafted into the military in 1950, after his service eventually gravitating to Chicago, where he played with saxophone titan Johnny Griffin and pianist Ike Cole (Nat King Cole's brother), among others.

The ears-wide-open, "space is the place" aesthetic of Sun Ra immediately appealed to Cohran's spirit of musical daring. But when Ra left Chicago in the early 1960s, Cohran stayed, playing multiple instruments in Abrams' Experimental Band (a precursor of the AACM).

On May 8, 1965—Cohran's birthday—the founders of the AACM met in his East 75th Street apartment to create the AACM as a means for presenting their own music, in their own venues, at a time when jazz clubs were shuttering around Chicago and across the country.

"We said: Why do we go through this?" Cohran told the Tribune in 2015 as he walked through "Free at First," an exhibition marking the AACM's 50th anniversary at the DuSable Museum of African American History.

"Why don't we do something about it?

"Our problem was we'd been studying instruments of other people," added Cohran, referring to traditional Western pianos, violins and the like. "We needed to study our own and to create our own."

Cohran did exactly that with the Frankiphone and, like other AACM progenitors, presented his Artistic Heritage Ensemble in venues that he found or created.

He took the idea a step further in the late 1960s, establishing the Affro-Arts Theater on South Drexel Boulevard as a nexus for music, drama, comedy, instruction and political activism. Khan and White learned there.

"Once you stepped inside the theater," Khan said in a 2013 Tribune interview, "it took you into a really high place spiritually."

Civil rights activist Stokely Carmichael appeared at the theater, the place subsequently shut down by Mayor Richard J. Daley.

A sign then posted on the theater marquee read: "We are closed by deceit—Philip Cohran & the Artistic Heritage Ensemble."

Cohran continued to rehearse, teach, perform, inspire and expand his universe, developing expertise in astronomy, nutrition and other seemingly far-flung disciplines.

Perhaps no ensemble was more profoundly influenced by him than the aptly named Hypnotic Brass Ensemble, staffed by his eight sons. The group started out performing on Michigan Avenue and at "L" stops in the 1990s, eventually moving to New York, appearing with Prince, winning a measure of international recognition and becoming the subject of the documentary film "Brothers Hypnotic," which aired on PBS' "Independent Lens" series in 2014.

Though the brass band's forays into rap and hip-hop veered far from Cohran's musical idioms, its questing nature reflected his ideals.

"One thing that our father always taught us to do was to keep the music for our people, for the people that need it, the people like where we came from that have nothing," Cohran's son Clef says in the film.

In 2014, Cohran—having just returned from sold-out concerts in Brazil—led his Kelan Zulu Ensemble at the Garfield Park Conservatory, singing, chanting, playing harp and otherwise conveying a kind of musical serenity.

On May 10, two days after his 90th birthday celebration, he performed at the Promontory, on South Lake Park Avenue, with Alexandre Pierrepont's Bridge project.

"He performed for an hour and a half, sang and recited a whole Paul Laurence Dunbar poem, verse for verse," recalled El'Zabar.

Said his son Tycho Cohran, "He was about his people, dealing with descendants of slaves and what could he do to help them get out of the predicament they've been in during the last 400 years."

A planned 50th anniversary celebration of Cohran's landmark recording "On the Beach" at 63rd Street and the lakefront already was scheduled for July 9. Now it "will be a celebration of the body of his work, but it will be a commemoration as well," his son said.

Cohran Honors Sun Ra

Aug. 16, 2008

Those fortunate enough to have seen pianist-bandleader Sun Ra in concert never will forget it. Leading an army of instrumentalists, dancers, acrobats, fire-eaters and whatnot, Ra turned every performance into a multimedia spectacle.

"Space is the place" he'd cry, insisting he was thousands of years old and traveling on a journey through the galaxies.

For all his stage antics, however, Ra—who merged high craft with deep spirituality—influenced generations of musicians. Among them, Chicagoan Kelan Phil Cohran was an ideal choice to stage a Ra tribute, presented Thursday night to an audience of 7,500 at the Pritzker Pavilion in Millennium Park.

But this was no mere imitation of Ra, which would have been pointless. Instead, "Kelan Phil Cohran and the Legacy of Sun Ra" evoked the spirit of Ra's work—while focusing on the substance of Cohran's.

A revered Chicago musician, octogenarian Cohran has taught and enlightened uncounted jazz artists, drawing inspiration from his own years with Ra's Arkestra, in the late 1950s and early '60s. But if Ra's work was explosive and fantastically complex, Cohran's radiated a serene majesty throughout Thursday's concert.

Assisted by a vocal choir called the Rainbow Ensemble, flanked by a corps of instrumentalists dubbed the Spiritual Journey Percussion Ensemble and accompanied by the dynamic Hypnotic Brass Ensemble, Cohran presided over a music as rich in texture as Ra's but considerably less frenetic. If Ra's art thrived on furious rhythm and futuristic dissonance, Cohran's harked back to African antiquity.

You could hear it in the simplicity of the phrases the Rainbow Ensemble sang, its chanted choral passages punctuated by imploring solos, including an impassioned one from Maggie Brown.

The Hypnotic Brass Ensemble punched out aggressive motifs, nobly evoking the brass bands that flourished in the prehistory of jazz.

Cohran sat at the center of the stage—and the action—playing harp, French horn, drums and more, reflecting on Ra between numbers.

"When I was playing with him, we starved to death," Cohran told the crowd.

"He was ahead of his time—that was his only fault."

There's some consolation, though, in knowing Ra has had a worthy artistic heir in Cohran.

CHAPTER 15

Muhal Richard Abrams

A Vital Influence

Nov. 2, 2017

In 1965, Chicago pianist Muhal Richard Abrams and colleagues formed an organization that would change the course of jazz and much more.

The Association for the Advancement of Creative Musicians dramatically redefined how individuals and ensembles could compose and improvise their works, and how they could take control of their own performances and recordings.

Abrams was integral to those achievements and influenced generations as composer, teacher, organizer and scholar. He died Sunday evening in his New York home with his wife, Peggy Abrams, and daughter, Richarda Abrams, at his side, they said. Muhal Richard Abrams, who was born in Chicago and launched his career here, was 87.

In co-founding the AACM, "He was able to create a community of artists who all respected each other, all shared the responsibility of playing with each other and all actually taught each other," said Wadada Leo Smith, an early AACM member whose "Ten Freedom Summers" was a Pulitzer Prize finalist in 2013.

"Muhal spent his life in service to us, his fellow musicians, composers and the world," said George Lewis, a MacArthur Fellowship winner

Fig. 8 Muhal Richard Abrams: As co-founder of the Association for the Advancement of Creative Musicians (AACM), Abrams helped alter the course of jazz in the 1960s and after. His innovations kept coming, including during this 2013 performance as part of Chicago's Symphony Center Presents Jazz series. Photo by Todd Rosenberg.

and author of the definitive study "A Power Stronger Than Itself: The AACM and American Experimental Music."

"He was a great teacher, but he also taught us to teach ourselves and to teach other people. . . . Now all four of the [AACM] founders have passed away, and we are on our own," added Lewis, referring to AACM co-founders Abrams, drummer Steve McCall, multi-instrumentalist Kelan Phil Cohran and pianist Jodie Christian. (Recording secretary Sandra Lashley also signed the AACM's articles of incorporation on May 8, 1965.)

Abrams attended DuSable and Wendell Phillips high schools and took classes at Roosevelt University and Governors State University, but he considered himself a mostly self-taught musician.

"He used to come to the Roosevelt sessions," remembered Joe Segal, who organized jazz performances at the school starting in 1947.

"He was one of many very fine pianists. He was straight-ahead," added Segal, meaning Abrams was playing in the bebop manner of the day. "I have some cuts of him playing. If I didn't tell you who it was, you'd never guess."

Abrams' keyboard prowess won him engagements with major figures who played Chicago, including Max Roach, Kenny Dorham, Hank Mobley, Ray Nance and Sonny Stitt.

But by the late 1950s and early '60s, the jazz landscape in Chicago was imploding because of changing musical tastes, the rise of rock 'n' roll, disappearing clubs and urban renewal.

Unwilling to give up on music even as opportunities for work were evaporating, Abrams in 1962 formed the Experimental Band, inviting fellow free thinkers to expand stylistic and expressive boundaries. Staffed by such rising figures as saxophonist Fred Anderson, woodwinds masters Joseph Jarman and Roscoe Mitchell, and drummers McCall and Jack DeJohnette, the Experimental Band drew inspiration from Sun Ra's Arkestra and set the stage for the emergence of the AACM in 1965.

"Not only did Muhal cultivate this community, but we were able to practice a discipline that the world has never seen from a musical organization," said trumpeter-composer Smith. "During those times we never received a single grant, never had any deep pockets from private donors. We walked the streets, posted signs, made mimeographed announcements."

Within a few years, the AACM was gaining fame and admiration in Europe and beyond, thanks to the travels of the Art Ensemble of Chicago and Anthony Braxton's trio. Early AACM bands such as Cohran's Artistic Heritage Ensemble and units led by Abrams, Christian, Jarman and Mitchell opened up new sonic possibilities. Freewheeling ensemble interplay, ancient and invented instruments, age-old New Orleans musical traditions, unabashed dissonance and Afro-centric musical rituals were behind the AACM's motto: "Great Black Music: Ancient to the Future."

"We had no idea the AACM would catch on as it did," Abrams said in a 1990 Tribune interview. "We simply were turning to each other for support, and that was all it took. The resources were within us."

In the late 1960s, Abrams also emerged as a co-founder of the nonprofit Jazz Institute of Chicago, which to this day programs the Chicago Jazz Festival and organizes educational events across the city.

"He came to the meetings, though he wouldn't let us put his name on as a board member . . . but he was very much part of it," said Harriet Choice, a co-founder of the organization and a former Tribune jazz critic.

Abrams also was involved in planning the massive Grant Park jazz concerts of the mid-1970s that led to creation of the Chicago Jazz Festival, in 1979.

By 1977, Abrams had moved to New York, establishing a chapter of the AACM there and developing into one of the most uncategorizable composer-pianists of the late 20th century. Jazz, classical, blues, avant-garde, folkloric and other musical languages coursed through his work—some meticulously composed, some invented spontaneously at the piano.

"He was a student of esoteric knowledge," said Lewis. "He went far beyond the standards of academically acceptable modes of thinking and of knowledge production and transmission.

"He was a tireless inventor, constantly searching for new information—voracious appetite and curiosity and love of learning."

Abrams' enormously wide view of music was unmistakable when he sat down at the piano, unfurling an epic sweep of sound and ideas. Strands of melody and harmony intertwined, orchestral splashes of color emerged from his fingertips, shades of Alban Berg and Claude Debussy met up with jazz riffs and blue-note figurations. It all attested to Abrams' vast knowledge of the breadth of Western and non-Western music.

"Muhal, in his later years as a pianist, he had this sort of hypertranscendental mode of performance," observed Lewis.

Meaning that his music welcomed anyone open to its far-flung influences.

Abrams was widely recognized for his achievements. He was the first winner of the Danish JAZZPAR Award, in 1990; won a National Endowment for the Arts Jazz Masters Fellowship, the United States' highest jazz honor, in 2010; and received an honorary doctoral degree from Columbia University in 2012.

And he never stopped championing bold new ideas in music, leading a new version of Muhal Richard Abrams' Experimental Band at the Chicago Jazz Festival in Millennium Park in 2015, to celebrate the AACM's 50th anniversary.

"The major issue is still reaching the public," he said in the 1990 Tribune interview, on the eve of the AACM's silver anniversary.

"Many musics have been exposed to the public over the past 25 years, so the situation is a little different, but not very much.

"In a way, it's the same as when we began."

Memorials for Abrams are being planned for Chicago and New York.

An Epic Statement

April 13, 1999

Anyone who doubts that the Loop is reawakening as an arts and entertainment destination should have headed to the Chicago Cultural Center on Sunday afternoon.

Hundreds of visitors poured into the glorious former home of the Chicago Public Library, some to see the Museum of Broadcast Communications, others to ogle photo exhibitions displayed throughout the venerable building.

But the day's key event was a piano recital by Muhal Richard Abrams in the Cultural Center's Preston Bradley Hall. The performance was not only a coup for the city's Department of Cultural Affairs, which organized it, but an indication of the quality of bookings that now define Cultural Center programming.

As a founding father of the Association for the Advancement of Creative Musicians (AACM), a Chicago organization that began to reenergize jazz in the mid-1960s, Abrams commands attention wherever he plays. Yet for more than a decade, Abrams—who long since moved to New York—has leaned toward classical composition and away from the freewheeling jazz improvisation that the AACM has represented.

So Abrams' recital, while rich in intricately stated ideas, only occasionally addressed the jazz-blues vocabulary at the core of both AACM philosophy and Abrams' Chicago years.

Even so, there was much to recommend in Abrams' performance, which unfolded in an uninterrupted sweep. Opening with a simple motif stated in single notes, Abrams eventually built immense, texturally thick blocks of sound. In an hourlong performance, he produced layers of melody, harmony, dissonance and color, in effect addressing the piano on orchestral terms.

In many ways, Abrams has developed musically as an internationalist, drawing upon everything from the moody Expressionism of the Austrian Alban Berg (much of Abrams' playing recalled Berg's pivotal Piano Sonata) to the lush Impressionism of Claude Debussy (with Abrams offering the whole-tone scales and intentionally blurred colors associated with turn-of-the-century France).

Add to this mix elements of African-American music (particularly in the use of left-hand ostinatos and occasional blue-note discord), and you have a composer embracing as much world music history as his fingers can articulate, which is quite a bit.

The thrust and direction of his music was apparent. This is a composer-pianist who relishes juxtaposing crisply stated bass lines and plushly layered chords, the paradox of brazenly dissonant chord clusters and traditional Western tonality.

For the most part, the progress of Abrams' ideas—and the inventive way he voiced them on the keyboard—kept his listeners interested. Yet Abrams ultimately may have offered too little contrast among musical themes to justify the length of this performance. And the sweetly diatonic tune with which he concluded his epic statement sounded a tad cynical, as if Abrams were determined to end his performance with something easy to digest.

Nevertheless, there was no denying the value of hearing Abrams' nearly encyclopedic command of music history in a solo setting.

CHAPTER 16

Willie Pickens

A Piano Titan

Dec. 14, 2017

On Tuesday afternoon, Chicago piano giant Willie Pickens was practicing in a rehearsal room at Jazz at Lincoln Center in New York.

Workers heard characteristically thunderous sounds emanating from the piano, said trumpeter Marquis Hill, whose band was preparing to rehearse with Pickens for a show Wednesday night at Dizzy's Club Coca-Cola at JALC.

"He was admiring the building, the practice room, super excited to be at the venue to come play with us," said Hill, a Pickens protege who won the Thelonious Monk International Jazz Trumpet Competition in 2014 and wanted to honor Pickens with this engagement.

"He was walking from the practice room to the club—which is on the same floor, around the corner—and they said he collapsed in front of the door on his way into the sound check.

"He was playing seconds, moments before."

Pickens suffered a fatal heart attack, said his daughter, Bethany Pickens, a prominent Chicago pianist and a music teacher at Kenwood Academy High School.

Willie Pickens was 86 and revered in Chicago—and around the

Fig. 9 Willie Pickens: The Milwaukee-born pianist based his career in Chicago, where his all-over-the-keys hyper-virtuosity made him a local treasure and an international touring attraction. Younger musicians from across the country and beyond came to Chicago to learn from him. Photo by Marc Monaghan.

world—not only as a colossal piano virtuoso but as a symbol of Chicago jazz. The muscularity of Pickens' work and his generosity in mentoring generations of young musicians placed him alongside such Chicago jazz icons as tenor saxophonists Von Freeman and Fred Anderson.

"Willie was about the future, and he used his technique to project that way," said New York-based pianist Jason Moran, a MacArthur Fellowship winner who often has said he studied Pickens' recordings as a student in Texas and sought out Pickens' performances in Chicago.

"He also used his energy to get kids into the music," added Moran. "I feel like all the work I've done in the past few years in Chicago has been because of my relationship to him."

Moran wrote the evening-length "Looks of a Lot" for the jazz band at Kenwood Academy, a school at which Pickens launched the music program in the 1960s. Moran and the Kenwood students performed the world premiere in Orchestra Hall at Symphony Center in 2014 and played the Washington, D.C., premiere last February at the Kennedy Center, where Moran serves as artistic director for jazz.

"I watched him play in his living room in his house, at the piano he knew the best," Moran said. "And he asked me to play something. I played something very small.

"And he played something very large, to show me what sound was. His hands were full hands."

Indeed, Pickens summoned immense masses of sound at the piano without succumbing to a percussive clatter. Add to this the extraordinary velocity he could achieve, as well as the melodic and harmonic ingenuity of his improvisations, and you had a pianist held in awe by colleagues and students alike.

"Willie Pickens was one of the foremost piano players in jazz," said Chicago pianist Ramsey Lewis. "He had technique, the knowledge of the instrument and jazz in general. . . . Although he wasn't tall, he was a gentle giant."

Born in Milwaukee on April 18, 1931, Pickens came to Chicago in 1958 because that "was where the action was," he told the Tribune in 1995. He quickly began sitting in on impresario Joe Segal's jam sessions.

"I remember vividly when he hit Chicago like a whirlwind," recalled Chicago vibraphonist-pianist Stu Katz.

"He sat in, and he was like nobody else. And remember, at that time we had Jodie Christian, John Young, Muhal [Richard Abrams], Larry Novak—tons of great pianists. And here comes this original who's totally different and fabulous, frankly."

Pickens met his wife, Irma, at one of those Segal jam sessions, the couple marrying in 1959, and Irma Pickens became a kind of ambassador for her husband at his Chicago engagements.

His work created a stir across the city, and in 1961 Pickens reached an international audience thundering at the piano in Chicago saxophonist Eddie Harris' hit recording of "Exodus," from Harris' "Exodus to Jazz" album. The record went gold and catapulted Harris, Pickens and friends to sharing a marquee with Duke Ellington at the Newport Jazz Festival, among other high-profile engagements.

But Pickens decided not to move to New York, Los Angeles or another jazz capital, feeling he already had found his home.

"Because I came to Chicago, I didn't have to go on the road—the road came to me," he told the Tribune in 2015. "Everyone came through Chicago or lived here, so I was working with [James] Moody, Dexter [Gordon], Gene Ammons, Roy Eldridge, Johnny Griffin, Johnny Hartman, Art Pepper, Max Roach, you name it. It was terrific for me because I could play with the greats at night but still stay in town and have a chance to raise my family."

In 1966, Pickens began teaching music at the Chicago Public Schools, launching the Kenwood program and teaching in other institutions as well.

By 1990, Elvin Jones—one of the towering drummers of the second half of the 20th century—invited Pickens to tour the world with Elvin Jones' Jazz Machine.

Pickens thought he'd take a leave of absence from his teaching job, but Irma Pickens told him, "'Just retire and go out on the road,'" Willie Pickens said in a 2016 Tribune interview.

"She wanted me to have that experience. She was the one that encouraged me."

The opportunity enabled Pickens to realize the high regard in which he was held around the world.

"The reactions were incredible," Pickens said in a 1995 Tribune interview. "When we were in Japan, I went into a shop to buy postcards; they didn't have what I wanted, but a bunch of teenage girls recognized me and said they could take me to a better store.

"So they took me down there, I found a bunch of cards, and before I could pay, they did—and said it was a gift from them. When I left, they came to the airport to send me off and brought me flowers. It was unbelievable."

Pickens circled the globe several times with Jones, who died in 2004, but the pianist remained a fiercely devoted teacher in Chicago.

In 1995, he became a founding member of the Ravinia Jazz Mentor Program.

"He was the heart and soul of it," said Lewis, artistic director of jazz at Ravinia. "The students and teachers and Ravinia bigwigs all looked up to him."

For more than two decades, Pickens "mentored thousands of young musicians" and was going to continue his work next week, said

Christine Taylor, director of Ravinia's Reach Teach Play Education Programs.

Pickens also taught for years at Northern Illinois University in DeKalb.

Though Pickens was under-recorded for an artist of his stature, he leaves behind some key documents, including his recording debut as leader, "It's About Time!" (Southport Records), which captured the volcanic power of his pianism; "Marian McPartland and Willie Pickens: Ain't Misbehavin'/Live at the Jazz Showcase" (Concord Jazz); recordings with Elvin Jones and E. Parker McDougal; "Jazz Spirit Volumes 1 and 2" (Southport Records), in which he reimagined sacred songs; and "A Jazz Christmas" (Southport Records), featuring the brilliant New Orleans trumpeter Nicholas Payton.

Spirituality played an important role in Pickens' life, with the pianist overseeing an annual Christmas benefit concert at Hyde Park Union Church.

Irma Pickens died in October 2015, at age 75, not long before her husband played his belated Orchestra Hall debut as bandleader in February 2016.

"She died just a few days before our 56th anniversary," Pickens said in a 2016 Tribune interview.

"I miss her dearly. She was just a bright spot in my life, just a tremendous part of my life.

"And I'm just floundering without her."

Pickens persevered, headlining NPR's "A Jazz Piano Christmas" at the Kennedy Center on a double bill with Renee Rosnes and Bill Charlap in December 2016.

"It means a lot—it's really, really big," Pickens said in a Tribune interview a couple of weeks before the Kennedy Center concert.

Playing the piano never lost its allure for Pickens.

"I can definitely tell my students and his students that he was on his way to practice before the soundcheck," Bethany Pickens said.

"He died doing what he loved to do."

In addition to his daughter, Pickens is survived by children David Pickens and Kiron Pickens and two grandchildren.

Funeral arrangements are pending.

Next for NEA?

May 13, 2015

Last month, the National Endowment for the Arts made a very good move, bestowing the country's highest jazz honor on a man who richly deserved it: veteran Chicago jazz impresario Joe Segal.

By presenting Jazz Showcase founder Segal with the NEA's Jazz Masters Fellowship during a ceremony at Jazz at Lincoln Center in New York, the endowment accomplished at least two valuable tasks: It saluted one of the country's most enduring jazz presenters and cast a spotlight on a jazz city whose legends it has not honored often enough.

Now that Segal, who recently turned 89, has received his $25,000 check, engraved glass trophy and Jazz Masters cap, it's time—past time, in fact—for the NEA to salute another larger-than-life jazz figure long based in Chicago: 84-year-old pianist Willie Pickens. For while the Jazz Masters Fellowships have tended to go to artists with global name recognition (at least in jazz circles), Pickens qualifies in areas that matter more.

Which is not to say that Pickens doesn't command the admiration of some of the greatest jazz musicians working today. MacArthur Fellowship winner Jason Moran, 40, speaks often of how, as a piano student in Texas, he studied Pickens' recordings and seized every opportunity he could to hear the master at work whenever Moran was in Chicago. Still does.

New Orleans saxophone virtuoso Donald Harrison not only makes sure that Pickens accompanies him whenever Harrison plays the Showcase, he paid extraordinary tribute to the master by giving up a portion of his stage time at the Chicago Jazz Festival in 2013 so that Pickens could have the Pritzker Pavilion spotlight to himself. Pickens proceeded to give the event one of its most thrilling moments, a two-fisted solo account of John Coltrane's "Giant Steps."

The piano probably is still recovering.

"Willie Pickens is one of the virtuoso pianists," Harrison told me in 2008. "He has phenomenal technique and harmonic invention. It's like playing with the swing-era guys, who have just a vast amount of knowledge."

But Pickens' sovereignty at the instrument and profound awareness of the sweep of jazz history tell only part of the story. The rest owes to the influence he has had on jazz in Chicago, and far beyond.

Remember Chicago tenor saxophone giant Eddie Harris' hit recording of "Exodus," from his "Exodus to Jazz" album, in 1961? That was Pickens thundering at the piano, the gold-certified album making Harris an international name and opening the door to high-profile engagements for Harris and Pickens at the Newport Jazz Festival on a marquee with Duke Ellington, and elsewhere. Other young pianists who found themselves in Pickens' fortunate position might have moved hastily to New York and pursued a life of international touring. Pickens, who had grown up in Milwaukee and came to Chicago in 1958 and stayed, raised his family here.

That family includes Bethany Pickens, a formidable jazz musician and teacher in her own right. But Willie Pickens' influence rippled far outside the Pickens home. In 1966, he began teaching in the Chicago Public Schools and that same decade launched the famous jazz program at Kenwood Academy High School.

Pickens' students surely benefited enormously from studying with a musician of his stature, but by 1990, one of the greatest drummers in the world, Elvin Jones, made Pickens an offer he couldn't refuse: come tour the world with him. Those lucky enough to have heard Jones' explosive percussion in tandem with Pickens' monumental pianism encountered one of the great partnerships in jazz.

"It meant the world to me," Pickens told me in 2012 of his tenure with Jones, which stretched to 1995 and, belatedly, gave the Chicago pianist the global attention he long merited. Audiences across Europe and beyond belatedly discovered what Chicagoans knew all along: the towering character of Pickens' pianism.

Pickens' devotion to the Chicago scene only deepened after touring the world with Jones. The annual Christmas benefit performances he presented at Hyde Park Union Church, the farewell concert he organized for Geraldine and Eddie de Haas at the Jazz Showcase in 2013 and his tutelage of generations of young musicians at Northern Illinois University in DeKalb, and elsewhere, echo in the musical life of this city and well beyond.

Like Chicago tenor saxophonist Von Freeman before him, Pickens has come to represent the big-and-muscular sound of the city itself. Considering Chicago's outsize role in the ongoing history of jazz, Pickens' therefore holds a valued place in the evolution and nurturance of the music.

What's it like to receive an NEA Jazz Masters Fellowship?

"It was great," says Segal, whose acceptance speech—as well as the rest of the ceremony and concert—can be viewed at arts.gov. "I saw a lot of people there that I knew."

Like Segal, Pickens has known them all.

Nominations for the 2017 class of NEA Jazz Masters can be made at arts.gov/honors/jazz/nomination (nominations for next year's class closed Dec. 31).

Surely Pickens ought to be next.

CHAPTER 17

Ramsey Lewis

The Music of His Years

Feb. 25, 1996

All eyes are on Ramsey Lewis, as he pulls the heavy black gloves off his hands and gently places his fingertips on the keys of his Steinway grand.

The Arctic temperatures outdoors have put a chill even in the recording booth, and between tapings Lewis slips his hands back into the gloves, hoping to keep his hands warm and his fingers nimble.

"How did that sound?" he asks the folks listening from the other side of the glass booth.

"That's not it, Pops," says the producer, who happens to be Lewis' 27-year-old son and business partner, Frayne. "Just read the music, man."

With the sixth of his seven children urging him on, Lewis finds himself not only immersed in a tough recording session but also opening the latest and perhaps final chapter of a tumultuous career.

Long adored by fans, praised and bashed by critics, embraced then discarded by the record industry, Lewis has taken about every blow and honor that the music business has to offer. He has won gold records and Grammys, and he has been dismissed as a has-been only to re-emerge as one of the most visible jazz musicians in America.

He may be bruised from the battle and a little tired in the legs, but after 40-plus years in the ring, he still comes out swinging.

Fig. 10 Ramsey Lewis: Chicagoan Lewis proved it was possible to make gospel-inflected jazz broadly popular. His classical training engendered vastly ambitious works, including this Ravinia Festival premiere of his 2009 "Proclamation of Hope."

Moreover, at nearly 61, an age when many folks are counting the days to retirement, Lewis has put his chips on one of the biggest gambles of his career: a gleaming, state-of-the-art recording studio that he has created on North Halsted Street, within eyeshot of both the city's glittering skyline and the Cabrini housing project where he grew up.

From this studio, Lewis isn't simply cutting records—he's also fighting for a piece of his legacy.

How else to explain the recent, creative surge in Lewis' musical life? By recording his first bona fide jazz album in years (to be released later this year on the Impulse label) and writing and producing the jazz soundtrack for a new HBO special airing this month, "The Journey of the African-American Athlete, 1875–1995," Lewis appears to be returning to his roots. In so doing, he's trying to remind listeners that, yes, he's still a jazz musician, not merely a commercial one.

That his new Ivory Pyramid studio also will record and promote undiscovered jazz talent in Chicago and beyond only underscores the point.

"As I get older, I get bolder," says Lewis, during a break between recording sessions. "If I had been as confident 10 years ago as I am now, I probably would have started sooner," he adds, referring to his return to his jazz roots.

But 10 years ago jazz still was a four-letter word in American popular culture, a music deemed unsaleable by the major record labels and unplayable by the foremost radio stations. From the mid-'60s to the mid-'80s—the prime of Lewis' career—the music he had revered since his teens had been pushed to the periphery of American life.

Jazz-inspired artists as formidable as Frank Sinatra and Tony Bennett had lost their recording contracts; jazz clubs as famous as Chicago's London House—where Lewis was a perennial favorite—had closed their doors for good. Lewis, in fact, presided over the demise of that fabled nightclub at Michigan Avenue and Wacker Drive, playing the sad last show on a freezing January night in 1975.

So Lewis, married and the father of seven, had to survive, and the way he chose to do so—by transforming himself chameleon-like from jazz piano virtuoso to easy-listening pop star—produced financial rewards and, not surprisingly, a degree of artistic self-doubt.

The roller-coaster ride that led him to that point would make a rich subject for an HBO special of its own.

Born the second of three children in a cramped apartment on South Evans Avenue, Ramsey E. Lewis Jr. at 4 years old literally threw a fit when he learned his older sister would be getting piano lessons.

"The word in the house was that somebody's going to take piano lessons, and it was going to be my older sister, because my father said he only could afford to send one of us," remembers Lewis. "So I just kicked the wall and fell on the floor crying until my father said I could go for lessons, too.

"But my new teacher, Ernestine Bruce, had this ruler, and if you didn't play the right note or have the right fingering, she'd go 'pop,' right across the knuckles.

"I didn't like it, so after about two or three lessons, I said, 'I'm through with music.' And my dad said, 'No you're not.'"

Ramsey E. Lewis Sr., an amateur church musician from Georgia who made his living in Chicago as a maintenance man, wasn't going to let his son off the hook quite so easily. Neither was the boy's mother,

Pauline Richards Lewis, who worked as a domestic in plush homes along the Gold Coast.

Often, recalls Lewis' elder sister, Rev. Lucille Jackson, "Daddy would go to the playground and usher Sonny—that's what Daddy called him—right back to the house and straight to the piano. Especially if Mama would complain, 'Ramsey hasn't been at the piano all day.'

"But Daddy also would take Sonny, and the rest of us, to the Regal Theatre to see [the pianist] Earl Hines and [the band leader-composer] Duke Ellington. There was a desire in our daddy's heart for Ramsey to become a great musician."

But it wasn't until Lewis had begun studying piano with Dorothy Mendelsohn at Chicago Musical College that he went along with the plan.

"Dorothy Mendelsohn would say, 'Ramsey, listen with your inner ear,'" the pianist recalls.

"And I'm 11 years old and thinking: 'Inner ear? My ears are out here.'

"And she'd say, 'No, you must listen from within, you must feel the music. You can make the notes sing.'

"Sing? You can make the piano sing? Really! I was amazed.

"So I got hooked. By the time I was 13 years old, I figured that I would tour the world playing classical music in all the Orchestra Halls and Carnegie Halls in the world."

Lewis' teacher, however, understood a grimmer reality.

"She told my parents, 'Being Black, he may not be able to make a living in classical music,'" Lewis remembers.

Indeed, in the '30s and '40s, "For a Black boy, the doors were not being swung open in classical music or most anything else," says Rev. Jackson.

Certainly not many kids growing up in the Cabrini housing project, a low-rise forerunner of Cabrini-Green, were going to make it to Carnegie Hall. Although Lewis remembers Cabrini as "a nice place with a flower garden in front that Mom was very proud of and a Victory Garden in back," the place was very near the bottom of the socioeconomic ladder.

For Lewis, and for a generation of gifted young musicians like him, the sole outlet and saving grace was jazz—the one musical arena into which Blacks were admitted and which they dominated. Singer Nat

Cole, piano titan Art Tatum, band leaders Ellington and Count Basie—those were the artists that Lewis was hearing on his father's record player at home and over the radio in the auditorium of Wells High School, at Ashland Avenue and Augusta Boulevard (Lewis was in the class of '53), and these were the sounds that seduced him.

"I met Ramsey in 1946 or '47, and he always was begging me to teach him how to play jazz and to let him play in my group," remembers Chicago musician Wallace Burton.

"Red Holt [the drummer] and I had started a group in '49, the Cleffs, and when our pianist left, I went over to Ramsey's house and asked Ma Lewis if he could join."

"And she said to me, 'Wallace, we're bringing Sonny up to be a Christian and a God-fearing young man,' so I had to promise I'd bring him home personally by midnight.

"That night we played our job at the Parkway Ballroom and—wouldn't you know it?—that was the night the union guy came out," adds Burton, recalling an era when union reps monitored performances to make sure union rules were being followed to the letter.

"When I spotted the union guy," continues Burton, "I put down my saxophone, rushed over to the piano, pushed Ramsey under the piano and started playing the keyboard myself, while the union guy counted heads. So that was Ramsey Lewis' initiation into jazz—from underneath a piano."

Lewis says he didn't play very well that night in 1950, but he was immediately drawn to the jazz life, watching couples swirl and swing around the dance floor before him.

By 1955, with Burton in the Army, the rhythm section—Lewis, Holt and bassist Eldee Young—began working as a trio, their bluesy, funk-tinged music rapidly earning them a following around town.

"We were playing this lounge on the South Side," remembers Lewis, "and we thought it was a pretty good gig, even if the waiters were keeping their knives and forks inside the piano. They literally were using the far end of the piano as the waiters station.

"Daddy-O Daylie [the legendary South Side jazz disk jockey] used to come by, and when he found out that they were keeping silverware in the piano, he went to the manager and said, 'You can't do that.'

"Then he told us we ought to make a record, and he set up an audition with us for Phil Chess," who, with brother Leonard Chess, recently had formed the revered Chess Records blues and jazz label.

The trio's debut album, "The Gentlemen of Swing," in 1956 didn't hit the charts, but at least it put the band on the map. Soon renamed the Ramsey Lewis Trio, the group by the late '50s was opening for jazz stars James Moody, Clark Terry and Ellington himself in joints all around Chicago.

What's more, the Ramsey Lewis Trio was acquiring a reputation in America's Black neighborhoods.

"I remember hearing their records on the jukebox in Washington, D.C., my hometown," recalls pianist Billy Taylor.

"They were into this bluesy Chicago kind of thing, and it was unlike anything I heard anyone else doing. In D.C., those were some of the most popular dance songs on the jukebox."

Already, however, Lewis and company were taking blows from critics. Though some picked up on the hip, dance quality of the music, "some of the so-called local jazz authorities couldn't pigeonhole us as offspring of [Thelonious] Monk or [Bud] Powell, so they weren't terribly nice to us," says Lewis.

"But the surprising thing was that when Dizzy [Gillespie], Duke [Ellington], Clark [Terry], Nat [Cole] or Oscar [Peterson] would come to town, they would hear about us, find us, listen to us all night, then go out to breakfast with us. And they'd say, 'That's good stuff—you guys should keep it up.'"

No doubt the catchy tunes, breezy swing rhythms and church-inflected piano playing had a lot to do with the trio's appeal. But there was more to it than that.

Recalls Holt, "We were a group of young cats, church cats, who were listening to modern music every day.

"I used to call on Ramsey sometimes at 3 o'clock in the morning, and say, 'Hey, Ramsey, we ought to do one of these soul tunes,' and then I'd hum it to him over the phone.

"The next day we'd play it, and he'd put in his classical thing, and we'd do our jazz-church thing, and it was like a marriage that was out of sight, the three of us.

"I tell you, we had a real closeness. We'd pack up the wives and the babies and go to each other's houses, it was a brotherly love thing, it was a God blessed thing.

"We ate together, we slept together, we learned how to do a lot of things together. We fit like a glove, and we loved each other."

Word of the trio's growing success had reached Burton, their former colleague, in the Army, "and when I came back to Chicago," recalls Burton, "I thought I would get back together with them. But Daddy-O Daylie, who was working as their agent at the time, said: 'They don't need you. They're doing fine without you.'

"It disturbed me at first," says Burton, who learned a painful lesson about the carnivorous world of show business.

Burton's loss must have seemed all the more imposing when the trio set the world afire with "The In Crowd," the title track of their 16th album.

"We had put it out in May of '65," says Lewis, "and by the time we were playing Detroit, in July or August, we got a call from Leonard Chess saying, 'You've got a hit.'"

"He said, 'Everybody wants it, and we're going to put it out as a single,' which was amazing, because there weren't a lot of jazz singles in those days. Still aren't.

"By October of that year, we did not believe it. Up until that point, all of our jobs were nightclubs, where you did three shows, six nights a week.

"Now, all of a sudden, we were getting calls for real concerts, where you go on at 8 o'clock and you're through at 10. And we're thinking, 'What's this all about?'

"We went from making $1,700 a week to making $10,000, $12,000 a week, all within a six-month period. It was really heady. Suddenly we didn't have to worry about where the next rent payment was coming from. We would go out to some restaurant, and I remember thinking that this was the first time I was looking at a menu without looking at the price column."

As Holt recalls, "It was the greatest time of my life. Those were some beautiful days.

"I remember we were in New York, taking a cab down Broadway, and you could hear 'The In Crowd' pouring out of the big speakers in the record stores. It was unreal."

Unfortunately, about a year after the trio finally hit the big-time with "In Crowd" and a similarly infectious pop tune, "Hang On Sloopy," the band came apart at the seams.

"At first, all the success was fun," recalls Lewis, "because people are lined up around the block to hear you play; Johnny Carson is calling you to come on the show; managers are inviting you to be on the 'Carnegie Hall whatever' concert. And then things started to happen, and we didn't deal well with it.

"Before, there were times when he had to share hotel rooms; now, all of a sudden, we don't have to. Before, there wasn't much else to do but perform at night and practice in the daytime. Now the daytime is all this other stuff, distractions, business meetings, tons of interviews.

"Success started affecting the music, and the feeling on stage started to change. It wasn't as comfortable anymore; it wasn't as much fun on stage as it had been."

Finally, the trio disbanded.

Today, three decades after the breakup, each of the players is reluctant to reopen the wounds of the past. Young closed off discussion entirely by saying, "It's water under the bridge."

Yet it seems inescapable that for Lewis' colleagues, immense personal disappointment followed in the wake of the trio's success.

Says Holt: "It came apart really after the hit. The lawyers and parasites came in, and the cats who were in charge said, 'You're going to do this and that.' And we said, 'No, man, it always was a three-way split [financially]; it should be that now."

Lewis, however, denies that money was the issue.

"It was all so trivial," he says. "I was getting $50 a week more for being the spokesman of the group. So I don't think it was about money."

Perhaps, then, it was about the spotlight, and how it tends to shine on the leader of a band, rather than the others.

"How do you think you feel when you're making a record," asks Holt, "and they take your drum solo, they cut it out, and you see the tape go straight onto the floor?"

From today's vantage point, "It all seems so trifling," says Lewis. "There were all these personality conflicts over things like whose name was going to go out front on the marquee, who got to do the interviews, who didn't get to do interviews.

"I thought we could overcome the problems, but we had been together for 15 years, and it was like a marriage—there was too much emotional baggage hanging around.

"And when it got to the point where it affected the music, we said, 'Bye-bye.'"

The split "was one of the worst things that ever happened to me in my life," says Holt.

Adds Young: "We had worked so hard on this music together, and when the group broke up, it was like a family breakup. I took it very hard."

So Young and Holt went their way as a duo, slipping into relative obscurity (both men are based here and tour the world as musicians, together and separately), and Lewis went his way as a star. If there is any lingering bitterness or remorse among these three men, they mask it well. They have even done reunion performances.

Holt, for instance, simply says, "Everybody [in the trio] was Christians, so we forgive."

With each season, Lewis' fame seemed to grow, thanks to radio-friendly hits such as "Wade in the Water," which he recorded with drummer Maurice White and bassist Cleveland Eaton. Clearly, he had come up with a cunning mixture of jazz, pop, gospel and blues that could delight some of the cognoscenti while entertaining the mass audience as well.

By the early '70s, as acoustic jazz was dying on the vine, Lewis segued to electronic keyboards, clearly chasing the pop trend of the moment. Sure enough, he scored a gold record in '75 with "Sun Goddess," an album that brought him perilously close to the sound, texture and intellectual weight of Muzak.

Thus by degrees Lewis' connection to the jazz tradition, to the music that first had made him a name, unraveled. With acoustic jazz all but banished from the marketplace, with rock 'n' roll overwhelming everything that came before it and with "jazz-fusion" the order of the day, Lewis pushed further into lightweight fare.

He sold millions of records, comfortably supporting his children and his wife, Geri, whom he had married in 1954.

Yet the cost to Lewis' reputation as a jazz musician was high. In any recent jazz encyclopedia worthy of the name, his bio entry is likely to be cut off after the '70s, as if he simply had ceased to exist as a jazz artist.

Today, though Lewis makes no apologies for the artistic direction he pursued, he acknowledges that his music of the late '70s and '80s amounts to something of a blur to him.

"In the '80s, when I was recording for CBS, there wasn't really a definite direction or definite musical goal," he says.

"Actually, I like both worlds," says Lewis, referring to the light dance music he played in the '80s and the more substantial fare on which his reputation originally was made.

"It's just unfortunate, I got kind of shoved over on that [light] side. And I allowed it.

"I mean, nobody makes you do anything. When you look back, you say, 'Wait a minute—you didn't have to.'"

When Lewis signed with the "jazz lite" record label GRP in 1991, after several years without a recording contract, some of the pianist's most ardent fans figured he truly was finished as a jazz musician.

But a couple of years ago, something happened, something barely discernible at first that became more apparent with each passing season.

Lewis was starting to open his live shows playing solo piano again with a technical virtuosity, a musical depth and a reverence for the jazz tradition that had been sorely missing from his work for years.

He began offering his audiences vast, poetic readings of "Body and Soul," "Lush Life" and other jazz standards worthy of his talent.

In other ways, too, he was turning his life upside down. Married to the mother of his seven children for 35 years, in 1989 he was divorced from Geri Lewis and the next year married his current wife and business partner, Jan.

In 1993 he became artistic director of the Ravinia Festival's Jazz in June series, taking up a post that for the two previous years had been filled by one of the certifiable giants of jazz, the late Gerry Mulligan.

And last December Lewis opened his new studio.

With his weekly radio show on WNUA-FM 95.5 (10 p.m. to midnight Saturdays) and his regular appearances on the "Jazz Central" program on the Black Entertainment Television network, Lewis has become one of the country's more visible spokesmen on jazz.

In this regard, he surely has been following in the footsteps of trumpeter and jazz advocate Wynton Marsalis, whose appearances on Public Broadcasting Service TV specials and directorship of the Jazz at Lincoln Center series in New York have helped make acoustic jazz fashionable once again. The question, then, is whether Lewis really is coming home to jazz or simply going with the in crowd.

"Here's what happened," says Lewis. "I did the two albums on GRP, 'Ivory Pyramid' and 'Sky Island,' which were what they wanted, and we sold records.

"And it was on the strength of selling those records that I was able to go back in and say, 'You know, this is fine, but there are other things on my mind these days.'

"So we renegotiated the contract several months ago. I'm still going to do records for GRP, but later this year I'm also going to release a record exploring the music of great American composers on Impulse." GRP acquired and revived that historic jazz label a few years ago.

"With Impulse I'll be able to record something personal, something special, something artistic, something where I won't have to worry about air play and about selling 10 million albums," says Lewis.

"The concept is to explore the music of great American composers—Duke Ellington, Charlie Mingus, Thelonious Monk, Aaron Copland, maybe Samuel Barber."

Whether Lewis' Impulse record comes off as planned, whether he can prove to the world that he's still a jazz musician remains to be heard.

To those willing to give Lewis the benefit of the doubt, such as his longtime friend and colleague Billy Taylor, the new and improved Ramsey Lewis is here to stay.

"This has been coming for a long time," says Taylor.

"He's been looking for a vehicle. A few years ago, he tried to open his own club," adds Taylor, recalling Ramsey's Place, which never opened for business.

"What has happened to Ramsey is something that happens to many of us at a certain time in our lives," adds Taylor.

"You've done the things you've wanted to do—now you want to do something else. You want to reassess."

For Lewis, the Ivory Pyramid studio may provide that opportunity. He hopes it will enable him to "spend most of my days at home, tour in the summer and spend the other nine months here in Chicago. "I want more time to write music, more time to practice, more time to explore jazz as well as European classical music.

"Basically, I think I've just started setting up a new period of my life."

"I guess I also started thinking about giving back," he says.

"That's why I do all the projects with kids at the Ravinia Festival," adds Lewis, who, with Ravinia's executive director, Zarin Mehta, and the Chicago Public Schools, two years ago established a Jazz Mentor program for young musicians.

"As for myself, all I'm hoping is that people will listen to the new Impulse record and say, 'Oh, so that's what Ramsey Lewis was about. He wasn't just 'The In Crowd.'

"I don't see myself as a Duke Ellington, where when I die this music is going to stay on forever and ever. I really don't.

"I'm just trying to make music and maybe help someone else along the way."

"Proclamation of Hope"

June 7, 2009

As Ramsey Lewis' fingers stroke the keys of a Steinway grand, a great swell of orchestral sound rises up around him.

Nearly two dozen musicians have gathered to rehearse for the world premiere of the most ambitious piece of Lewis' career, an evening-length homage to the Abraham Lincoln bicentennial titled "Proclamation of Hope." But just a few months ago, Lewis didn't know if he would be healthy enough to finish writing the work, let alone play the piano for its unveiling Friday night at Ravinia in Highland Park.

Lewis, 74, had spent several months last year battling a disorder of his pancreas, "the longest I've ever been away from a piano since I was 4 years old," he recalls after the rehearsal in Ravinia's Martin Theatre. "I just didn't know how it was going to be at the piano afterward. Maybe I was afraid."

During the treatment and recovery that silenced him from September to November, "there was a part of me that was missing," adds Lewis, a lifelong Chicagoan. "There was a part of me that was not being fulfilled."

So when he was strong enough to return to the piano and resume work on "Proclamation of Hope," last December, Lewis poured his frustrations and anxieties—as well as a lifetime of musical experiences—into it. The result is a vast, eight-movement work that not only addresses Lincoln's legacy but pushes beyond it.

For in the midst of Lewis' illness and recuperation, America elected its first African-American president, altering not only the nation's history but, on a more personal level, the progress of Lewis' opus. And what Lewis originally intended as a celebration of Black music in America (and Lincoln's role in igniting it) eventually blossomed into an exploration of the links between presidents Lincoln and Obama.

In effect, Lewis during the past year unexpectedly found himself at the intersection of three powerful currents: his attempt to compose an epic work, his battle for his health and his awe at the ascent of an African-American (and fellow Chicagoan) to the White House. These three themes inspired "Proclamation of Hope," says Lewis, and changed his understanding of his life and his art.

That Lewis even was undertaking such a Herculean composition would have seemed improbable just a few years earlier, for the classically trained pianist had spent his career performing and recording succinct jazz tunes. With the possible exception of "A Gospel Celebration," which Lewis led at the Ravinia Festival in 1996, Lewis rarely had worked on a large canvas.

But Ravinia president Welz Kauffman pointed Lewis in that direction, when Kauffman commissioned the pianist to compose a solo piano work in 2006. Lewis, the longtime artistic director of jazz at Ravinia, pleased Kauffman immensely with "Clouds in Reverie," inspiring Kauffman to ask for a more extended piece: Lewis' original score for a Joffrey Ballet world premiere, "To Know Her. . . ." That gorgeously lyrical piece—in which Lewis' trio accompanied Joffrey Ballet dancers in choreography by Donald Byrd—won critical accolades in 2007 and set the stage for Kauffman to dream bigger still.

"I had been thinking about Ravinia celebrating the 200th birthday [of Lincoln]—how would that take shape, what it would look like?" remembers Kauffman, who approached Lewis with the idea in summer of '07.

"My idea was we would look forward, celebrate this man [Lincoln] with a couple of new pieces," adds Kauffman, who also commissioned choreographer Bill T. Jones to create a Lincoln ballet, which will be staged in September.

Recalls Lewis: "Welz said, 'I want you to do something for the Abraham Lincoln bicentennial, and I want you to take the whole evening.'

"Well, to compose something for two hours, that's more than a notion," adds Lewis, who was somewhat daunted by the invitation.

Says Jan Lewis, the pianist's wife, business partner and muse, "He was excited but very serious about it, very wary of it, because the scope of it was so big."

Pianist Lewis immediately began immersing himself in all things Lincoln, devouring books, traveling to Springfield and spending days at the Chicago History Museum ogling Lincoln memorabilia. But the music, which he started to write in spring of last year, "was slow coming," Lewis says.

It wasn't until Lewis realized he was inspired by specific moments in Lincoln's life that the music started to pour out of him. Events such as Lincoln witnessing the brutality of a slave auction and Lincoln dying at the hands of an assassin moved Lewis profoundly.

Unfortunately, the music was interrupted last September, after doctors "found a spot on my pancreas," says Lewis. "And, of course, when anybody talks about a spot on your pancreas, everybody gets very concerned.

"So they did a biopsy, and they found that it was not cancer cells at all—there was no cancer to be found. But they couldn't explain what those cells were.

"So not wanting to take a chance, they treated them as if they were cancerous."

The grueling operation, called the Whipple procedure, precipitated further health complications, including a blood clot on Lewis' lungs, which extended his period of hospitalization and recuperation.

"We were wondering how he would be afterward," says Jan Lewis.

Though Lewis' pancreas problem was deemed "totally resolved," he says, it wasn't until December that Lewis returned to his Lincoln composition, and by then the White House was preparing to change hands.

This altered the course of Lewis' tone poem.

"The last movement was going to be a sort of culmination of blues and gospel and jazz, but something unusual happened—200 years after

Lincoln was born, and a few years after he freed the slaves, a political dream came true."

The event gave rise to the work's finale, "16/44: A More Perfect Union," the numbers referring to the Lincoln and Obama presidencies. In this movement, the motif Lewis wrote to evoke Lincoln gives way to a new one: "Obama's Theme: Hope."

Ultimately, what Lewis had conceived as a tribute to Lincoln morphed into a sweeping narrative on the epochal way Lincoln changed America.

"When Obama was elected, we were able to make this shift," says Scott Hall, Columbia College Chicago's director of jazz studies and the arranger-conductor of Lewis' piece.

"The fact that Obama is president gave us a landscape to write off of. It's like a musical blog. . . . I think it did change the approach toward the second half of the piece, and I think for the better, too, because the subject of Lincoln—everything about his life is so dark and heavy and serious," adds Hall. "Writing about Lincoln as a jazz group is a daunting task, for two hours of music. So once Obama became a part of the picture, it made it possible for us to go through the history from there to today."

To intensify the experience, Lewis enlisted Michael Coakes to assemble historic images that will be shown at key moments in the piece. Scenes of slavery, drawings and photos of Lincoln and a juxtaposition of Lincoln and Obama will help drive the narrative arc of the piece, says Hall.

Not surprisingly, the process of composing this work under stressful circumstances has changed Lewis.

"I don't want to use the phrase 'slowed down,' but he just seems calmer, and very trusting of me and others," says Hall, the arranger-conductor. "It seems he has grown even more patient."

Lewis acknowledges as much.

"Doing the Lincoln work, and looking at his life, and then going through six weeks in the hospital and all the recovery afterward, I definitely took a hard look at my life," says Lewis, who plans to cut back from doing up to 70 concerts a year to roughly half that, so he can pursue long-delayed travel with his wife.

"When I came out of the hospital, and as I was finishing the Lincoln project, it just made me look deeper into everything," adds Lewis. "And there's a sense of appreciation that comes to play in this."

What effect Lewis' experiences during the past year will have on the music remains to be heard, but during rehearsals the simplicity and directness of the music, as well as its melodic pull, are unmistakable.

"I think this piece defines his whole feeling of his history and his culture—the Black culture, how painful a history it was," says Jan Lewis. "But the piece ends with such hope. . . .

"And I think it helped define a lot of things in Ramsey's mind about who he is and where he came from."

CHAPTER 18

Dee Alexander

Spreading Her Wings

Dec. 30, 2007

She was everywhere in 2007:

Attracting throngs to Millennium Park; swinging joyously outside the South Shore Cultural Center; pushing into experimental music at the Velvet Lounge; improvising buoyantly at the first Hyde Park Jazz Festival.

But it wasn't merely the frequency of Dee Alexander's performances, or just the stylistic breadth of her work, that distinguished her. Perhaps more important, she sang with such interpretive depth and dramatic power as to force listeners to re-evaluate the music she makes. Though Alexander has been performing in her hometown for decades, in the past year she took on the most daring projects of her career and made them sing.

"I think this year was some kind of metamorphosis for me," says Alexander, invoking precisely the right word to articulate what happened to her, and her music, in '07.

"Chicago always has been my home, but this year I started to spread my wings."

In more ways than one. Geographically, Alexander performed outside the U.S. to critical acclaim, joining several local colleagues in a tour to Poland, organized by the non-profit Jazz Institute of Chicago.

Fig. 11 Dee Alexander: Equally persuasive as experimenter and tradition bearer, Alexander veers between musical complexity and easy accessibility. Her prolific performance career at home and around the world has made her virtually the face of Chicago jazz today. Photo by Marc Monaghan.

Yet even if Alexander hadn't received robust ovations in Eastern Europe, where she immediately was invited for a return trip in '08, her increasing artistic prowess yielded several of this year's greatest jazz performances.

Consider her breakthrough moment at Millennium Park last summer, when she unveiled "Sirens of Song: Dee Alexander's Tribute to Nina Simone and Dinah Washington." Tearing into Simone's "Mississippi Goddam"—an outcry against the racism of the South—Alexander unleashed every bit of anger that Simone intended, and then some. The gravel in Alexander's voice and the grit of her delivery pointed to a musician who didn't just sing a song but rejuvenated it.

The same artist, however, expressed the joy, optimism and technical acuity one sooner associates with Ella Fitzgerald, during a standing-room-only show at the Hyde Park Jazz Festival.

How can one artist prove so convincing in these diametrically opposed contexts, and several others?

Perhaps the long years Alexander has spent in relative obscurity has enabled her to develop her art in full, outside the glare of publicity and the artistic compromises of the music industry. Performing in low-profile venues at night and holding day jobs all the while, Alexander has been free to experiment with music and learn her own capabilities.

The influence of past Chicago masters such as Light Henry Huff, whose transcendently spiritual music she re-imagined in a South Side field house last June, informs every note she sings. But now she stands as a significant artist in her own right, carrying forth the traditions of Chicago jazz—and building upon them.

Not surprisingly, the increasingly obvious skill of her work has meant that her schedule has picked up dramatically, with forthcoming European tours and a first recording date in the offing.

But it's the music, she says, that still moves her most.

"Sometimes it gets so overwhelming to me—I get this feeling in my chest, and then I'm crying," says Alexander.

"When people come up to you, they're in tears, and they say, 'You've really touched my soul, you've touched my heart'—that's the greatest accomplishment that any artist can have."

A New Freedom

Oct. 15, 2016

For the past quarter century, jazz lovers have wondered how Chicago singer Dee Alexander managed to nurture an international career while holding down a full-time job at the University of Illinois at Chicago.

Not only working 9-to-5, that is, but turning in performances that pushed out the definition of what a jazz singer can be. For Alexander happens to be as persuasive in mainstream repertory as she is in the outer reaches of the jazz avant-garde, as illuminating in music of Duke Ellington as in the concepts of the Association for the Advancement of Creative Musicians (AACM).

If Alexander could do all that while working at UIC for 25 years, you wondered what she might be able to achieve if she didn't have to clock in at her day job.

Alexander and her admirers are about to find out, for she recently retired from UIC and celebrated that turn of events Thursday night at the Jazz Showcase. Sounding sumptuous of voice and exuberant of spirit, Alexander announced the news to her audience, underscoring the point with a rousing performance of "We'll All Be Free."

The anthemlike song, of course, addresses deeper aspects of freedom. But by performing it immediately after delivering the news to the crowd—"Guess what? I'm free!"—Alexander seemed determined to express her newfound liberation in the best way possible: through music.

Her scat singing in "We'll All Be Free" reminded listeners of the technical acuity of Alexander's art, the singer throwing off fast-flying notes with as much clarity as velocity. Like all top-notch jazz singers, Alexander commands sounds and effects that are unique to her, and the sheer inventiveness of her solo flights in "We'll All Be Free" pointed to the scope of her imagination.

She opened the evening on a rather different tack, singing what amounted to a mini-homage to Frank Sinatra. "All or Nothing at All" was one of Sinatra's earliest hits and practically a credo for the man, Sinatra reconceiving it throughout an extraordinarily long career.

Not surprisingly, Alexander reshaped the song to suit her own artistic needs, but the way she stretched phrases across the bar line and dug into the subtext of the lyrics reminded listeners of how much jazz singers today still owe to Sinatra's innovations.

"Once I Loved" dates from the classic "Francis Albert Sinatra & Antonio Carlos Jobim" album of 1967, and Alexander sang the Jobim ballad with the slow-and-easy tempo and subtle bossa nova feel it requires. The most luxuriant sounds emerged when Alexander turned to wordless vocal improvisation, her honeyed low notes and stirring, nearly vibrato-less high pitches a feast to hear—and not easy to dispatch at this unhurried pace.

Next year will mark the centennial of Thelonious Monk, a composer-pianist of towering importance and profound idiosyncrasy. Alexander offered a sneak preview of forthcoming tributes with "Ask Me Now," recast via Jon Hendricks' ingenious lyrics as "How I Wish." Carmen McRae sang definitive versions of this Monk piece and others, but Alexander finessed the off-kilter accents and melodic twists and turns with apparent ease, getting to the core of this music.

She ended her first set with Light Henry Huff's "Live," a signature song for Alexander and a testament to how much Huff meant to her as composer and mentor. Backed here and elsewhere by a band Alexander rightly called her "A Team"—with pianist Miguel de la Cerna, bassist Junius Paul and drummer Ernie Adams—Alexander spun one unexpected riff after another.

It made you realize anew that even as she was working her day job, she always really was free—whenever she stepped in front of a microphone.

CHAPTER 19

Reginald Robinson

Ragtime Blues

May 1, 2005

It's standing-room-only on a late February afternoon at tony Occidental College in Los Angeles, where some 200 students are about to learn that genius can come in unexpected forms.

The guest lecturer is from the very un-tony West Side of Chicago. He seats himself at the piano, gently places his fingers on the keyboard and proceeds to reel off ragtime tunes of astonishing complexity. In just a few beats his hands become a blur, the instrument begins to shake, and the kids find themselves swaying in their seats.

Between numbers, each of which draws a clamorous ovation, the pianist weaves a lecture. His subject is ragtime, and he traces the music's evolution from the classic works of Scott Joplin to the ferociously difficult and ornate original rags that he is unfurling on this balmy California day.

Seldom, if ever, have the students at Occidental, where tuition and lodging hover at $40,000 a year, received tutoring of this sort. The visiting professor, after all, dropped out of high school and taught himself his art before going on to compose a stack of certifiable, state-of-the-art ragtime masterpieces.

Fig. 12 Reginald Robinson: The Chicago pianist's 2004 MacArthur Fellowship earned him the sobriquet "genius," but that status was long apparent from his strikingly original compositions. Robinson has breathed new life into the seemingly dead art of ragtime, proving it holds fresh possibilities.

"How much did you get for the MacArthur 'genius' award?" one of the students inevitably asks, referring to the MacArthur Foundation Fellowship that the pianist received last fall.

"Half a million dollars," replies 32-year-old Reginald R. Robinson, with a demure grin. "And that's half a million more than I ever had before."

Indeed, just before Robinson learned last September that he had won one of the most lucrative and prestigious awards in the country, the gas in his West Side apartment was cut off and overdue notices from the electric company were piling up.

He was so broke and despondent that he'd given up practicing piano, ceased composing new music and very nearly stopped believing that he could make a living in ragtime—an art form that had been dead for roughly 80 years until Robinson came along and decided to try to breathe life back into it.

That a young man whose childhood was punctuated with shootings and other inner-city horrors—a kid who failed 7th grade before eventually bailing on the Chicago public schools—should emerge as the leading hope of a long-lost art form would seem remarkable enough. But that he taught himself practically everything he knows about music, spending years decoding notes and chords, only underscores the magnitude of his achievement.

Yet on this day, as on most others, his focus is not on his arduous journey but on its goal, the music.

"A lot of people think ragtime is hokey," concedes Robinson, who stands about 5 feet 8 inches but produces the colossal sound of a much larger man. "But in my mind, it's deeper than that. . . . You can hear every emotion; all of life is in it."

Certainly all of Robinson's life is.

Above all else, Reginald Robinson remembers two things about his turbulent childhood—the gang-bangers who repeatedly broke into his family's third-floor apartment in the Henry Horner Homes, and the ice-cream truck that chimed a lilting, syncopated melody as it rolled slowly along West Lake Street in the crushing summer heat.

If the violence scarred Robinson, the ice-cream truck's mechanical jingle may have saved him.

Robinson recalls jumping every time he heard gunshots fired in the streets. "I mean, almost anything you can imagine was going on over there. One time, some guy was trying to break in while we were at home! We were looking at him, and he was looking at us."

Another time, the Robinson family—two parents and six children—returned home from a movie to find their apartment being ransacked. "These guys had everything all over the place," says Robinson. "The front door had melted. I guess they used some kind of heating apparatus or something to get in."

Amid the chaos, Robinson sought refuge in music wherever he encountered it—on the radio, on the LPs that his folks played at home, ranging from Bach to Basie. And even from that ice-cream truck, with its twinkly little tune that was written by ragtime legend Scott Joplin—though back then Robinson had no idea who wrote it, nor had he ever heard of Joplin.

In fact, Robinson never thought about that song-Joplin's indelible "The Entertainer"—until one Friday afternoon during his second tour of 7th grade in 1986. A group of Chicago jazz musicians from the Urban Gateways program was playing at Robert Emmet School, in the Austin neighborhood, where Robinson's family had moved a few years earlier.

To Robinson's amazement, one of the musicians began playing the ice-cream truck song. The music evoked pleasant memories that stood out against an unsettling childhood and awakened in him an overwhelming desire to capture those sounds, to make them on his own.

"Something really was pulling me into that music," says Robinson. "It's strange to me; I'm still trying to figure that out."

Though he may never determine exactly why Joplin's melody—it had regained prominence in the Oscar-winning 1973 film "The Sting"—changed him, he knows that he had never felt anything like it before or since. In that beguiling little tune, he found a purpose for his young life, a way to bring some order out of the anarchy surrounding him.

"It just did something to him, it excited him so much," says his mother, Janet. "He came back home and told me all about it."

The 13-year-old Robinson immediately began rifling through dictionaries and other books at home, searching for any reference to "ragtime" but finding none. So he wrote the word down on a piece of paper to ensure that he wouldn't forget it before Monday, when he was able to look it up at school.

Every day after that he wandered to the back of the classroom to thumb through the pages of a dictionary until he arrived at "ragtime," reading the definition over and over, writing it down, memorizing it, absorbing it.

The text cited Joplin as "the king of ragtime," and soon other books pointed Robinson to "The Sting," which used Joplin's music as a backdrop and sparked a brief revival of interest in ragtime in the 1970s. Robinson found a videotape of the film and played it repeatedly to study its score. Then he moved on to Charlie Chaplin and Buster Keaton silent films, which similarly featured ebullient ragtime piano music as accompaniments.

Each day, his obsession deepened. "I was on a hunt," says Robinson. He begged his parents for a piano and eventually got a small electric keyboard, which he hammered constantly. His playing was crude, as the tapes he made of himself show, the fledgling pianist inventing snippets of melodies akin to nursery-school songs.

Meanwhile, the violence of the neighborhood constantly bumped up against Robinson's life. The house that the family bought in 1987 on the South Side had more space than anything they had before, but the new neighborhood didn't seem to be any less dangerous than the ones they left behind. Drug deals and armed violence remained fixtures of everyday life.

It got so bad that Robinson's mother decided she had to walk her kids to the front door of their schools and pick them up in the afternoon to ensure their safety. Even when Robinson was a teenager, his mother accompanied him to the steps of Tilden High School.

"The young people that went to that school began to carry guns," she recalls. "Reginald saw several of his classmates get shot, and it made him not want to go back."

He dropped out during his freshman year and retreated into his bedroom, teaching himself piano on an old Jensen spinet his mother had acquired from a neighbor. Someone had put stickers on each key with the name of every note, so Robinson was able to read the long runway of otherwise inscrutable black and white keys.

From morning until night he struggled at the piano, trying to find chords where the unskilled hand strikes only dissonance, working to pick out melodies from a seemingly infinite range of possibilities. When he wasn't hitting the keys, he was listening to recordings by Joplin, Louis Chauvin, Tom Turpin and others, trying to re-create on his piano the intoxicating sounds they had invented a century earlier.

For three years, Robinson rarely left his bedroom. And through the sheer intensity of his focus and the depth of his gifts, he began to play ragtime.

"He played continuously, over and over and over, until one day it turned into music," says his mother.

Adds elder brother Marlando Robinson, "I couldn't believe what he was accomplishing. One day he put on a tape of something for me, and I said, 'Was that Joplin, Handy or Chauvin?'

"And he said, 'No, that's me.'"

A skeptical Marlando marched Reginald over to the piano, insisting that he demonstrate this feat live, not on a cassette player.

"His hands flew so fast, you couldn't even see them," recalls Marlando, still somewhat incredulous.

In those three years—a blink of an eye in the course of most musicians' training—Robinson had remade himself from a kid who didn't even know the word "ragtime" into a creator of original tunes.

Though at age 16 he still had a lot to learn about writing a first-class composition—how to create multiple themes, how to switch from one key to another, how to replicate and even extend the formal structures of Joplin and other ragtime greats—Robinson surely had found his voice.

Yet he was dissatisfied that he still stumbled at reading music, that he couldn't accurately put his compositions to paper, that almost everything about the nuts and bolts of ragtime music eluded him—except how to create it and how to play it.

So he got a job at a silkscreen shop in the neighborhood to pay for a few music lessons at the now-defunct American Conservatory of Music, in the Loop. At his first session, his instructor was as skeptical as his brother Marlando had been.

"He played a number of his pieces for me, and I just couldn't believe he had created them, because he hadn't had any lessons," remembers his instructor at the conservatory, Ted Bargmann.

"For a teacher, it was hard to believe. But then I realized it was true—he showed me the music. The stems on the notes were going in the wrong direction, some of the rhythm notations weren't correct, but these were basically the notes he played. It was some kind of miracle."

But Robinson was just getting started. Deciding that neither Bargmann nor anyone else could teach him how to create ragtime any better than he already was doing, he again holed up in the bedroom of his parents' house.

In a burst of creativity, he wrote nearly a dozen compositions of unusual complexity and harmonic sophistication, even though he didn't know the names of the chords he was creating or understand the musical devices his ear was leading him to.

He saved up enough money to buy another used piano and added that to the other one in his bedroom, placing his bed between the pair of instruments. Night and day the young man literally was surrounded by music.

To help him connect with the spirit of the ragtime age, he pulled the red velvet curtains down from his parents' living room and hung them in his bedroom, conjuring the ambience of the old-time brothels where ragtime music emerged. Sometimes he took the shade off a lamp and placed the fixture on the floor so that it cast moody shadows across his room, the play of light and half-light helping him imagine that he was living in the gaslight era.

"It was like mentally transporting myself out of where we are now and into another zone," says Robinson. "Like I'm no longer in the present—I'm in 1907."

The result of these efforts was groundbreaking, even though almost no one outside the Robinson home knew it. The surging rhythms of "The Strongman" (composed in 1990), the poetic phrases of "Troubador Serenade" (1990), the sturm und drang of "Nile River Ripples" (1991) and the rhythmic swagger and bawdy chords of "Poker Face Blues" (1992) heralded the arrival of a new kind of ragtime, an art form that had essentially atrophied after Joplin's death in 1917.

Even the titles of Robinson's pieces reflected his fertile imagination. "Boogie Man Creep," "The Hustler's Two-Step" and "Ebony Venus" evoked exotic worlds of sound and image.

Though pianists such as Dick Hyman, Max Morath and others long had played the old tunes nobly, and a couple dozen latter-day ragtimers wrote retro music of their own, no one was crafting compositions as intricate and original as Robinson's.

Perhaps because he never was taught the rules of harmony and theory, he was not constrained by them, building his oft-fanciful compositions on unanticipated chord changes, unusual bursts of dissonance, unorthodox turns of phrase and unexpected clashes of traditional and contemporary techniques.

Feeling ready by the early 1990s to bring his ragtime creations into the world, he began seeking out other Chicago musicians, finally lucking out in 1992 when he met the brilliant pianist Jon Weber, who long has ruled over the lounge of the Four Seasons Hotel. Though commanding an encyclopedic knowledge of jazz history, Weber was stunned at the freshness of Robinson's art.

"'Where'd you study?'" Weber recalls asking. "And Reginald said, 'I didn't.'

"He was 19 years old then, and these scores, they were so precise and so fastidious, I could hear exactly how they sounded by looking at them. And I'm thinking, 'I can't believe this humble man has produced all this.' It was almost like he was living in another time; he was living, breathing, dreaming that bygone period."

Weber soon realized that Robinson had perfect pitch, a gift that surely had enabled him to learn music and master composition without benefit of a teacher. Weber became his first and most ardent champion, paying for studio time so that Robinson could record his bulging catalog of original works.

Weber brought dozens of cassette tapes of the studio sessions to sell at Robinson's low-key, Sunday-afternoon debut at Uptown's Green Mill Jazz Club in September 1992. The tapes practically flew out of Robinson's hands, inspiring him to bring a copy to Bob Koester, owner of the respected, Chicago-based Delmark Records.

"What he was playing sounded totally original," says Koester, who immediately signed Robinson to a recording contract.

"He wasn't just playing ragtime like most of these guys play it," a reference to the buttoned-down, note-perfect, often-anemic renderings of many players a generation or two older than Robinson.

Perhaps because he had learned ragtime as its original creators had—on his own, without formal training, note by grueling note—Robinson's music sounded all the more authentic, credible and true.

Not surprisingly, Robinson's recording debut in 1993, "The Strongman," earned lavish praise from critics, musicians and scholars.

Dick Hyman, for decades one of the country's top interpreters of ragtime and other early-American styles, remembers being caught off guard by the quality and depth of Robinson's original works. "Reginald," says Hyman, "had so absorbed all the classic rags that he could write them as well as the old masters could."

And play them. His version of Joplin's "Maple Leaf Rag," which opens "The Strongman," became something of an instant classic. "I don't think there's anyone in the world that plays a piece like 'Maple Leaf Rag' who comes as close to Scott Joplin's piano roll as Reginald does," says Trebor Tichenor, one of the leading scholars of the genre.

Within months, Robinson was taping Marian McPartland's "Piano Jazz" radio show and broadcasting live, nationally, during a New Year's Eve double-bill with Weber at the Green Mill.

But just as Robinson's career was taking flight, it began to sink in how marginal ragtime was in the spectrum of musical tastes at the turn of the 21st Century. He was paid a $1,000 advance from Delmark for "The Strongman," and got only $2,000 up front for its follow-up,

"Sounds in Silhouette" (1994)—not exactly a big-time payday for work he had spent years creating, even including modest royalties.

And though various ragtime festivals booked him when he was a novelty on the scene in the early 1990s, Robinson's engagement calendar never filled out.

"I simply had no money," he recalls of what he terms his first great "slump," in 1995. "I was at a really low state, where I was just trying to look for a [day] job, and ended up going from door to door in the Loop, trying to put in job applications. I was borrowing money from my mother just to try to live."

He began working as a day laborer for a packaging company in Elgin, serving food at a Loop restaurant, washing autos at a car-rental place downtown—anything to support himself and his music.

The $3,000 advance he received for his third and most ambitious Delmark CD, "Euphonic Sounds"—which made history by including a fragment of a Scott Joplin tune Robinson discovered while scrutinizing an old photograph—did not pull him out of debt. The bills only mounted after he moved out of his parents' house in 1999 to live with a girlfriend in Uptown.

Why couldn't a pianist of such distinction and achievement earn even the barest subsistence wage with his music?

"You've got to remember that 98 percent of any jazz musician's life is worrying about how to make the rent or a car payment," says Weber, a veteran of the financial squeeze. Robinson's position was all the more precarious because he had chosen to work in one of the most arcane subsets of jazz.

"He was in a strange spot. He should have been playing all the ragtime festivals, but there's a lot of latent racism there," says Koester, describing an insular milieu that features white performers playing for mostly white audiences. Robinson, with his urban-looking cornrows and ragtime iconoclasm, couldn't crack this nostalgia-based circuit.

"He should have been playing the jazz festivals, too," adds Koester, "but [they] generally turn their backs on traditional jazz."

There was another, deeper reason why Robinson was overlooked by the very music world that is starved for talent of his caliber, and that's the stigma of ragtime itself.

Born in the post-slavery era when Blacks were suffering profoundly, ragtime was used as the backdrop for minstrel shows and other demeaning entertainments.

"Even when ragtime was popular, there definitely was a 50–50 split about it in the Black community," notes Tichenor, the music scholar. "Eubie Blake said his mother told him to 'take that ragtime out of my house,' knowing where ragtime came from." In other words, the sporting houses and streets.

Jelly Roll Morton, who started out as a ragtime piano player in the brothels of New Orleans' Storyville vice district, literally was kicked out of his family's home as a teenager and left to fend for himself when his grandmother found out he was playing the illicit music.

Associations of this sort, of course, have nothing to do with the inherent value of the music, as Robinson has proved, but the aura lingers. Many audiences and musicians, including a number of African-Americans, "would rather put that part of the past behind them, and who could blame them?" says Hyman. "That's why what Reginald has done is such a brave act of individuality, to go against this attitude the way he has."

As the 20th Century slipped into the 21st, Robinson spent the hours away from his temporary day jobs composing tunes for his next—and still unreleased—album. Aptly titled "Man Out of Time," the homemade CD contains one intricate ragtime opus after another, each a world of pitch and rhythm unto itself.

The recording, a milestone in the maturation of his art, culminates in "The 19th Galaxy," a ragtime tour de force that reaffirms Robinson's position at the front lines of the art form.

Reluctant to take the recording to Delmark, where he had received so little money for his previous efforts, he shopped the CD elsewhere but could find no takers.

He moved out of his girlfriend's place in 2003 and into affordable housing for artists on the West Side, but he still found himself slipping into financial ruin. Only a cash gift from a friend made it possible for him to take his piano with him. The future looked bleak.

"Man, here I am again," he told himself. He looked for janitorial jobs, stockroom gigs, anything that could provide steady money. Even menial jobs were hard to find. Meanwhile, he felt himself losing his will to write music and practice the piano. "It was just not fun anymore," he says.

Out of desperation, he took his "Man Out of Time" CD to Delmark last year. Koester offered him a $2,000 advance, which Robinson urgently needed but ultimately declined to accept, saying it would amount to "signing my soul away" for a pittance.

On the day the MacArthur Foundation telephoned, Robinson was lying in bed, chilled to the bone because the gas had been cut off, wondering what he would do when the electricity went next.

When Daniel J. Socolow, director of the MacArthur Fellows program, told Robinson that he was a winner and would receive $100,000 annually for the next five years, he wasn't sure he hadn't dreamed it. For hours afterward, he kept checking his caller ID to make sure it really was the MacArthur Foundation that had phoned.

He went to the bathroom to splash his face with the icy cold water coming from both faucets, then spent the next couple of days chewing over what had happened before telling anyone else.

Finally, he went to his mother's house on the South Side and asked her to come for a drive with him. They had traveled all the way to the suburbs before he pulled over and said, "Don't jump out of your skin, but I just won the MacArthur Award."

Janet Robinson was familiar with the prize and its mysterious ways—the foundation secretly seeks out and researches potential candidates before selecting winners whose lives will be changed.

On hearing the news, Robinson's mother couldn't catch her breath.

"I was surprised, I was ecstatic," she recalls. "Oh, man, tears just came to my eyes."

Suddenly, Reginald Robinson, ragtime pianist, was back in business, a development that posed interesting problems of its own.

For starters, the years in which he hadn't composed any music and the months in which he hadn't touched a piano meant that a great deal of his art had escaped his fingertips. To this day, he says, he struggles to recapture the pieces he once tossed off with ease, to relearn his virtuoso technique.

"The MacArthur thing kind of caught me off guard," says Robinson. "I'm getting engagements now where there used to be nothing, and so

I'm being pushed to get my music up. That music on 'Man Out of Time,' I have to learn it again."

After the lecture at Occidental College, students swarm around Robinson, asking to buy the CDs he brought and imploring him to autograph them.

Later that day he ventures to Hollywood, which he never has seen, and asks me to photograph him with a disposable camera Robinson just bought. The setting is the famous corner of Hollywood and Vine, along the Hollywood Walk of Fame, where the beehive tower of Capitol Records looms nearby. Then on to other celebrated sites.

On practically every block, Robinson wants another picture to prove to his family—and, perhaps, himself—that he really was here, a kid from some of the toughest parts of Chicago, who literally played his way out of there.

Even so, Robinson is quick to point out that he's "still half literate," as far as music is concerned. "I still do not know simple things—simple terms in music, I still don't understand."

He goes to a Los Angeles video store to see if he can pick up any of the science-fiction films he devours in his spare time. Like ragtime, he says, these films take him to other places, far away from his everyday life.

For the most part, though, he spends his waking hours consumed with music—reading books about it, listening to recordings, practicing the piano, honing his compositions. Most of his life, in fact, plays out in his apartment, his never-ending immersion in ragtime music interrupted periodically with trips to the concert stage or visits to his family's South Side home.

Though he hasn't decided exactly what he's going to do with the MacArthur money, he knows what he wants to accomplish: "I want this ragtime music to be accepted, to be back in the mainstream," he says.

There's one more thing Robinson wants, and has wanted, since he heard the ice-cream truck music played by real musicians in the 7th grade: He wants to compose the ragtime masterpieces that are still left unwritten—the music that he says wafts quietly through the ether, waiting for someone to capture it.

"I always had this thought in my mind that these melodies, if I listen long enough in silence, that I'll hear this music that's not yet written down—I mean that," he insists.

"I think that there are things Scott Joplin never got a chance to write down, and things that many other ragtime musicians never got a chance to write down.

"And I can catch that—if I listen."

Invisible Man?

Jan. 24, 2010

Five years fly fast when you've got $500,000 to spend as you please.

But now Chicagoan Reginald Robinson's five years are up: His prestigious MacArthur Fellowship "genius" grant, dispensed in annual installments of $100,000 (with no strings attached), just ended.

So, the pianist-composer needs to figure out what to do with the rest of his life. And at 37, that could be another half-century or so of trying to scrape together a living by playing, of all things, ragtime music.

And not just any ragtime, but his own lushly beautiful, startlingly original rags—compositions with beguiling titles such as "Ebony Venus" and "The 19th Galaxy," "Ballerina Figurine" and "Four Horsemen of the Apocalypse."

The genius of these works—and literally dozens more like them—earned Robinson the MacArthur grant, which delivered him from pennilessness: Just before he received the MacArthur call, in late 2004, the gas had been cut off in his South Side apartment for unpaid bills and the electricity was going to be next.

Five years later, Robinson has worked mightily to get his life on track and to champion ragtime, the art form that turned a high school dropout into one of the most original musical voices this city has produced. Yet even though Robinson has used his MacArthur funds to self-release two stunning CDs—the aptly named "Man Out of Time" (2006) and the new three-disc set "Reflections" (2010)—he realizes that he hasn't been able to make a dent in popular consciousness.

Both Robinson and his ethereal ragtime compositions remain obscure to all but a small group of devotees fortunate enough to have heard them.

"Even with the MacArthur 'genius' title . . . I'm invisible," says Robinson in a characteristically gentle, soft-spoken voice.

"Like, take 'Man Out of Time,'" adds Robinson, referring to a recording 11 years in the making. No major record label was willing to release it—even after the MacArthur—notwithstanding some high-powered representatives who tried to place it for Robinson. So, the pianist used the first wave of his grant money to produce the CD, though he had to learn the intricacies of mastering recordings and dealing with manufacturers to do so.

"It's a great CD. I know it was," says Robinson. "The reviews were very good. . . . But it's still invisible. You need publicity and promotion, or no one knows who you are."

The inconvenient truth here is not simply that the pop-rock industry has no room for the age-old art of ragtime—that's a given. But even the world of jazz, which blossomed out of ragtime's innovations, generally turns its back on the radiant music Robinson has devoted his life to.

"It's a music that's out of sight. It's totally ignored," says Bob Koester, owner of Chicago-based Delmark Records, which released Robinson's first three CDs, "The Strongman" (1993), "Sounds in Silhouette" (1994) and "Euphonic Sounds" (1998).

"We put out other ragtime records, too, and they sell terribly."

Among the reasons may be the stigma that still clings to ragtime, which many listeners understandably associate with a grim chapter in American race relations. Born on plantations and disseminated in minstrel shows, ragtime long has been synonymous with awful racial stereotypes, thanks in part to the unconscionable lyrics attached to its indelible melodies.

"It is the unwholesome words and not the ragtime melodies that many people hate," ragtime king Scott Joplin said in 1913, using the race vernacular of the period: "Ragtime rhythm is a syncopation original with the colored people, though many of them are ashamed of it."

That sentiment may be widespread.

Of course, the public buys what it wants, and the market decides what's popular. But Robinson's against-all-odds quest to revive an art form that atrophied after the death of Joplin, in 1917, seemed to get a new shot at life with the MacArthur grant. Or at least Robinson thought so.

After winning the award, one of the most revered in America, Robinson aced engagements in prestigious venues such as the Hammer

Museum in Los Angeles; the Greenbrier, a National Historic Landmark in West Virginia; and the Auditorium Theatre in Chicago, where in 2007 he performed the world premiere of "Concerto for a Genius," in which Chicago composer Orbert Davis orchestrated four of Robinson's solo piano works.

None of these appearances likely would have happened without the MacArthur. The pianist also has crisscrossed the United States to film a documentary-in-progress on the life, death and resurrection (he hopes) of ragtime.

Most important of all, perhaps, Robinson has penned several original compositions that extend the expressive possibilities of ragtime. The idiosyncratic chord progressions of "Footloose" and the structural innovations of "Freedom Dance" (both included on the new "Reflections" set) attest to Robinson's unyielding musical curiosity.

Yet the obstacles remain formidable, for both Robinson and ragtime. There still isn't a great deal of demand for a ragtime piano player specializing in complex, though hauntingly lyrical, original works. And unless the world is galvanized anew by another popular film such as "The Sting," which in 1973 rejuvenated interest in the music of Joplin, ragtime will continue to subsist beyond the periphery of most listeners' consciousness.

This puts Robinson in a peculiar position, atop a tiny, shrinking field. For he not only stands as America's leading composer of 21st century ragtime but also has emerged as a world-class expert in the field. It was Robinson who discovered a fragment of hitherto unknown music by Joplin, making history by recording it for the first time, on his CD "Euphonic Sounds."

So although Robinson—a self-taught pianist—has toiled mightily for all he has achieved, he'll have to struggle to make a living in ragtime. Yet few are better positioned to do so.

"I think he's ready to own the genre," says Davis, the composer-conductor who long has been a mentor to Robinson. "He's a ragtime master. . . . There's got to be a way for him to incorporate that, in a business sense.

"I'd love to see Reginald get a college degree or an honorary doctorate in this. That may be the missing link in explaining why he's not on a tour of universities across the country as the ragtime scholar.

"I'm not sure he knows what is the next step."

If Robinson's post-MacArthur journey seems steep, it's nothing compared with what he has overcome to reach this point.

When he was a child in the Henry Horner Homes, on the West Side, gangbangers repeatedly broke into his family's third-floor apartment.

But in seventh grade, Robinson's life abruptly changed when a group of musicians—led by Davis—came to Robert Emmet School, in the Austin neighborhood, and played Joplin's "The Entertainer." Robinson was transfixed by this music and soon began to teach himself to play the piano. Though the street violence plaguing the South Side neighborhood where his family had moved, in 1987, led Robinson to drop out of Tilden High School, he spent his days and nights studying ragtime, alone, in his room.

When he began playing his music publicly, in the early 1990s, listeners were struck by the originality and lyric sheen of his work, as well as his prodigious keyboard technique. Yet until the MacArthur checks started rolling in, in 2005, Robinson plowed ever more deeply into debt.

Now he stands at the start of the rest of his career, his finances organized, his challenges and possibilities before him.

Though he's reeling from the death of his father, Mose Robinson, last month, he takes solace in his relationship with his 11-year-old daughter and his coming marriage to singer and public school teacher Sondra Davis (who appeared on his "Euphonic Sounds" CD).

The end of the MacArthur money convinced Robinson to sell the house he had bought after he won the award and move into an apartment. He also has gotten rid of his grand piano, meaning he'll now return to practicing at the Harold Washington Library Center or other public places where he can find an instrument to use.

In some ways, then, he's returning to the way he lived before the MacArthur, but without the financial desperation and buoyed by a national reputation—albeit in rather narrow circles.

"I have the dream of my music being in theater and film," says Robinson, who believes that when ragtime music accompanies a narrative story, it's not invisible anymore.

"That's the only way the music I create will survive," says Robinson, whose work deserves no less.

CHAPTER 20

Patricia Barber

Reaching "Higher"

June 2, 2019

Barreling down the highway from a Minnesota gig the night before, Patricia Barber sounds exuberant.

"Minneapolis is one of my favorite places to play in the United States," says Barber, speaking via cellphone, both hands on the steering wheel, she assures me.

"That's because they understand English very, very well."

Meaning that Barber's songs—though easy enough to enjoy when listening nonchalantly—are uncommonly rich in content and reward close attention. Every syllable, every chord change, every whispering vocal turn sends a message, and if you dare to breathe, you may miss it.

Nowhere has that point emerged more succinctly than in "Higher," her newly released recording and a high point in a discography stretching back decades. For though the Chicagoan has penned song cycles before, the one that stretches across the first eight tracks of "Higher" represents her singular art distilled to its essence.

Tightly compressed lyrics, transparent musical textures, infinitesimally subtle vocal shadings, moments of unexpected silence and multiple layers of subtext define "Angels, Birds and I . . . ," a suite at least five years in the making.

Fig. 13 Patricia Barber: Longtime Barber devotees have seen an unassuming Chicago singer-pianist evolve into one of the most original jazz composers of our time. Her meticulously crafted art songs and song cycles uplift these genres; her crystalline pianism and liquid vocals enchant the ear.

When you think of the song cycle's title, it's clear what links the angels, birds and Barber—singing, of course, each producing it by nature. Except in Barber's case, an extraordinary amount of art, craft, sweat and technique goes into every ultra-polished vignette.

Consider the song "Higher," which launched Barber's venture into creating this cycle, the singer-pianist having first performed an embryonic version of the tune at the University of Chicago's Logan Center in 2014.

"In a few tautly compressed sentences and a gently ascending melodic line, Barber just hints at her subject matter: nothing less than death and transformation," I wrote in my review of the work-in-progress. "Played with zero sense of pulse, its phrases seemingly suspended in air, 'Higher' drifts into the listener's consciousness, then disappears, like a soft breeze that's gone before you knew it was there. As it now stands, 'Higher' is sheathed in mystery, its haiku-like verse telegraphing a message that's only partially discernible."

Having developed, reworked, honed and performed the song ever since, Barber has rendered the message of "Higher" clearer, if you listen intently enough.

"I wrote 'Higher' for my mother," who died in 2009 at age 90, explains Barber. "I'm asking her to lift her voice and take wing—to leave her body and the pain behind."

The lyrics evoke the story:

And you my true love / Have been stilled by pain / Grounded in silence / On earth you'll remain.
Until an air / Blows in like spring / You'll be young again / Raise your voice, take wing.

Even before Barber began working on "Higher," she had started to liberate herself from traditional jazz chord progressions and from the tyranny of relentless backbeats. "Higher" took her deeply into another realm.

Or, as a friend told her while she was developing the piece, "You're getting dangerously close to the art song," Barber told me in 2014.

In truth, she already was there.

"This all started with 'Higher,' and then I started thinking about the singer thing," says Barber, meaning the theme that eventually would come to define the slowly emerging song cycle.

"Then 'Surrender' was second," she adds, referring to a song about music's seductive power to overcome our resistance. "Then I thought: OK, this is what I'm interested in—singers and music. And at some point in there, halfway through the song cycle, that's when I hooked up with Renee Fleming, and we did a tour together on half the song cycle."

Chicagoans will remember star soprano Fleming partnering with Barber at the Harris Theater in December 2015, for "Higher: Renee Fleming and Patricia Barber Perform the Music of Patricia Barber." Fleming, a jazz singer early in her career who eventually became one of America's most beloved operatic divas, would drop by the Green Mill Jazz Club to catch Barber's Monday night sessions whenever Fleming was in town working at Lyric Opera.

The friendship and partnership that ensued inspired Barber to pen for Fleming "The Opera Song," a verbal and musical tour de force about a disillusioned officer worker who imagines herself an opera star. On the new album, it unfolds practically as a miniature three-act opera in itself, not only in Barber's recording but in a kind of bonus track featuring soprano Katherine Werbiansky.

Add to this the personification of music that Barber conjures in her "Muse" (dedicated to Fleming), the wicked social satire she expresses in "The Albatross Song," the yearning for the sweet sound of birds after a long winter in "High Summer Season"—among others—and you have a work unlike anything else heard in either jazz or classical realms these days.

"The way I see it, it has been an evolution," says Martha Feldman, a professor at the University of Chicago's Department of Music who's married to Barber and served as associate producer of the new album.

"The evolution is ultimately a harmonic one, but the harmonic one is inseparable from the poetry and the melodic thinking. I guess I would say that definitely by the time she did 'Mythologies,' in 2006, she'd already [broken from] some of the traditional jazz forms."

Feldman was referring to a stunning album in which Barber crafted a quasi-Schubertian song cycle inspired by Ovid's "Metamorphoses," complete with choral music and passages of hip-hop.

"I think that 'Smash,' in 2013, was an experiment with line lengths and syllable counts that was pushing that further forward. But by the time she got to 'Higher,' she was really directly working on writing jazz that kind of evolves out of voice leading," adds Feldman, referring to a method of composition in which the unfurling of melodies reflects the text's cadences, and vice versa.

It takes great labors and vast swaths of time to achieve this economy of poetry and concision of musical structure, which surely helps explain why it has been six years since Barber's last studio CD, the aforementioned "Smash."

"It really took me that time to write this music," says Barber. "When you look at the time it takes to write books," it's not so surprising, she implies.

"And I'm dealing with the words as well, which is not something most [jazz musicians] do. Fitting these words into new harmony, or fitting new harmony around these words, or as they perhaps come together, is difficult. It looks small.

"And I guess if it's short, it seems easy. It wasn't easy."

Along the way, Barber has sought help from a friend and mentor to whom she has dedicated the song "Surrender," Pulitzer Prize-winning composer Shulamit Ran, a professor in the University of Chicago's Department of Music.

"I took some lessons from her," says Barber. "What she showed me, she didn't tell me in words—it's hard to explain harmony that way. What she showed me at the piano really stuck with me and opened up a whole new vista."

Ran long ago was smitten by Barber's musical innovations as singer, songwriter and pianist.

"I heard her at the Green Mill, and I thought to myself, 'This is fantastic,'" Ran told me in 2014, on the eve of Barber unveiling the early version of "Higher" at the Logan Center.

"This was just really amazing music of tremendous imagination and very personal, very, very daring. . . . And then I had the realization that [musical] categories are not nearly as important as the level of imagination and creativity."

So Barber now stands at the newest pinnacle of a long, tough, winding journey. She first came to wide attention when she was toiling as a singer-pianist at the long-gone Gold Star Sardine Bar on North Lake Shore Drive. When I first reviewed her there, in 1990, a Valentine's Day blizzard had forced her to walk 2 miles from her apartment to make the set because no cabs were available.

"It's easy to understand why Barber is on her way up," I wrote of that indelible evening. "You will not hear Dick Rogers and Earle Hagan's 'Harlem Nocturne' sung more intimately or with greater languor. Barber knows how to stretch a vocal line without distorting it, and—like the best jazz singers—she dispatches lyrics with utter clarity."

But Barber was brave enough—and musically and intellectually astute enough—to break out of the lounge-entertainer persona and aspire toward something more complex, rarefied, sophisticated and autobiographical via her songwriting. It was a struggle.

"To be doing what she's been doing all these years means you don't have a [steady] paycheck, you don't have health insurance from any outfit," says Feldman.

Yet Barber persevered, her efforts rewarded most recently with her election to the American Academy of Arts & Sciences.

"Maybe a month ago, I was getting up, and I went to turn off the porch light in the morning, as I do every morning," says Barber.

"And there was a FedEx letter. I opened it up and read it—I didn't have my glasses on. I figured this is an organization that was asking for money.

"So I made myself an espresso, put my glasses on and read it and said: 'Oh my God, this is for me!'"

What's the significance of this?

"It means that people have been listening," says Barber.

Or as she noted in a Facebook posting when writing about what happened at a recent Academy reception: "I did not expect to be welcomed so warmly, people taking my hand, saying, for instance, 'Hello Patricia, I'm George in astrophysics—so happy to see you here. I'm a fan.' History, linguistics, biogenetics, musicology, math, literature, chemistry, economics, philosophy, political science and on. They acted like they knew me, and they do know my work."

This development "really means a lot," says Feldman, also a member of the Academy who "didn't watch the process, which is confidential. . . . It means that she's gotten this very broad affirmation from a very broad group of people."

But also an elite group of achievers who presumably have recognized the uniqueness of Barber's art, the value of her contributions and the distinctiveness of each of her albums.

"You feel that each new adventure she goes on, it's like a deep dive," says composer and University of Chicago professor Augusta Read Thomas, who invited Barber to open the Ear Taxi Festival in 2016 at the Harris Theater. In that performance, Barber sang portions of the then-still-evolving "Angels, Birds, and I . . ." cycle.

"It's a little bit like she's on the high dive, and she dives deep into these huge adventures, because she needs to," adds Thomas. "And we get to have the benefit of it in such beautiful pieces of art that she makes."

So "Higher" may be more than just Barber's latest offering. It could be a foreshadowing of deep dives yet to come.

A New Take on Art Songs

Dec. 9, 2015

Chicago jazz singer-pianist Patricia Barber never will forget the first time soprano Renee Fleming stepped into the Green Mill Jazz Club to hear her, a few years ago.

Barber knew full well that Fleming ranks among the world's most admired sopranos, a marquee performer at Lyric Opera of Chicago, the Metropolitan Opera in New York and houses far beyond.

"I was so nervous," recalls Barber. "I can't breathe. I can't sing. There's no way I can sing for this woman."

But, of course, Barber did sing and play the piano, speaking to Fleming afterward.

"We started talking about mucus," adds Barber, "which is very common among singers to talk about. She was showing me how to hold my tongue when I was opening up a big mouth."

Clearly, the two bonded, their mutual admiration deepening over time, and their relationship reaching a new plateau with Monday night's world premiere of "Higher: Renee Fleming and Patricia Barber Perform the Music of Patricia Barber" at the Harris Theater for Music and Dance. After the Chicago performance, the historic program will travel to the Kennedy Center, in Washington, and National Sawdust, in Brooklyn.

Ever since that first time Fleming heard Barber, the diva became increasingly intrigued with Barber's work, dropping in often at the Mill and catching Barber's shows on the road, whenever the two globe-trotting artists happened to be in the same town at the same time. Gradually, Fleming began performing some of Barber's hyperliterate, musically sophisticated songs in recital, Fleming realizing that this work stands apart from the usual love-song cliches.

"I was sitting there [at the Green Mill] a year ago, and I said, 'My God, these are art songs,'" recalls Fleming, aptly describing the high craft and layered meanings of Barber's best compositions. "This is really something special."

As a singer, continues Fleming, "Her sound, it's interesting. It's very pure, she has impeccable pitch. She's actually a really fabulous musician.

"I don't feel she leads with her singing. I think it's the music, and it's so powerful."

Indeed, though Barber remains best known as a vocalist of ethereal allure and a jazz pianist of sleek elegance, the music she has written during the past decade-plus may be her greatest contribution. The bittersweet wit of "The Swim" and the searing eloquence of "Scream" (both from her 2013 album "Smash") and the vivid imagery and delicate tone painting of "Snow" (from her 2008 album "The Cole Porter Mix") point to the evocative nature of her writing. And who else but Barber would pen a Schubertian song cycle inspired by Ovid's "Metamorphoses" (documented on her 2006 album "Mythologies")?

More recent Barber songs, such as "Higher" and "Surrender," have shown Barber delivering increasingly subtle and ambiguous messages, her work appealing to anyone who values lyrics that carry multiple meanings and music that illuminates them.

How fitting, then, that a singer of Fleming's stature should hear the potency of these songs and want to build an evening out of them.

"The 'Mythologies' project, especially . . . this is off-the-charts sophisticated," says Fleming, who sees similarities between Barber's art and the world of Western art music.

"There's something almost reverential in the atmosphere in her concerts, or her club dates," explains Fleming. "People are there because they know the work and want to hear it again and again. That sounds like classical music. She's really a composer who happens to play and sing her own music."

It's critical to note, however, that Fleming does not come into Barber's world as a highbrow singer dabbling in jazz. On the contrary, Fleming recordings such as "Christmas in New York" (featuring jazz artists Wynton Marsalis, Brad Mehldau and Gregory Porter) and "Haunted Heart" (with jazzmen Bill Frisell and Fred Hersch) attest to her long-standing fascination with an idiom that Tony Bennett calls "America's classical music."

"I started as a jazz singer, actually, in college," says Fleming. "And I sang [with] a trio for two years every weekend, which was not just an education in jazz but in performance. And I've remained an avid fan and listener. I still listen a lot more to jazz than to anything else."

But neither Fleming nor Barber has taken on anything quite like the "Higher" project, which seems likely to draw each artist well outside her comfort zone. Barber, after all, never has performed an evening-length program with an operatic vocalist of Fleming's stature, and Fleming says she never has sung a recital of works by a contemporary composer with that composer at the piano (pianist Craig Terry also will accompany Fleming during part of the program).

The concert marks the launch of an ambitious performance series, "Renee Fleming: To the Edge," produced by the Harris Theater in association with Lyric Unlimited (Fleming serves as Lyric Opera's creative consultant). Future endeavors are yet to be announced.

Not surprisingly, both Fleming and Barber realize they are venturing into potentially dangerous waters.

"It is intimidating," says Fleming, whose far-flung artistic projects around the world do not suggest an artist who's easily daunted.

Barber says she has "a strange kind of concern": becoming a bit too emotional at hearing her own music given life by Fleming's remarkable instrument.

"I think if I wait until the performance to hear this set, I might cry," says Barber. "And a singer can't cry, because [then] you can't sing."

Still, the prospect of being moved to tears by another artist's rendering of your compositions seems like a welcome problem.

In any event, each singer seems to be helping the other to build this concert, which also will include some holiday repertoire.

When Barber heard Fleming rehearsing "Let It Snow, Let It Snow, Let It Snow," for instance, "I said maybe there shouldn't be so much emphasis on the 't,'" recalls Barber, referencing any classical singer's inclination toward ultra-crisp enunciation.

"So she writes down a 'd'" on the score," to achieve a more colloquial effect.

Fleming, meanwhile, has recorded for Barber the pronunciations of various classical terms that appear in Barber's "The Opera Song," which they'll sing together during this evening.

"She's still correcting me on the German pronunciation, the Italian pronunciation—I need coaching on this," says Barber.

All of which only heightens one's interest in this program, a rare convergence of two artists—each at the pinnacle of her field—and daring to meet the other on less-familiar musical turf.

"I think these kinds of collaborations are very important," says Fleming. "Our audiences will come together. My audience will hear her and vice versa."

And perhaps all of us will hear something we've never heard before.

CHAPTER 21

Kurt Elling

Raw Talent, Naked Ambition

March 23, 1997

The club, a Chicago jazz landmark, is packed to overflowing, the noise level almost at a roar.

All at once the band lets loose with a couple of combustive swing tunes, and then, as if out of nowhere, the trumpeter steps up to the microphone and launches into a terse soliloquy.

"As you know, we're the JazzMasters, but tonight we've got a little surprise for you," says Chicago jazz veteran Paul Serrano. "We've discovered an amazing young cat who truly can sing. So we thought we ought to present him to you while we still could afford him."

And with that, the young, hungry, unknown young man takes the mike from Serrano and, as if with the flick of a switch, lets loose a torrent of sound, hitting his unsuspecting listeners directly between the eyes and ears. The weird sound effects, ferocious scat singing, hysterical tempos, bizarre facial expressions, comical one-liners and other forms of verbal and visual mugging may be way over the top, but they jolt the crowd.

It has been a long time since anyone under 30 walked in and electrified Joe Segal's Jazz Showcase, a fabled club that over the last half

Fig. 14 Kurt Elling: The Chicago vocalist made a spectacular recording debut with "Close Your Eyes" at a fortunate moment—the mid-1990s, when major record labels were signing young talent and emerging male vocalists were in short supply. He remains a powerful force.

century has presented such jazz deities as Charlie Parker, Dizzy Gillespie, Art Blakey, McCoy Tyner . . . the list goes on.

So on this night, everyone in the house is thinking the same thing: Who is this kid, and what planet did he come from?

: : :

Just three years after that astonishing set, which took place on a frigid January night in 1994, Chicagoan Kurt Elling—not yet 30 years old—has become the most buzzed about young jazz singer in America. And trumpeter Serrano's crack about presenting him "while we still could afford him" may well have been the most prophetic comment the trumpeter ever made.

Six months after the Showcase debut, the nakedly ambitious singer was signed by Blue Note Records, arguably the most prestigious label in jazz. In short order, Elling was nominated for a Grammy Award (Lena Horne aced him) and embraced by critics coast to coast (the Los Angeles Times raved about his "gleaming instrument," The Washington Post his "venturesome spirit," The Boston Globe his consistent "boldness").

With all this fuss, "CBS Sunday Morning" hustled to Chicago last year to film him crooning at his favorite haunt, the rambunctious Green Mill Jazz Club in Uptown; Down Beat honored him with coveted berths in its Readers Polls (Elling ranked 9th last year for Record of the Year, 7th for Best Male Singer); and Hollywood film producers began eyeballing him, clearly seduced by the young man's chiseled good looks and his ravenous appetite for success.

Not bad for a divinity school dropout whose academic career at the University of Chicago went up in flames in 1992, whereupon Elling redirected his studies in some of the South Side's smokier jazz clubs.

How a burned-out divinity student became America's most accomplished and promising young male jazz singer—and what that early blush of success has done to him—might someday make an intriguing motion picture, something like "The Jazz Singer" meets "What Makes Sammy Run?"

: : :

If Elling had succeeded at the U. of C. Divinity School, where he had enrolled as a master's degree student in 1989, he probably would be preaching from a church pulpit or a university lectern right now, rather than from a bandstand. Surely his father's career as a Lutheran church organist in Rockford, where the Chicago-born singer grew up, and his paternal grandfather's work as a circuit-riding missionary in Canada, gave young Elling an abiding respect for theology.

But to his regret, Elling did not win standing ovations from his professors at the U. of C.

"About two-thirds of the way through I started to see the train pull out of the station and leave me behind," Elling recalls today.

"I was white-knuckled all the time, because you've got about 40 books per class in every 10-week quarter, and you never catch up, you're never on top of it, unless you're one of those people who's peculiarly gifted to do that.

"It was a real slam to me at the time. It was a real surprise, because I had spiritually devoted myself to what I thought was my calling, and I was still foolish enough to think that because I had devoted myself to the thing and had prayed about it and had tried to make it right, that it would be given to me to do this.

"And it wasn't given to me to do. So when I left, I was really disheartened and really angry."

Unlike many angry young men, however, Elling had a release. In fact, during the entire time that he was drowning in divinity school, he was learning to swim in a decidedly less devout setting: Chicago's jazz joints. The first week he arrived in town, Elling dropped in at Milt Trenier's Lounge, a past-its-prime, Vegas-style watering hole that reportedly held jam sessions for aspiring performers.

"The 'session' comprised a piano player and three other people in the room—one of them a call girl, one of them a low-life gangster, and the other one me," Elling remembers, with a chuckle.

"After I sang that first night, the first thing out of the owner's mouth was, 'I'm going to give this kid a job.'

"And I stupidly said: 'I'll work for free.'"

For the next year and a half, Elling rarely took home more than $7 in tips on any given night, but he came away with crucial information about the vocalist's art.

Even then, "He was one of the most accurate singers that I have worked with," says Karl Johnson, still the house piano player at Trenier's (which, in another era, was the fabled Chez Paree, a mob-run joint where Frank Sinatra, an Elling hero, often worked his magic).

"Kurt's pitch, his rhythm, his concept of the music he was doing were really accurate," adds Johnson. "He was in the very basic root of his own style, so we just rehearsed and rehearsed a lot."

So much, apparently, that by the time Elling bolted from the U. of C. ("in the middle of the night," he says, "because I had to break a lease"), he was ready to take on the South Side jazz joints, where the (mostly Black) audiences know their jazz top to bottom.

"I think the first time I met Kurt was at Alexander's," says Serrano, referring to a steak joint on East 79th Street, where the JazzMasters offer up down-home jazz every Thursday night.

"That's really a Black-vibe joint, and most of those people have a history of growing up with jazz, and going to bebop dances when people like Lester Young and Billie Holiday were playing the Sutherland Lounge.

"The amazing thing was those folks at Alexander's just ate him up. He showed them that he was comfortable on stage with Black jazz, and he seemed to have a direct 'in' to the music. He wasn't making it artificial, and it was amazing that he could scat like that, that he could be so exuberant and do just about anything [vocally] that he wanted to.

"Very few singers can really scat, you know, and with Kurt, even back then, it was just shoop-a-doo-be-doo."

: : :

Elling didn't come by his mercurial vocal technique quite so easily as it might have seemed. On the contrary, he had been singing in church as far back as he could remember, training his instrument all the way through Lutheran elementary and high schools in Rockford, as well.

By the time he reached Gustavus Adolphus College, a small liberal arts school in St. Peter, Minn., Elling was accomplished enough to tour Europe with the Gustavus choir, soloing in everything from Ralph Vaughan Williams to J.S. Bach.

Combine that lifelong classical training with the plush texture and amber color of his baritone, add a nascent interest in jazz (which Elling discovered at Gustavus), and you had the makings of a fine young swing singer.

The world, however, overflows with fine—and utterly indistinguishable—young singers.

But Elling had much, much more. For one thing, he had spent his college years (including an eight-month stint at The University of Edinburgh) studying Kierkegaard, Rilke, Hegel, Proust, Kenneth Rexroth and similarly weighty thinkers, and he began bringing their texts and ideas to his jazz tunes.

Thus in a number such as "These Clouds Are Heavy, You Dig?", Elling dared to offer a hipster's account of Rilke's deeply metaphorical story "How the Thimble Came to be God." In a cool, laid-back tempo, Elling crooned: "Just then a wise old woman cloud happened along/ And she asked the little cloud, 'What's wrong?'/ And the little cloud replied, 'God's gone.'/ But the older cloud knew right away/ So she said to the little one, 'Here's your thimble, I found it today.'"

Bolder still, while most jazz singers invent melody lines and vocal effects, Elling began to improvise his lyrics, as well—"ranting," as he calls it, or creating "poetry on the fly."

In the midst of a performance of the old chestnut, "Everything Happens to Me," for instance, he might burst into singing a laundry list of mishaps that had befallen him yesterday or 20 years ago. At the climax of "Delores Dream," he might head-trip his way through a recollection of lost loves and crumbled romances, singing all the while.

It was a bizarre, unexpected, stream-of-consciousness form of singing that sprang naturally from Elling's theological background and took audiences utterly by surprise.

"There's this Charlie Mingus tune called 'Sue's Changes,' and during his solo, Kurt started getting into one of his made-up song stories," remembers Laurence Hobgood, who first heard Elling sitting in on saxophonist Ed Petersen's Monday night sessions at the Green Mill in 1991. Hobgood was the pianist; the music was outrageously avant-garde; and Elling fit in perfectly.

"The amazing thing was that Kurt wasn't speaking this story that he was making up—he truly was singing it," adds Hobgood.

"Now you might assume that 'Sue's Changes' refers to chord changes. But in Kurt's made-up song, it turns out Sue was a baby and the changes referred to Sue's diapers.

"It wasn't so much funny as it was beautiful, and, by the time Kurt got to the end of it, there were people in that crowd literally crying, it was so beautiful."

Though Elling was living in what Hobgood calls a "one-room hovel" in Hyde Park for $150 a month and feeding himself—barely—by moving furniture and working as a bartender, he also was writing profound lyrics and forging exquisite songs with Hobgood. By wedding his texts to Hobgood's tunes or writing lyrics to fit famous instrumental solos (a technique known as vocalese), Elling was creating a music at once fresh and familiar, distinctly autobiographical yet deeply reminiscent of pioneering vocal work by Mark Murphy, Jon Hendricks, Eddie Jefferson and King Pleasure.

Equally important, by collaborating with such brilliant young Chicago players as Hobgood and drummer Paul Wertico (guitarist Pat Metheny's percussionist for more than a decade) as well as such esteemed veterans as South Side saxophonists Von Freeman and Eddie Johnson, Elling was crafting a sound unique to this town. Its aggressive swing rhythms and lusty ensemble blasts, its full-bodied tone and rip-roaring sense of experimentation somehow caught the rough and rambunctious spirit of '90s Chicago jazz as well as anyone had done.

A less ambitious artist might have been content to refine and perfect that formula over the next few years, but Elling was chomping at the bit.

"He kept saying, 'We've got to do a demo tape, we've got to do a demo tape,'" recalls Hobgood. "And I kept saying, 'Wait a minute, now hold on a minute.' I just didn't think he was ready."

Finally, in mid-1993, Hobgood agreed to produce the demo for the still green young singer, and the race was on.

Elling had persuaded a friend to part with several thousand dollars to fund the tape. Then he managed to find a friend who knew a West Coast jazz manager. The manager listened to the tape and passed it to Blue Note president Bruce Lundvall, who could hardly believe his ears.

"I was about to drive to my dentist's office," Lundvall recalled in 1995, "I grabbed my bag of tapes, and I spotted one that just had arrived from this same Kurt Elling [whom Lundvall had just read about in the Chicago Tribune], which was kind of a wild coincidence.

"So I put the tape on while I was driving, and while Kurt was singing 'Close Your Eyes,' I was thinking: 'This is really nice. He can sing.' Right after that came 'Delores' [with Elling's searing, indelibly autobiographical lyrics to a Wayne Shorter tune], and now I was getting very interested.

"And as the tape went on, with all these new and strange ideas, I started thinking: 'This guy is unbelievable, very fresh. He's coming out of an early tradition but doing something very modern with it. He's got a voice that's terrific.'"

Four days later, Lundvall had jetted to Chicago to catch Elling at the Mill and, after hearing one explosive set, announced that he was going to sign the young man.

: : :

From that moment forth, Elling's career was airborne, and no one seemed less surprised than Elling himself.

"The field was wide open," says Elling, who indeed announced himself at a moment when the jazz world was sorely lacking in charismatic young male vocalists.

"I mean, Frank [Sinatra] already was an older cat, Joe Williams was an older cat, Mel Torme was an older cat, and you had all these cats who had really had their time," adds Elling, clearly smitten with the jazz patois of the '50s.

"And as you looked around the jazz world, there were a lot of great young women, but in terms of men, there's just a very small number."

How strange, though, that in the age of Wynton Marsalis—when the CD bins are crowded with work by young male trumpeters (Nicholas Payton, Marcus Printup), saxophonists (David Sanchez, Joshua Redman), pianists (Marcus Roberts, Eric Reed) and so on—the scene is almost devoid of emerging male vocalists.

"I think it has to do with the fact that for young boys, it's OK to be, say, a drummer," says Elling.

"You can be a drummer and be a man. In second grade, you can be a trumpet player and be a man. You can even be a saxophone player and be a man.

"But singing isn't valued very much in American society as something that men do. At least not jazz singing."

When Elling's debut album, "Close Your Eyes," came out in 1995, he quickly found himself playing stages from Montreux to Montreal, from Paris to San Francisco. The jazz world hungered for a fresh male voice, and the kid from Chicago was wowing them with his instrument, his technique, his versatility, his looks, his swagger and, above all, his attitude.

"I remember we were opening for Michael Brecker in Malta," says Hobgood, "and the president of the country—the president of Malta!—is sitting out in the front row.

"We finish the song, and Kurt goes to the microphone, and he says, 'All right. Wow, this is really beautiful. I guess your president is with us tonight, and that's beautiful.'

"And then he looks over at the president, and he says: 'You have one very happening country on your hands here, my friend.'

"That's a direct quote. And I'm sitting here thinking, 'Oh my God, he just ticked off the president of Malta.'

"But the president gets up, puts his hands up in the air like a boxer, and the place goes wild.

"That's Kurt. That's pure Kurt."

Part comedian, part crooner, part hipster, part beatnik for the '90s, Elling surely was one of a kind, a breath of fresh air in world awash with clones of Sinatra (Harry Connick Jr.), Nat Cole (John Pizzarelli), Joe Williams (Kevin Mahogany) and on and on.

So Elling, an utterly unknown quantity in '94, was heading for stardom just a year later.

The experience could turn the head of any young performer, and though Elling coped with the attention as well as one might expect, changes were afoot. Soon Chicago club managers were reporting that the singer no longer was returning their phone calls; tales of Elling's control-freak tendencies in the recording studio seeped out.

And though Elling was developing his technique and his art with astonishing speed, he also started to bring a palpable narcissism to the stage. The way he posed beneath the spotlight, gesturing grandiosely and perpetually running his fingers through his hair, suggested the antics of a preening rock star more than a serious jazz musician.

The L.A. Weekly observed as much earlier this year, noting after an Elling show in Hollywood's notorious Viper Room (where River Phoenix died of a drug overdose): "The man must have spent 20 of his 28 years in front of a mirror. This kind of chilled ham is palatable only when offered on a platter clearly marked 'outrageous kitsch,' but Elling shows no signs of conscious camp."

And though Elling early on won favorable press notices in most major American cities, his repeated forays into New York have generated indifference at best, unalloyed hostility at worst. Perhaps it's no surprise that a performer as increasingly cocky as Elling would fare so poorly in the capital of cockiness.

"Once when he came to New York, I invited all these people who never had heard of him," remembers a veteran of New York's jazz industry. "I told them, 'You're going to like this guy, he's different; he's an acquired taste.'

"And Kurt comes on stage with his usual bravura, and they were a little taken aback. I had one particularly famous musician in the house, and he was angry that I even got him down there."

When Elling played Carnegie Hall, on a triple-bill with Dianne Reeves and Rachelle Farrell, New York Post writer Chip Deffaa chastised his "occasionally clumsy attempts at humor" and declared that "Elling hasn't been blessed with a great voice—in terms of tonal richness, strength or flexibility" (though he allowed that Elling "uses it honestly").

Even veteran Mark Murphy, Elling's idol as a singer, remarked in a radio interview that "there's a kid in Chicago who's stealing my gig," referring, no doubt, to Elling's artistic debt to the older singer.

And Will Friedwald in the Village Voice lamented that Elling offers "ideas so esoteric even repeated listenings don't clear them up."

In part, the press barbs may be credited to East Coast chauvinism. Even the aforementioned insider acknowledged that "You can't come in here cocky and say, 'Look at this, man—I'm hot stuff.' That's not going to work for a New Yorker.

"You have to really prove yourself.

"When a new artist comes in and does a great job, the [New York] critics will put the knock on him the first time and then, maybe, praise him the second time. It's a New York thing."

: : :

Yet Elling, who has dreamed of wooing a mass audience "beyond jazz" ever since he was signed by Blue Note, absolutely lusts for the approval of the New York press, the very contingent that has given him the cold shoulder.

"I'm confident that as soon as we have New York, we have the rest of the world," says Elling.

"So I think that as soon as we make it there, we're going to have a lot of work, and I'm going to have to really be on top of it for the duration, or at least the next wave is going to be a lot more massive."

In his pursuit of that recognition, Elling will spend approximately a month blitzing New York clubs in May, a campaign similar to the one he conducted last year in Los Angeles.

"I think that it's only right that there be somewhere in the world where I haven't made it yet," says Elling, who may overestimate his success.

"New York has the most intense fraternity; membership is difficult to obtain there."

This time, though, "We're going to be there long enough that [the critics] are going to have to come out and deal with us, because we're going to have a lot of people, and people are going to be talking about us, and they're going to be digging it, and they're going to get the word on the streets, and the people will do what the critics haven't done yet."

What Elling, in his youth, doesn't yet understand is that in music enduring reputations are earned slowly, over time, and with artistic achievement, not swiftly, via shrewdly orchestrated media blitzes. The faster he tries to dance for the approval of others, the less likely his work will carry meaning for those who already admire it. And the wider an audience he seeks to seduce, the thinner his music is likely to become.

"When I walked into Kurt's one-room apartment in Chicago a couple of years ago, I saw that this was Kurt the artist," says Richard Elvee, chaplain of Gustavus College and an Elling mentor.

"But if things work out, I imagine he might finally end up looking at Lake Michigan from some expensive high-rise.

"But when you're in that high-rise, is the artist still there? Does the muse still sing?"

That's the question Elling faces, as he chases success. Having been married since October to Jennifer Carney, a dancer who toured the country for three years in Andrew Lloyd Webber's "Phantom of the Opera," Elling must decide how much of his personal happiness and artistic self-esteem he's willing to link to critical approval and media adulation.

For the moment, though, Elling—who turns 30 on Nov. 2—is still a very hungry man, and it shows every time he prowls the stage.

"I'm going to be happy 30 years from now when there's a kinder, gentler Kurt on stage," he says.

"I won't have any problems with the fact that I will have mellowed. "But right now, I'm just a really aggressive cat."

Coming Home to Chicago

Oct. 18, 2020

Twelve years ago, jazz singer Kurt Elling left Chicago for New York.

Three months ago, he returned.

The move, says Elling, was prompted not by the pandemic, which has devastated New York, but by a longstanding desire to move back to the city where he launched his career.

Still, with many New Yorkers having left the city—as documented in various press reports—one has to wonder whether the pandemic was the catalyst that finally triggered the move.

"Jennifer and I had talked about moving back every year that we lived in New York," says Elling, referring to his wife, Jennifer Elling. "It was always a question of when was going to be right.

"The catalyst was that my daughter got into an arts high school" in Chicago.

Also in the mix: "Family concerns, grandparents wanting to enjoy them while they're young and healthy," explains Elling. "It just happened that the pandemic hit on the summer that we had already planned to come home.

"It made the move certainly more challenging and more dramatic. But it was 11 years coming, since we only thought we were going to be there [in New York] for a year."

Before the move, Elling was identified as a Chicago singer whose art had been shaped on the bandstand by hometown giants such as saxophonists Von Freeman, Eddie Johnson and Edward Petersen. Elling's long New York tenure dulled that profile, which he now seems intent on sharpening.

When Elling began presenting his local "Porch Concerts" online over the summer, and when he recently opened his "25th Anniversary Virtual Concert Tour" online, his between-song commentary embraced his ties to this city and its globally admired jazz scene.

So why had he resettled in New York?

"I think it's all too common for jazz musicians who are coming up to want to test their mettle" there, says Elling. "We want to see if you can find a place in New York that is yours.

"I wanted to have something of what I think are sacred spaces—a neighborhood that belongs to me [and] friends that I made myself and not just from passing through. As much as I love Chicago, New York has always been a force to be reckoned with."

Quite apart from geography, however, Elling—like most musicians in the United States—temporarily has lost the home that's central to his art: the stage. He played his last bona fide public concert in March in California, just before the coronavirus lockdown, and—again like most colleagues—has been contemplating the toll of that loss.

"As it has been for a lot of musicians, it's been a psychological challenge," says Elling. "I was upwards of 200 nights a year on the road before the pandemic. And to have that avenue of communication, vocation, sustenance so completely cut off, so suddenly—I think the hardest part for me has certainly been that I can't engage my vocation.

"I need to sing for certainly emotional reasons, for spiritual reasons, physiological reasons, for the sake of my sense of self in the world, for friendship's sake. If I'm not out there, some of these people I see only on these gigs."

"I count my blessings," adds Elling, who this year released the album "Secrets Are the Best Stories."

"I'm not out on the street. I'm not scrambling in the way a lot of musicians are. I was able to take a step back for a second and try to figure out what I could contribute, rather than just claw my way through something."

What he came up with was the aforementioned "25th Anniversary Virtual Concert Tour," a series of Friday-night livestreams from the Green Mill Jazz Club. That's where then-Blue Note Records President Bruce Lundvall first heard Elling and decided to sign him in the summer of 1994.

I heard Elling several months before Lundvall did and also was struck by Elling's work.

"The other 'find' of the evening was newcomer Kurt Elling, a singer who instantly—and justly—won over the huge crowd at the Jazz Showcase," I wrote of a January 1994 performance. "His high-speed scat in music of Thelonious Monk [with ingenious lyrics by the great Jon Hendricks] and his unexpected whimsy in the old torch song 'Everything Happens to Me' utterly disarmed his listeners."

A week later, Elling told me of his surprise at how Chicago musicians had begun embracing him.

"When I began studying at the U. of C. [two years ago], I started sitting in with musicians in South Side places like Alexander's Steak House and the New Apartment Lounge," Elling had said. "And I couldn't believe it, but musicians like Eddie Johnson and Von Freeman and Ed Petersen and Paul Serrano kept pushing me on. . . . So I'm a singer now.

"I'm still trying to figure out exactly what it is I'm doing [vocally]. I'm living in a basement, hustling for work, singing for society bands, trying to pay off student loans and eating sparingly. But this is the best time to be a jazz singer.

"I mean, how many young male jazz singers are there now? Hardly any because they don't teach jazz in the schools. So maybe the field is open."

Elling was right about that, considering the dearth of great male jazz singers then and now. His first Blue Note album, "Close Your Eyes," emerged as the most exciting jazz debut recording of 1995, propelling him to the front ranks of that era's jazz vocalists. Several brilliant subsequent albums followed, as well as some decidedly less interesting work.

But Elling certainly was performing on all cylinders during his first "25th Anniversary Virtual Concert Tour" performance Oct. 9. Though his vocal tone was a bit nasal and even at its best not exactly plush, his scat singing proved thrilling and his range of repertoire wide.

The Green Mill's online concerts, which also include a "Saturday Night at the Green Mill" series featuring other artists and hosted by Elling, are likely to benefit both singer and venue.

"It helps keep the joint at the forefront," says Green Mill club owner Dave Jemilo. "It's seen all over the world, and it's coming live from the Green Mill.

"It's not like you're putting on a slick show. It's like you're putting on a gig."

Yet the production values—featuring warm lighting and unobtrusive camera work—exceed much of what we're encountering online these days.

It all comes across as Elling's somewhat belated but explicitly stated love song to Chicago, a city he has been reevaluating since his return.

"A lot has changed," says Elling. "Most of the important things are still the same. Some of the saddest things are still the same.

"We still have the obvious problem with guns and gun violence in town. The city is still as beautiful aesthetically as it's ever been, if not more so. . . . I'm hopeful."

Why?

"Because Chicago is an incredibly resilient and tough city," he says. "And I think that a lot of the brain drain or monetary drain that front-line New York is suffering just now, we're not going to have as much because Chicago is an economically more livable city to begin with."

Chicago, adds Elling, has been "my dream city from my earliest memories. It's the sparkling, magnificent, architectural and artistic and culinary capital on the beautiful Lake Michigan. And with COVID treating the world the way that it is, and cities having to circle the wagons, I want to be home and help defend my city."

With music.

CHAPTER 22

Ken Vandermark

"Genius" Grant

June 23, 1999

Considering that he plays in at least a dozen bands and on more than 40 recordings, Chicago avant-garde musician Ken Vandermark was bound to be in transit when he received the news: He has won a 1999 MacArthur "genius grant" worth $265,000.

Even so, the windfall in dollars and prestige, announced late Tuesday, carries unmistakable poignance, since Vandermark is in the midst of a characteristically low-budget, zero-frills tour—16 cities in 16 nights, by car, with Vandermark and his band sleeping on the floors of friends' apartments.

The man's relentless, guerrilla-style approach to playing unabashedly radical music has made him one of the most talked-about jazz musicians to emerge in Chicago during the last decade. Down Beat, a revered jazz magazine, in January aptly referred to Vandermark as "a bright, articulate, unflinchingly committed tenor saxophonist, clarinetist, composer and bandleader whose presence has been a major defibrillator for the city since he set up shop here in 1989."

And though Vandermark can't say precisely how many ensembles count him as a member or exactly how many CDs he has cut—"It must be a few dozen by now," he guesses—the 34-year-old artist clearly has thrived as an outsider.

But with his MacArthur Fellowship, Vandermark, one of 32 individuals honored this year, finds himself in an unexpected position. He's a lifelong iconoclast suddenly embraced by the cultural establishment, or at least by one of its best funded outposts, the John D. and Catherine T. MacArthur Foundation in Chicago.

Having flourished artistically, if not financially, as a revolutionary out to obliterate the stylistic boundaries that separate jazz, alternative rock, avant-garde classical and other genres, Vandermark now stands among several regal jazz figures who have won the same award. The honor roll includes such long-established artists as bebop drummer Max Roach, free-jazz pioneer Ornette Coleman, piano titan Cecil Taylor and heavyweight composer- improviser Anthony Braxton.

Suddenly, Vandermark may no longer be on the outside looking in.

"To be honest, I'm kind of afraid," says Vandermark, speaking by phone from his parents' house, outside Boston, where he stopped briefly during an east-of-the-Mississippi tour. "When I look at the other winners who work in similar music, like Max Roach and Cecil Taylor and the rest of them, those are people I'm in awe of, and I'm really overwhelmed by even being put in the same sentence as those people.

"So I'm really floored by this news. These guys, by the time they were my age, they were changing the face of the music. I feel like I'm still really a student."

Though it will takes years to know for certain if Vandermark's often brazenly dissonant sounds also have redirected the course of jazz and related musical languages, there's no question he has energized the improvised music scene in Chicago more than any other single figure of the '90s.

"Ken has been a force in spearheading this music, that's for sure," says Chicago tenor saxophonist Fred Anderson, an elder statesman of the avant-garde who collaborated with Vandermark on the recording "DKV Trio" (Okkadisk).

Adds Chicago drummer Hamid Drake, a longtime Vandermark partner on disc and on stage, "Just the amount of projects he works on has had a huge effect on music in Chicago, and even as far away as Europe, where he has played a lot."

Anyone who frequents such Chicago clubs as Anderson's Velvet Lounge on South Indiana Avenue or the Empty Bottle on North Western Avenue (where Vandermark regularly performs and helps curate a Wednesday night new-music series) will have heard his eruptions on tenor saxophone and clarinet.

Moreover, a small but devoted group of record buyers knows Vandermark from the decidedly unorthodox musicmaking of bands such as the Vandermark 5 (currently the focal point of his work), the Aaly Trio (with saxophonist Mats Gustafsson), DKV Trio (with Chicagoans Kent Kessler on bass and Drake on drums), the Crown Royals (a funk- tinged outfit), Cinghiale (a duo with fellow reed madman Mars Williams) and others.

Yet Vandermark is the first to acknowledge that his artistic ascent in Chicago owes at least as much to the city's burgeoning new-music scene as it does to his own drive and talent. In that regard, his MacArthur award could be considered an acknowledgment of the vibrancy of new music in Chicago at the turn of the century.

"I don't have a good answer for why all this is happening in Chicago right now, but for some reason there's this incredible confluence of a lot of different elements going on," says Vandermark, who closes his current tour Friday night at the Empty Bottle. The performance will celebrate the release of the newest CD from the Vandermark 5, "Simpatico" (on Atavistic).

"You have a pool of musicians in roughly the same age group [their 30s] who have been working hard and communicating with each other," continues Vandermark. "You have labels like Okkadisk and Atavistic documenting the work, you have radio stations like WNUR-FM 89.3 and WHPK-FM 88.5 playing the music, and, most important of all, you have people coming out to hear the music.

"All that activity has brought a lot of national and international musicians to Chicago to play and record, so there's this influx of outside information feeding the local scene."

But it's important to remember that Chicago wasn't always so welcoming to Vandermark, who arrived here in 1989, disenchanted with life in Boston.

"In the beginning, he couldn't find anyone to play with, he couldn't find many gigs, paid or unpaid, so for the first few years he just practiced like crazy and wrote music non-stop, because there wasn't much else for him to do," says Ellen Major, Vandermark's wife since 1996 and a pediatrician at Children's Memorial Hospital.

"I remember going to his occasional shows in these horrible dives, and no one would be in the audience but me and my friends."

By spring of 1992, Vandermark was ready to move back to Boston in defeat. But Chicago musicians Kent Kessler and Michael Zerang persuaded him to stay, their partnership eventually forming the core of what would become the Vandermark Quartet.

Equally important, composer Braxton, another MacArthur winner, encouraged him to keep up the fight.

"I played Braxton a cassette of a trio, and he was incredibly complimentary about what we were doing," Vandermark says. "Braxton has had a major impact on me, and to hear him say, 'I think you're doing something interesting' gave me license to think, OK, I'm not crazy, maybe there's some merit here."

Though it's difficult for any musician to establish roots in a new city, Vandermark's difficulties in part may have been because of the still nascent quality of his musicmaking. Granted, there was no denying the sheer size of his sound and the bravura of his technique during shows he played with Hal Russell's NRG Ensemble.

But the relentlessly loud, rhythmically repetitive nature of Vandermark's work at the time pointed to a musician hungry to make a splash but seemingly less interested in developing a variety of ideas in sound. It wasn't until the mid-'90s that Vandermark began to show a more substantial expressive range.

"The early quartet material was interesting, but it didn't have a fullness or depth I was looking for," says Bruno Johnson, owner of the Okkadisk label, which has released several Vandermark recordings. "That first started to come through with [Vandermark] groups like Caffeine [in 1994]. That's when he started getting a sense of voicing for other instruments.

"Actually, the same thing happened with [past tenor saxophonists] Coleman Hawkins and Ben Webster, who realized, as they got older, that there's beauty in playing ballads and other things with less energy and display."

By 1996, a show Vandermark played at the Empty Bottle with such profound South Side musicians as tenor player Ari Brown, drummer Avreeayl Ra and bassist Harrison Bankhead affirmed the young musician was beginning to find a lyric voice to counterbalance the manic energy for which he was best known. In 1997, his writing for the Brotzmann Tentet proved at once idiosyncratic and masterful, and last month, during the Empty Bottle Festival of Jazz and Improvised Music, Vandermark's playing opposite Gustafsson in the Aaly Trio established them as the most dynamic and musically versatile tenor pairing in cutting-edge jazz.

Nevertheless, financial concerns never have been far off for Vandermark, who didn't leave his day job at the School of the Art Institute's Video Data Bank until last year. Says Johnson: "I've seen Ken play five hours for $10."

Yet Vandermark has steered clear of more lucrative jobs closer to the commercial mainstream, instead reveling in cutting-edge jazz, alternative rock, avant-funk and beyond.

"When I was growing up, music constantly was being played on the stereo at home all the time, and the attitude was wide open," says Vandermark. "My parents would play Stravinsky, Duke Ellington, Sly and the Family Stone, whatever.

"And their attitude wasn't: 'Stravinsky is great European music, Ellington is a great American composer,' and so on. Their approach basically was: 'This is music, and there's no separation at all among different kinds of music.'"

Vandermark nonetheless found himself drawn most intensely to his parents' jazz recordings. He took up trumpet in 4th grade and "played it terribly until 11th grade," when he switched to tenor sax and began writing original tunes.

As a film major at McGill University, in Montreal, Vandermark relished analyzing cinema, but his fascination with music inexorably took over. By the time he graduated in 1986, he was ready to plunge into the Boston music scene.

After 10 years in Chicago, this city still holds a spell on him, for in interviews with out-of-town media he consistently talks up the virtues of working in a town where minds are open, rent is cheaper than on the coasts and audiences thrive on new ideas.

Though he hasn't yet decided what he's going to do with more than a quarter-million dollars, a number of possibilities leap to mind.

"I'd like to do a tour with [multi-instrumentalist] Joe McPhee and Kent Kessler, I'd like to do an outing with [drummer] Paul Lovens, and I'd like to do a U.S. tour with the Brotzmann Tentet," says Vandermark, who also hopes to help Johnson release recordings that are lingering in the can at tiny Okkadisk.

"And I'd like to be able to pay all these musicians to at least stay in a motel. That would be great. These guys have to put up with extreme conditions to work with me—this is not a commercial music, and it doesn't generate a lot of money.

"But it really would be nice to give them what they deserve."

Sounds Never Heard Before

Sept. 8, 2002

Time is running out, and Ken Vandermark knows it.

The European musicians who staff the biggest, most ambitious musical project of his career—his Territory Band-3—soon will be arriving in Chicago for rehearsals, and he needs to spend practically every waking hour completing the scores.

So he sits in the basement of his North Side home—sheet music scattered everywhere, a boom box churning various bleeps and blips—trying to come up with ways of notating sounds so new and original that symbols for them have not yet been invented.

Ready or not, Vandermark and his groundbreaking Territory Band-3 will take the stage at the Chicago Cultural Center on Sept. 22 (coincidentally Vandermark's 38th birthday), headlining Chicago's fourth annual World Music Festival. Vandermark, whose experimental music won him a MacArthur "genius" award in 1999, never has enjoyed such mainstream visibility at a city-sponsored music festival, and he knows how much is riding on this performance, as well as follow-up dates in Germany, Sweden, Norway and Austria.

"I think it'll fly, because over and over I've seen audiences come to concerts eager and willing to have their expectations challenged," says Vandermark, whose Territory Band concept is nothing if not challenging. With its outlandish mixture of acoustic, electronic, improvised and composed music, as well as its daring use of long silences, sharp dissonance and extremes of loud and soft, it brazenly defies easy categorization or description.

Musical experimentation on this scale would have been impossible, says Vandermark, without the $265,000 he's receiving from the Chicago-based John D. and Catherine T. MacArthur Foundation, which is distributing the funds to him over a period of five years. Unlike many fellowships and grants, however, the MacArthur "genius" awards come with no strings attached—recipients are free to spend, invest or sock away the money as they see fit.

"Our feeling is that the individual rather than the foundation is in the best position to know what to do with the money," says Daniel Socolow, director of the MacArthur Fellows Program, which will announce its next group of winners on Sept. 25.

To date, the list of MacArthur artists, scientists and scholars has included such well-known figures as pianist Stephen Hough, composer Bright Sheng, choreographer Bill T. Jones and Chicago director Mary Zimmerman, as well as others virtually unknown to the general public.

"Some have used the money to buy time off from the universities or institutions where they work, some have bought studios and equipment, some have used the money to go into totally different directions than what they already were doing," adds Socolow, emphasizing that MacArthur Fellows are chosen in a years-long, secret process by unnamed nominators and that no one may apply for the award.

"The fellowship is not for what they've achieved but what they may achieve," Socolow says. "We're guessing at their potential."

Vandermark wasted no time using part of his money to create the Territory Band, an ensemble that stands out for its sheer size (12 musicians), its arsenal of instruments (including double percussion and electronics) and its novel approach to big-band writing and improvisation.

As Vandermark sweats over a new score, for instance, he writes in a fashion that probably would startle traditionalists. The angular lines, zigzags and arrows he uses to trace the progress of the music hardly conform to standard musical notation. The musical themes he has penned are so spare and the written instructions for the musicians so cryptic (such as "overtone wall with electronic feedback") that one wonders how the players have a clue as to exactly what it is he wants.

"But I'm specifically trying to keep things ambiguous, and to keep the notations on the score to a minimum," says Vandermark, who indeed compresses all of the information for a 10–15 minute piece onto a single page of score paper.

"The idea is to give them a setting in which they can play what they want, what they do best, but based on a sketch that everyone in the band is using as a starting point."

In some ways, the process is not so far removed from the techniques of classic big-band leaders such as Duke Ellington, who created themes that he felt best suited his players, then encouraged them to riff on the material during solos.

But Vandermark has gone further out on a limb, giving his players freedom to improvise en masse, as well as in instrumental sections and in solos. Some of the most creative musicmaking, then, takes place onstage, when the players respond to one another, while the audience tries to make sense of the swirl of sound that results.

"It's a blast to play, but it's definitely not easy," says bassist Kent Kessler, a longtime Vandermark collaborator. "In fact, it can be very difficult, because you're hearing so much sound around you all at once, you're constantly shifting gears from one section of a piece to the next, from one group of instruments to the next, and even from one style of composition to the next.

"Plus you've got guys of five different nationalities trying to come to terms with each other and trying to give Ken what he wants."

That, in itself, is a formidable task, since Vandermark acknowledges that he has found it difficult to get the sounds in his head onto the page. The first time around, the music that the band plays in rehearsal may seem to him light-years away from the way he thought it would sound, which means he needs to revise the notation or simply drop pieces that aren't working the way he wanted.

For five days straight, Vandermark and friends will plow through this music in rehearsal, creating what Kessler calls "planned structures" rather than "compositions" in the usual sense. These musical landscapes will allow players to improvise freely in some passages, to play a loose-limbed backup in others.

This kind of high-wire musical act would not be possible, Vandermark says, without the "creative improvisers" he has convened for the occasion, including British drummer Paul Lytton, German trumpeter Axel Dorner and several Chicago radicals, among them reedist Dave Rempis, cellist Fred Lonberg-Holm and trombonist Jeb Bishop. It's their input during rehearsals, as much as Vandermark's ideas on paper, that make possible the Territory Band, and its unusual brand of large-ensemble, electro-acoustic improvisation.

It wasn't until Vandermark won the MacArthur prize, however, that he was able to dream of a project as large-scale, artistically ambitious and, therefore, as costly as the Territory Band. The cash made it possible to bring to Chicago the international roster of musicians Vandermark wanted for the project and "to treat them in the way they deserve to be treated—in other words, to pay them," Vandermark says.

Even so, many of the players will crash in Vandermark's home for the week's worth of rehearsals and performances, to make the MacArthur money stretch further.

From the start of Vandermark's Territory Band experiment, it was obvious that he was onto something.

The band's stunning debut at the Empty Bottle, in February 2000, attested to the stylistic range and technical acuity of its personnel (then nine musicians), who conveyed some of the muscular swing rhythms and frenetic virtuosity of the "territory bands" that toured the Midwest and the South in the 1930s. But unlike the great, lusty ensembles of Andy Kirk, George E. Lee and others, Vandermark's alternative version reveled in the unconventional, non-chordal musical language of today's jazz avant-garde.

Moreover, the band's first recording, "Transatlantic Bridge" (on Chicago-based Okka Disk), proved that the debut concert was no fluke, with critics around the world struck but its originality. "Vandermark is just as capable of deeply reverent traditional bopping as he is of totally pushing the envelope," wrote critic David Keenan in The Sunday Herald in Scotland. "He combines both here, with ferocious soloing tied up in big-band action."

When Vandermark unveiled his Territory Band-2, as he dubbed last year's incarnation of the ensemble, he expanded the lineup to a dozen musicians, including the brilliant Chicago electronics improviser Kevin

Drumm. Thus the ensemble started to merge acoustic and electronic sounds more daringly than virtually any other experimental band.

Yet despite the originality of the venture, or perhaps because of it, the Territory Band remains something of a luxury for Vandermark, his players and its fans. The MacArthur money has allowed Vandermark to gather the ensemble once a year for an intense rehearsal-performance period, the musicians then going their own ways, until it's time to regroup.

But the band may be on the verge of something bigger, thanks to the marquee engagement on the World Music Festival's opening weekend, the release next week of the band's newest recording, "Atlantis" (also on Okka Disk), and the forthcoming European tour, which includes a spot on the prestigious Berlin Jazz Festival.

Given a chance to be heard at prominent venues around the world, an ensemble as pioneering and virtuosic as this could gain momentum rapidly.

"This band means a great deal to Ken, so it would be great if people around the world stood up and noticed," says Bruno Johnson, owner of Okka Disk and a longtime champion of Vandermark's work.

"The MacArthur money gave him the chance to do something that most artists can't do, which is to advance his music in ways that would have been impossible otherwise. And that's just what he's doing."

Yet Vandermark's journey is not easy. Sitting in his basement, he pours his third cup of coffee, hoping the influx of caffeine will help him make sense of the notes, lines and squiggles he has been penciling all day.

"The band sure is bigger than anything I've done, the scores are more complicated, the demands on the musicians are great," he says, sounding nearly overwhelmed by the challenge he has undertaken.

"So this may be the most important thing I've done," he adds.

"It's certainly the most expensive."

CHAPTER 23

Orbert Davis

The Turning Point

Nov. 24, 1995

On this Thanksgiving weekend, few Chicago musicians will be giving heartier thanks for their blessings than Orbert Davis, who at age 35 has seen life from the bottom and the top.

Five years ago, Davis was lying in a hospital bed, barely able to breathe from a stormy bout with the asthma that he has endured all his life.

Today, he's one of the fastest-rising jazz trumpeters in the business, recent winner of the $10,000 top prize in a major jazz competition and star of an upcoming national television program.

"I remember thinking in the hospital how odd it was that every penny that I make comes from blowing air through a piece of metal," says Davis, who learned early in life never to take for granted the simple act of breathing.

"But even in the hospital, I never really feared losing the ability to play the trumpet, even though I couldn't touch the instrument all summer" of 1990, adds Davis. "I just had this faith that if God would allow me to get well, then I knew I'd be stronger than before."

Though Davis had to rebuild his trumpet playing and his breathing technique "from square one," as he puts it, he indeed came back to music with remarkable force and vigor. He may have been a little-known

Fig. 15 Orbert Davis: The brilliant Chicago trumpeter has extended his influence well beyond his horn via the Chicago Jazz Philharmonic. The CJP has become the country's leading Third Stream institution, intertwining jazz and classical languages via Davis' visionary compositions. Photo by Paul Natkin.

Chicago trumpeter before his illness, but immediately afterward he embarked upon a journey that would turn his life around.

Two months ago, for instance, Davis ventured to New York to beat a national field of competitors in the Cognac Hennessy Jazz Search, one of the more lucrative contests in jazz.

Three weeks ago, he played a brilliant trumpet-and-strings concert that was taped live by a small army of cameramen for broadcast early next year on the Black Entertainment Television cable network.

And last weekend, Davis made musical history playing the role of Miles Davis (no relation) in one of the first live performances of "Sketches of Spain" since Miles' legendary recording of 1960. The standing-room-only crowd at the Park West gave the younger Davis the kind of ovation more typically reserved for his late, lamented namesake.

Those are just the highlights. Since jump-starting his life and his career five years ago, Davis has become:

- First trumpeter with the Chicago Jazz Ensemble, a nationally noted repertory jazz band that will make its New York debut next year with Davis as soloist.
- Director of the Greater Chicago High School Jazz Orchestra at Columbia College Chicago, where he has been artist-in-residence since last year.
- Instructor in the Ravinia Jazz Mentors program, which coaches gifted young musicians in the Chicago public schools.
- Solo recording artist on his debut CD, "Unfinished Memories" (Copia), which has received extensive national airplay since its release last year.

The marvel, however, is not how much Davis has done but how well he has done it.

"Orbert is technically an extraordinary player," says William Russo, who conducted the Chicago Jazz Ensemble in the "Sketches of Spain" concert. "He's up there with the best, he's up there with Wynton [Marsalis]. Certainly he's far beyond almost any other trumpeter I can think of, technically speaking, and he's a fiercely hard worker."

So what makes Orbert run? And why would a fellow whose prospects "didn't look too bright," as Davis puts it, try to devour the world whole?

"Orbert always has been like that, at least since he was a freshman in high school, which is where I met him," says Mark Ingram, the trumpeter's partner in Orbark Productions, a commercial music firm they own.

"Even back then, when we were into Top 40 and practicing pop tunes, during every break in rehearsals Orbert would be listening to and studying someone else's records. Every minute, every second he would be working on something else."

Yet Davis came to the trumpet comparatively late in life. Born in Chicago and reared in Momence, near Kankakee, he started noodling on the trumpet at age 10 but didn't begin formal lessons until high school.

A shrewd elementary school teacher in Momence, Charles Danish, saw the youngster's potential and drove him to Chicago every Saturday morning to study at DePaul University.

"Mr. Danish never charged me a dime, not for gas money or anything," recalls Davis, still a bit incredulous at the man's generosity.

Recalls Danish: "I first had heard Orbert play when he was in 6th grade, and by the time he was in 8th grade, his playing just about knocked me off my chair."

Davis eventually took his undergraduate degree from DePaul in classical trumpet, but it wasn't until years later, in 1985, that he became wholly smitten with jazz. The love affair began in a small and obscure South Side club called The Other Place.

"I was working with [saxophonists] Andy Goodrich and Ari Brown, Fridays through Sundays in the wee hours of the morning—that was the training ground," Davis recalls. "Andy took me under his wing, told me what records to buy, what I should be playing.

"I started listening to [trumpeters] Freddie Hubbard, and then Lee Morgan, Blue Mitchell and Clifford Brown. And I also was into Stevie Wonder."

Those musicians obviously represent a galaxy of styles and sounds, yet they share a fervently lyrical way with a phrase as well as a formidable technical equipment. The description befits Davis, as well.

It wasn't until after his illness, however, that Davis started to achieve his goals. Though he had been working just as hard before his sickness as after, something happened, something clicked that made listeners, critics and other musicians take notice.

"I think what happened was that getting ill actually gave me a chance to start over, from square one," says Davis. "I really had to start all over, but this time it was as a more experienced musician.

"And by starting again, I suppose I started playing better. Maybe it's because of all the time I had spent away from playing, I started getting serious about writing music and arranging, and that probably helped my playing, too."

Whatever happened, the results were unmistakable. For those who have been listening to Davis regularly since 1990, the man's playing has been getting more polished, more technically audacious and more distinctive with each season.

Davis reached a new high point in '94, when he achieved a longtime dream by fronting a jazz rhythm section and a classical string unit in his "Strings Attached" show at the Green Mill Jazz Club. Rarely has any musician played the triple role of soloist, conductor and arranger in such a setting.

The project quickly captured the attention of Black Entertainment Television, which committed to airing the video version.

In September, when Davis won the Cognac Hennessy contest, there was no doubt that his star was ascending.

"After they announced that my band won, I got this big embrace from Grover Washington Jr.," says Davis, referring to the noted saxophonist who headed the competition jury at the Bottom Line club in Greenwich Village.

"But the funny thing was that even as I was realizing that I had won this contest, all I could think about was the 'Strings Attached' taping coming up. I wasn't so much thinking that I just won 10 grand, I was thinking, 'Hey, this will help pay the musicians for the taping.'

"So I really haven't had the time to pat myself on the back. I've been too busy."

Therein may lie one of the dangers ahead for Davis. Russo, who hired him at Columbia and remains one of his staunchest supporters, says point blank that "Orbert is working too hard."

Others, also, have noted that in his zeal to perform, he may be stretching himself a bit thin.

Some observers also are wary of Davis' flirtation with commercial studio work. Though his "Unfinished Memories" CD has been popular on radio, its slick studio sound has inspired mixed comments from critics who enthusiastically have applauded his live jazz performances.

"I fear," says one observer who asked not to be named, "that Orbert may be leaning a bit too much toward commerce and away from jazz."

Davis passionately disagrees.

"The goal that Mark and I had in starting our commercial music business never was to become megarich," says Davis. "I've simply always loved pop music and still do.

"As for my workload, I actually cut down and changed my whole performing life when I got married," in 1993, to a pediatrician.

"I used to play parties every Saturday night, and I just completely stopped doing those kinds of jobs when we got married."

Regardless of what his critics believe, Davis appears to have found the rhythm that's right for him. That much was obvious last weekend, during the "Sketches of Spain" concert.

Playing Miles Davis' extensive, 45-minute solo part, the young trumpeter gave one of the more mesmerizing performances of his career. If there were a couple of bloopers early on, he quickly settled in to the elegaic spirit of the work and the poetic style of the trumpeter for whom composer Gil Evans wrote "Sketches."

"To be honest, at first I didn't want to do that concert, though I never told Bill [Russo] that," says Davis. "I listened to the record, which I had owned forever, and I just realized that you never can sound like Miles.

"But then I started to think of it more as an acting situation in which I'm portraying Miles. That would be the challenge, and since I like challenges, I decided to do it.

"When you think that just a few years ago I was in the hospital unable to breathe, and five years later I'm onstage playing Miles Davis—it's the kind of thing that can make you pretty humble."

The Chicago River Gets Jazzed

May 27, 2013

The reversal of the Chicago River more than a century ago helped transform a polluted, disease-ridden city into a sprawling, modern metropolis.

It also wiped out vegetation, sank land masses and triggered flooding along the Illinois River and beyond, as Chicago sent its human waste and other detritus—from stockyards, tanneries and whatnot—downstream toward St. Louis.

That epic tale, and the engineering feat that made it possible in 1900, long ago became part of the can-do lore of this city. But Friday evening, it took on a new form as a jazz symphony by Chicagoan Orbert Davis, whose five-movement work told the story in emotionally gripping ways. With historic, black-and-white images from the turn of the previous century projected onto a screen above the stage of Symphony Center, Davis led his Chicago Jazz Philharmonic in the world premiere of "The Chicago River."

The piece traced the narrative of a city on the make with grandeur and introspection, jazz rhythm and symphonic gesture. As bold and brawny as the city it sought to portray, the work lived up to its enormous subject matter, even if "The Chicago River" did not push into unfamiliar or innovative musical languages. Davis, in other words, has written more complex and daring scores than this, by far, but none as mature, concise, finely crafted or expressively profound.

Inspired by Richard Cahan and Michael Williams' book "The Lost Panoramas"—which published rediscovered photos documenting the reversal of the river's flow—Davis' opus opened just as the tome does: with idyllic scenes of the Illinois River. As the audience savored bucolic images of downstate locales, the orchestra played a pastoral music of comparable serenity. Winds and strings shaped lovely phrases, the music proceeding unhurriedly, like the gentle flow of the waters. Titled "A Lost Panorama," this opening movement turned back the calendar to a much slower, more peaceful time and place.

The city of Chicago, flexing its muscles in the aftermath of the great fire of 1871, changed all that, pouring into the river blood and guts and waste—the byproducts of an urban colossus in the making. Davis achieved his most brilliant tone painting in this portion of the story, evocatively titled "Brewing the Toxic Stew": The rumbling low-register writing, thick-as-mud textures and snarling, smarting dissonance produced a vivid sonic portrait of all this muck. Accompanying photos of so much putrid material oozing into the river heightened the effect.

This odious brew could not be allowed to continue to befoul Lake Michigan, where the river emptied and Chicago drew its drinking water. Cholera, typhoid fever and other waterborne diseases were killing people, hence the audacious plan to reverse the river. Davis' "Retrograde" movement ingeniously captured the optimistic spirit that enabled a young city to take on nature itself, the music upbeat, up-tempo and exuberant. Better still, it drew upon the early ragtime rhythms of the period, thereby evoking not only the flavor of the era but its musical syntax.

In the symphony's penultimate movement, "Fortress of Solitude," Davis ventured away from the storyline of Cahan and Williams' book, instead looking inward, toward his own youth growing up in Momence, alongside the Kankakee River.

As a boy who harbored dreams of someday becoming a jazz musician in Chicago, Davis often practiced his horn at riverside, and his somewhat melancholy fluegelhorn solos in "Fortress of Solitude" reflected not only his longings back then but also the bittersweet fate of the rivers themselves.

Chicago's triumph in reversing the waters' direction, after all, wreaked havoc elsewhere, and Davis' plaintive horn lines—set against a simple string backdrop—eloquently expressed this dichotomy. Recall the lyric poetry of Samuel Barber, as in his "Adagio for Strings" or "Knoxville, Summer of 1915," and you're hearing the tap root of Davis' music here.

It would be difficult to overstate the dramatic power of Davis' final movement, "The Seventh Wonder," its title referring to the nickname accorded Chicago's engineering triumph. But as he did with all the preceding movements, Davis built this one subtly, its crescendos gradual, its rhythms pulsing but not rushed, its degree of orchestral detail remarkable to behold.

Saxophonist Steve Eisen held the most prominent role here, his solos not looking to the past (as in the work's earlier ragtime references), but to the present, in the form of intricate phrase-making, blues-drenched phraseology and unabashed bursts of dissonance.

Clearly Davis was evoking Chicago of today, his choice of tenor saxophone as the lead voice a clever one, considering that this instrument, above all others, has come to epitomize Chicago jazz (just as the trumpet long ago became the signature jazz instrument of New Orleans). As "The Seventh Wonder" brought "The Chicago River" to a finale, Eisen unleashed a storm of ideas, the orchestra providing dramatic punctuation in the form of slashing fortissimo chords. And in one of the most persuasive closing passages Davis ever has written, he extended the conclusion of the work with a series of climaxes, giving drummer Ernie Adams an extended solo before Eisen, Adams and the orchestra alternated exclamatory statements.

When a final shot of the Chicago River today suddenly appeared on screen—gleaming high rises stacked alongside the river—the audience instantly erupted with applause. It would have been impossible not to.

It's critical to note, however, that notwithstanding its storyline, "The Chicago River" had a great deal to say on purely musical terms. Like all great pieces of program music, from Beethoven's "Pastoral" Sixth Symphony to Berlioz's "Symphonie Fantastique," Davis' "The Chicago River" ultimately needed no narrative or images. The music spoke searingly for itself.

In performance, Davis may have erred in encouraging the audience to applaud after particular solos from the Chicago Jazz Philharmonic, thereby interrupting the flow of the music. And Davis could have pushed the last movement, at least, into more bracing, experimental territory. Moreover, the shorter pieces Davis and the Philharmonic offered in the brief first half of the concert felt like a mere warm-up for the main event, complete with technical flaws from particular instrumentalists.

But those are minor quibbles in an evening that really was about "The Chicago River," which was commissioned by Symphony Center as part of its ongoing "Rivers" series. The piece now stands as the most masterful work Davis has written—quite an accomplishment, considering the copiousness of his pen.

CHAPTER 24

Kahil El'Zabar

Still Pushing Boundaries

Nov. 2, 2003

Perhaps because he unleashes so much galvanic energy onstage and off, the brilliant Chicago percussionist-activist Kahil El'Zabar always has seemed like a young man on a crusade.

But next weekend, El'Zabar, who has been a dynamic force in music in Chicago and beyond for roughly three decades, turns 50, a milestone not only for him but for this city's perpetually expanding avant-garde scene.

Were it not for El'Zabar—who has advanced the art form through innovative recordings, self-styled music festivals and relentless promotion of like-minded colleagues—Chicago's famously experimental music scene would command less edge and acclaim than it currently enjoys. For in the fervor of his performances and the restlessly itinerant nature of his work, El'Zabar has been a messenger for the Chicago jazz avant-garde, giving listeners around the world a taste of its artistic daring, technical prowess and remarkable accessibility.

So when a figure of El'Zabar's stature announces that he's about to qualify for membership in AARP, musicians and audiences take notice.

"Kahil's 50?" asks a slightly incredulous Von Freeman, an octogenarian Chicago jazz legend who still considers El'Zabar something of a youth.

"Well, he's got a long way to go."

Adds Tatsu Aoki, a comparably adventurous Chicago bassist and bandleader, "Kahil may be turning 50, but his mind is still fresh with ideas."

That's an understatement, considering the projects El'Zabar has in the works, including the forthcoming release of a plushly self-published coffee-table book, "Modern Jazz Masters," with text by El'Zabar and photographs by Bill Tucker; a bulging schedule of concerts across Europe; and the emergence of a new music company, JUBA Collective, which El'Zabar hopes will give avant-garde jazz musicians fresh opportunities in publishing, recording and performance.

Yet even the indefatigable El'Zabar is pausing for a beat or two to note the anniversary.

"In most cultures, 50 means that you are at the first stage of being an elder, and, of course, it's the half-century mark, so I guess the number does have significance," says El'Zabar, speaking in a Near West Side loft decorated with enormous abstract oil paintings and crowded with musical instruments.

"In turning 50, I've come to realize that I'm a part of the last generation [of Chicago jazz experimenters] who grew up in the 1960s, when this music had an organic relation to the turbulence of the times.

"And now to look at it in retrospect and think of how many of my colleagues we've lost—Lester Bowie, Fred Hopkins, on and on—and I realize that my generation has reached a crossroads."

Indeed, many artistic triumphs and personal losses lie between the 1960s and today. The towering achievement, of course, was the ascent of the Chicago-based Association for the Advancement of Creative Musicians, founded on the South Side in 1965. With jazz clubs closing and jazz record labels dramatically cutting back as teen-oriented rock 'n' roll overwhelmed the marketplace, the visionary Chicago instrumentalists of the AACM decided to take control of their own careers. They staged concerts in churches, school auditoriums and any other decent venues they could find; they recorded their music on tiny indie labels that would not dictate how art was to be made; and they booked their own tours across the country, Europe and beyond.

Thanks to AACM pioneers such as pianist-bandleader Muhal Richard Abrams, saxophonist-clubowner Fred Anderson, visionary reedist-composer Roscoe Mitchell and others, the young El'Zabar and his colleagues could see that, in Chicago at least, it was possible to produce important, experimental music and survive as an artist.

If the AACM effectively rejuvenated the art of jazz, which in the '60s was facing an artistic crisis to match its commercial decline, the organization also spawned generations of free thinkers more committed to art than to profits. Contemporaries such as El'Zabar, Ernest Dawkins, Malachi Thompson, Edward Wilkerson Jr. and others began following the lead of their AACM elders, developing new ways of addressing the fundamentals of jazz improvisation and composition.

If Dawkins' explosive New Horizons Ensemble, Thompson's quasi-orchestral Africa Brass and Wilkerson's majestic 8 Bold Souls represented fascinating re-inventions of long-standing jazz traditions, El'Zabar's Ethnic Heritage Ensemble took an equally intriguing path in the late '70s, digging deeply into ancient rituals of African music and liberating itself from the conventions of traditional jazz instrumentation.

"In many places where we first played, I was laughed at for having a band that used one African drum and two saxophone players," El'Zabar says.

"Presenters would say, 'You've got be kidding. Where's the piano? Where's the bass guy?' "

Yet the Ethnic Heritage Ensemble proved to be one of El'Zabar's more prescient efforts, its emphasis on reaching back to African cultural roots (as did other AACM bands, such as the Art Ensemble of Chicago) foreshadowing the ways in which jazz musicians today embrace various facets of world music.

In other bands, as well, El'Zabar developed unique methods for merging past and present, articulating gripping beats on hand-held percussion and chanting in mesmerizing, wordless vocals, while surrounding himself with great blasts of dissonance from all manner of horns. Even in his most daring ensemble, the Experimental Band—a radical large unit that uses no scores but improvises according to directions from El'Zabar, its conductor—it's the fusion of ancient and modern, African and American that drives the project.

"I've always felt that Kahil's music has been a little different than the 'free jazz' avant-garde that many people associate with Chicago," says bassist-bandleader Aoki.

"To me, his music has always been about bringing the roots of African music to Chicago. It's a more down-to-earth approach to improvising, because it brings your ethnicity into the mix, and it allows the whole community to get something very important out of the music."

Community always has been central to the identity of El'Zabar, who recalls a childhood surrounded by Black artistic, social and political giants.

Born Clifton Blackburn, Jr., on the Great Lakes Naval Training Center, he grew up next door to Mamie Till-Mobley, the mother of Emmett Till (whose racially motivated murder in Mississippi in 1955 made the 14-year-old victim a civil rights martyr). The Blackburn family, keenly aware of the tenor of the times, took their son to speeches by Malcolm X and Dr. Martin Luther King, Jr., and to picnics where Freeman, Gene Ammons and other neighborhood jazz stars played their horns.

When the teenaged Cliff Blackburn realized that most of his musician friends used African names, he recalled that his uncle—a contemporary and follower of Nation of Islam leader Elijah Muhammad—had given him the name Kahil, which means "force of light." To this the emerging musician eventually added "El'Zabar," which means "teacher," making him "Force of light, the teacher," a name he clearly has lived up to.

For El'Zabar has been an important figure in illuminating great Black music for listeners of all levels of sophistication. Disenchanted with the short shrift that organizations such as the Chicago Jazz Festival and the city's mainstream clubs gave avant-garde music, El'Zabar created events such as the Underground Fest and the Express Your Self Fest, each an excursion into the outer reaches of jazz experimentation. In ventures such as the long-shuttered Rituals club, in the South Loop, the Ascension Loft Series in various Chicago spaces, and the Traffic series he developed at Steppenwolf Theatre, El'Zabar has given uncounted musicians a setting in which to reach adventurous audiences.

"He's what I would call an organizer—someone who makes things happen," says Anderson, who himself runs one of the city's best forums for avant-garde music, the Velvet Lounge, on South Indiana Avenue.

"Kahil organizes, he advocates, he takes care of business."

Which is precisely what El'Zabar hopes to do on a greater scale as he passes his 50th birthday, on Nov. 11. The JUBA Collective firm he has established with business partners (the acronym stands for Joint Universal Breath Ascending) is a for-profit venture that will make recordings, produce books and otherwise promote new ideas in Chicago jazz, El'Zabar says.

If the forthcoming products convey the esthetic appeal of the JUBA Collective's first release, the "Modern Jazz Masters" book, the enterprise could be onto something.

"After spending the last 30 years in the non-profit sector as administrator, performer, educator and producer, I've seen the limitations of only depending on the not-for-profit ideology," says El'Zabar, who believes that if the AACM pioneers proved that artists could take charge of their careers, their 21st Century heirs should take control of their finances.

"I've now come to believe that the artists, themselves, have to attempt entrepreneurial experiments. We have to control not just our art but our businesses," says El'Zabar.

"So that's the next step that I'm looking at.

"The next 50 years should be interesting."

Trafficking in Creativity

Oct. 19, 1997

When he was growing up on the South Side of Chicago, Kahil El'Zabar was immersed in the sounds of Black culture.

In storied venues such as McKee's, the Pershing Room and the Regal Theater, the young man heard groundbreaking artists who would set the tone and direction for his life.

"If you could imagine going to the Regal Theater in 1958 and '59, you could see [trumpeter] Lee Morgan, [singer] Jerry Butler, [comic] Dick Gregory, the Staple Singers when they were still doing gospel, the Ramsey Lewis Trio when it was just starting out—it was almost overwhelming," recalls El'Zabar.

"In my own neighborhood of Chatham, I would see [tenor saxophonist] Von Freeman and his brothers George [a guitarist] and Bruz [a drummer], as well as Herbie [Hancock] and Jack [DeJohnette] and many more. The musical culture was prevalent everywhere you turned, and it didn't matter if you were talking about jazz or gospel or blues or soul or whatever.

"It was all great music presented as a class act by performers who dressed well and spoke well, and it taught me as much about excellence as it did about music."

El'Zabar must have learned his lessons well, for in addition to developing an important career as bandleader (he heads the Ritual Trio and Ethnic Heritage Ensemble) and percussionist (he has worked with everyone from archetypal Chicago tenor saxophonist Gene Ammons to innovative multi-instrumentalist Roscoe Mitchell), El'Zabar has brought the freewheeling spirit of South Side experimentation to an unlikely location: Steppenwolf Theatre.

The Traffic series, which El'Zabar curated last year at Steppenwolf (where it reopens Oct. 27), represents something more than just a provocative lineup of musical experimenters. By bringing to a single stage poets, actors, dancers and avant-garde instrumentalists—often in unexpected combinations—El'Zabar has drawn upon the freewheeling creative spirit of the South Side in which he was raised.

It is a part of the city that made jazz, blues and gospel into musical idioms that would be embraced around the world, thanks to the work of artists such as Ammons, Pops Staple, Thomas A. Dorsey, Louis Armstrong, Earl "Fatha" Hines, Muddy Waters, James Cleveland, Mahalia Jackson and hundreds more. Though the heyday of the South Side may be past, the fact that so many of the world's great musicians still live there (or maintain ties to those who do) has given El'Zabar the essential elements with which to build Traffic.

By featuring legendary and emerging South Side artists, in tandem with performers from other parts of the city and far beyond, El'Zabar has created an arts series that speaks volumes about Chicago and has no counterpart anywhere in America.

Last year, for instance, Traffic presented poet Ntozake Shange reading her evocative writings in a beguiling, sing-song fashion, while El'Zabar, trumpeter Lester Bowie and others riffed brilliantly alongside her. On other Traffic evenings, legendary Chicago guitarist David "Honeyboy" Edwards sang haunting, turn-of-the-century repertoire and reminisced (with Studs Terkel) on his friendship with blues pioneer Robert Johnson; and up-and-coming Chicago guitarist Fareed

Haque collaborated with several comparably cutting-edge players in the most exciting show Haque yet has played in his hometown.

That all of these performances were broadcast on WBEZ-FM only added to the impact.

"When we were first thinking about starting an interdisciplinary arts series, everyone said we should check with Kahil," remembers Martha Lavey, Steppenwolf's artistic director. "They said he's the guy who has connections with the major artists, and, boy, were they right."

Indeed, because El'Zabar has known all of these players for longer than he probably cares to remember, he was able to persuade them to appear in risky, unconventional settings they might not have been willing to explore otherwise.

As a teenager, after all, El'Zabar was playing in a sextet led by Muhal Richard Abrams, a towering pianist-composer who was one of the founders of the Association for the Advancement of Creative Musicians. Thereafter, El'Zabar came to know and work with Henry Threadgill, George Lewis, Chico Freeman, Douglas Ewart, Malachi Favors, Fred Hopkins, Anthony Braxton and dozens more, all pioneering artists who helped redefine avant-garde jazz during the past three decades.

Inevitably, each had to make a choice: Stay in Chicago or move on to the East Coast (as Abrams and Freeman did), the West Coast (Braxton) or beyond (Threadgill, who lives in India).

For El'Zabar, the choice was a simple one—continue to flourish in Chicago.

"I stayed for a lot of reasons, but mostly because I had seen so many great musicians stay here and still become known around the world," explains El'Zabar. "Ramsey Lewis, Malachi Favors, Gene Ammons, George Hughes, Eddie Johnson and so many others stayed rooted in Chicago, while great players like Malachi Thompson and Fred Hopkins moved to New York but eventually returned home.

"I think they all knew the same thing that I found out early on: There's this incredible creative well in Chicago, and it runs extremely deep. Deep enough, in fact, to nourish a musician for a lifetime."

What often was lacking here, however, was an adequate number of places where musicians could learn and perform, particularly with the demise of dozens of jazz clubs beginning in the mid-'60s. From this vacuum came the AACM, which was created on the South Side, in part, as an organization that could help musicians stage concerts, exchange ideas and educate new generations of musicians.

One of these students was El'Zabar, who remembers that his AACM mentors taught him something more than just new approaches to harmony, theory and instrumentation.

"Roscoe [Mitchell] always emphasized listening to Bird [Charlie Parker], and Muhal [Abrams] constantly talked about Fletcher Henderson and King Kolax," says El'Zabar.

"They taught us about Earl 'Fatha' Hines, how he ran a band, and the unusual voicings that he used that led directly to bebop. You had to learn all those things, how to put on a combo, how to play blues, soul, bebop, whatever."

That training enabled El'Zabar to survive as a working musician, but like many AACM alums, he also worked as cultural activist, staging concerts and arts festivals across Chicago and elsewhere in the States. The Underground Festival that he has presented periodically over the past decade often has outshone the Chicago Jazz Festival it was meant to complement; the Express Yourself Fest he presented last year brought to Chicago such estimable players as New York saxophonist Murray and New Orleans pioneer Kidd Jordan, each collaborating with some of the most sophisticated avant-gardists in the city.

None of these efforts, however, had the kind of financial and marketing muscle required to make a major impact. Instead, they were quixotic projects that El'Zabar and a few colleagues staged despite the odds.

And that's what made the emergence of the Traffic series so fortuitous—for Steppenwolf, for El'Zabar and, most of all, for music in Chicago.

"I know what it's like to muscle a production into existence, and I know how hard and how draining it is," says Steppenwolf's Lavey. "Give an artist like Kahil the support he needs, however, and you would be amazed at what can happen."

That's precisely what Steppenwolf did with Traffic, giving El'Zabar a first-rate performance space and the kind of marketing and advertising support he hadn't seen (or probably dreamed of) in his life. With the help of Lavey and Steppenwolf marketing director Tim Evans, El'Zabar last year put together an eight-event series that took off "like no one really imagined it would—we were astonished," says Evans.

Indeed, most of the events were sold out; the rest reached about 90 percent capacity, remarkable figures for a series featuring unexpected collaborations among artistic innovators.

The success led Steppenwolf to expand Traffic to 10 events this year, with all on the mainstage (a few last season had been in the studio). But it's the nature of the programming that captures the imagination, with El'Zabar and friends having come up with a series that seems—on paper, at least—even more adventurous than last year's. That the season will open with a "Tribute to the AACM" featuring three major bands (on Oct. 27) and continue with a concert appearance by the Art Ensemble of Chicago (Dec. 15) and a new version of Stravinsky's "The Soldier's Tale" (with new libretto by Kurt Vonnegut) suggests that Steppenwolf is becoming the epicenter of bold new ideas in Chicago music.

"This is just the beginning," says El'Zabar, whose words might seem boastful, if not for the achievements of last season and the promise of the new one.

"If we can get audiences this excited about new music after just one season, imagine what we might be able to do after three, or four, or five."

One hardly can wait to find out.

CHAPTER 25

Art Ensemble of Chicago

Neglected at Home

Dec. 14, 1997

They are celebrated in concert halls from New York to Paris, they're in demand at jazz festivals in Europe and Japan, but the pioneering musicians of the Art Ensemble of Chicago rarely perform in the city whose name they carry around the world.

Apart from anniversary celebrations of the AACM (Association for the Advancement of Creative Musicians) in 1990 and '95, as well as an appearance at the Chicago Jazz Festival in 1988 in Grant Park, one of the most famous avant-garde units in the world barely has been heard or seen in its hometown.

So when the Art Ensemble of Chicago makes its debut on the Traffic series of Steppenwolf Theatre on Monday, it will be creating musical history, and not just because the concert will be taped for a forthcoming live recording. For the first time in recent memory, the Art Ensemble—a group that merges elements of theater and performance art with avant-garde music-making—will perform in a top-notch Chicago auditorium (the Steppenwolf mainstage) worthy of its art and its reputation.

The question is why local audiences have had so few opportunities to hear a Chicago band so widely revered?

Fig. 16 Art Ensemble of Chicago: The groundbreaking band took the spirit, message and innovations of the AACM around the world in the 1960s. It's shown here in 1990 at Merkin Hall. Left to right: Roscoe Mitchell, Famoudou Don Moye, Lester Bowie, Malachi Favors and Joseph Jarman. Note: Although the banners announce the group's 20th anniversary, they were being reused to celebrate its 25th. Photo © Lauren Deutsch.

"Is that revered or feared?" asks Famoudou Don Moye, the exceptional percussionist of the Art Ensemble since 1970.

"We work more in Bosnia than we do in Chicago," adds Moye, exaggerating only a bit. "We work more in New York and California than we do in Chicago. It has to do with the politics of the powers that be. Things aren't like they used to be—we won't work in the conditions we used to work in 20 years ago—we're older."

Specifically, Moye means this: In the early days (the late '60s and early '70s), the Art Ensemble—like all the breakthrough bands affiliated with the AACM—worked for a pittance at almost any available venue. And though there's no shortage of such places in Chicago today, major concert halls that pay musicians well and treat them accordingly (with proper lighting, sound and other technical support) are not particularly interested in avant-garde fare.

"This ensemble should be at Symphony Center," says Kahil El'Zabar, artistic curator of Steppenwolf's Traffic series.

But a group as adventurous as the Art Ensemble, which excels at using novel instruments and African-based musical forms, is not likely to turn up at Symphony Center, where the emphasis is on mainstream entertainment (at least so far as its jazz bookings are concerned).

With Chicago lacking a midsize jazz presenter on the order of, say, the Knitting Factory in New York, the Art Ensemble finds itself mostly cut off from the very city that defines it.

"Another part of the problem is that when artists from Chicago gain major notoriety," adds El'Zabar, "our sense of familiarity with them sometimes makes us forget their importance in music.

"Sometimes, we may see Malachi Favors [the Art Ensemble bassist] at the grocery store, and we may forget that he is one of the brilliant innovators of music."

At this point, though, says Moye, "We're not bitter about that—I got over that in the early '80s.

"I used to get into these conflicts with the [musical] establishment, but then I started backing off of confrontational situations, because it wasn't producing anything positive.

"Now we direct our energy at projects that come to us and not at projects that didn't happen."

Even so, Moye can't help noting that Chicago, in particular, and the United States, in general, have not embraced the Art Ensemble the way Europe and Japan have done. Foreign concert tours in which the Art Ensemble has teamed with South African singers or fronted symphony orchestras or honored Chicago's blues tradition have not been seen in the U.S., a loss both for the Art Ensemble and for culture in America.

If you doubt it, consider the breadth of the Art Ensemble's achievements during the past three decades. Beginning in the late 1960s—when multi-instrumentalist Roscoe Mitchell collaborated with trumpeter Lester Bowie, saxophonist Joseph Jarman and bassist Malachi Favors (with Moye joining as percussionist in 1970, in Paris)—the Art Ensemble has established a distinctive musical and theatrical vocabulary that helped rejuvenate the art of jazz improvisation.

Its huge inventory of ancient, invented and conventional instruments; its African-inspired wardrobe and face painting; its merging of ancient African chant, pre-swing rhythm, nascent New Orleans jazz and outlandishly modern dissonance jolted audiences in Paris in 1970 and around the world thereafter. On recordings such as "The Art Ensemble: 1967–68" (a five-CD set documenting the beginnings of the music, on the Nessa label) as well as "A Jackson in Your House" (featuring Bowie, Mitchell, Jarman and Favors, on Affinity), "Live" (documenting a historic 1972 Mandel Hall concert, on Delmark) and "Fanfare for the Warriors" (with pianist Muhal Richard Abrams, on Atlantic), the Art Ensemble offered arresting new sounds. Latin, African, funk, jazz and shades of contemporary European classical elements merged in a music at once harmonically complex yet texturally transparent.

These and other recordings (on the ECM and DIW labels) traced the perpetual evolution of the band, which essentially grew out of the mid-'60s experiments of various AACM bands.

"The '60s was a difficult period in jazz, with the music divided into separate factions," remembers Chicago Jazz Ensemble conductor William Russo, referring to the pitched cultural battles between the avant-garde and the traditionalists (last summer, Russo's band performed with the Art Ensemble at two Italian jazz festivals).

"But even amid all the problems of the '60s, it was apparent that the Art Ensemble was important because of the way the musicians used color and content. They're real artists, serious and completely devoted, and they have a sense of spiritual and moral underpinnings to their art."

Indeed, just as the titles of Art Ensemble recordings such as "Art Ensemble of Soweto" (DIW) and "Urban Bushmen" (ECM) allude to the social undercurrent in their work, the music itself evokes the breadth of the Black musical tradition in America. "Great Black Music, Ancient to Modern" may be the motto of the AACM, but nowhere does it apply more directly than to the Art Ensemble.

When Moye, Favors, Bowie and Mitchell take the Steppenwolf stage, no one in the audience will be able to predict what will happen musically. But regardless of which direction these artists take, they surely will be drawing upon the legacy of the past three decades and exulting in the very fact of their survival.

"As professionals, we have to keep finding a way to perform, because that's what we do," says Moye. "I can't go changing my life because of not being accepted.

"Motivation comes from doing what we did in spite of almost insurmountable odds. Our quest is simply maintaining the high standards we were crazy enough to establish 30 years ago.

"Now we just try to live up to them."

Return to Mandel Hall

May 3, 2004

The Art Ensemble of Chicago isn't just a band—it's a way of life.

That's why this magnificent organization can flourish for decades, despite changing musical tastes, an imploding recording industry and, most significant, the deaths of two vital ensemble members.

Without the soulful bassist Malachi Favors, who died in January, and the ebullient trumpeter Lester Bowie, who died in 1999, the Art Ensemble that played over the weekend at Mandel Hall by definition was not the same unit that famously performed there in 1972. That historic date yielded "Live at Mandel Hall," an album that remains a landmark in the ever-deepening canon of the jazz avant-garde.

Yet the band's performance before a capacity audience on Friday night, recorded live for a forthcoming "Return to Mandel Hall" CD, proved as majestic, sonorous and charismatic as the band had been 32 years earlier.

At the very least, the Art Ensemble has undergone a profound and remarkably persuasive transformation, its surviving members—multi-instrumentalists Roscoe Mitchell, Joseph Jarman and Famoudou Don Moye—now joined by exceptional young Chicago trumpeter Corey Wilkes, nimble bassist Jaribu Shahid and the magisterial percussionist Baba Sissoko.

It's inarguable that these three artists significantly have altered the sound of the Art Ensemble. Trumpeter Wilkes is less brash and brazen than Bowie (who isn't?), yet Wilkes' quicksilver technique and deeply burnished tone on trumpet, fluegelhorn and pocket trumpet give the band an alluring, slightly muted sheen in the upper registers. Bassist Shahid does not try to mimic the deep well of sound that was Favors' signature (how could he?), but Shahid's rhythmically propulsive playing added palpable drive and momentum to the proceedings.

And then there's Sissoko, who—judging by this revelatory performance—restores to the Art Ensemble a spiritual center that one might have thought was forever lost with Favors' death. Sissoko's radiant personality, profound vocal chant and astonishing virtuosity on hand-held African drums enrich this band's already profound esthetic link to the musical rituals of ancient Africa.

If Sissoko, Wilkes and Shahid have changed the tonal palette of the band in intriguing ways, Art Ensemble stalwarts Mitchell, Jarman and Moye have retained the sonic splendor and radical fervor of old. Joined by their new colleagues, the veterans reaffirm the band's reverence for age-old Black musical traditions and relentless curiosity for outlandish new sounds.

The evening began auspiciously, with a shimmering, free improvisation in which all the players except Sissoko explored the unique tintinnabulation of a battery of modern, traditional and invented percussion instruments. When Mitchell, Wilkes and Jarman then picked up their horns to produce searing, blues-drenched exhortations, there was no question that the Art Ensemble—despite its losses—was alive and well and swinging in Chicago.

Mitchell turned in volcanic solos on alto saxophone and a particularly thunderous eruption on bass saxophone on his "Tech Ritter and the Megabytes." Jarman disarmed the audience with sweet plainsong chant on his "Za-za Ohm," and the entire band conveyed a palpable sense of hope and healing on the perennial closer, "Odwalla."

Long may they thrive.

EPILOGUE

Not Enough Time

Somehow, more than 40 years of covering music for the Chicago Tribune wasn't quite enough time to get to everybody and everything. Or maybe it's just that the past century-plus of Chicago jazz is so wide in stylistic reach, so deep in talent and so profound in innovation that a lifetime of work can't cover it all. Not even close.

Looking back on all the jazz giants I've met, interviewed and reviewed, I'm surprised to realize that I never wrote a freestanding piece on at least two masters: singer-pianist Nat "King" Cole and tenor saxophonist Gene Ammons. For no Chicago singer-pianist attained a wider following than Cole, and no Chicago tenorist delivered as visceral a sound as Ammons.

Yet their work echoes through mine, in the many times I referenced them while writing about other artists: Cole's and Ammons' achievements provided a benchmark by which to assess and understand the music of their successors. In Cole's case, his work as pianist and singer may have been so ubiquitous as to render writing a column or two almost superfluous, like penning a piece about the air we breathe. With Ammons, the situation was reversed—he has been nearly forgotten, except by every musician who wants to understand what the tenor saxophone can say in its most rhetorically urgent voice.

And though I've long considered Morton and Armstrong the root source of Chicago jazz, I must note that other great musicians migrated to Chicago even before these two giants (Morton himself visited Chicago long before the '20s). Perhaps none was more virtuosic and versatile than pianist-singer Tony Jackson, who came here in 1905 from New Orleans, where he had left Morton in awe.

Jackson was the "world's greatest single-handed entertainer," said Morton, who did not often rate other musicians above himself. "Could play and sing from opera to blues in its correct formation, knew everything that probably was ever printed."

Alas, scant record of Jackson's genius survives, apart from his inextinguishable song "Pretty Baby," a delicate but indispensable keepsake of a vanished era. Had Jackson—who died in 1921—lived long enough to record his memories, as Morton did during his Library of Congress sessions with Alan Lomax in 1938, a chapter of jazz pre-history would have been forever preserved.

So we're lucky to have what Morton, Armstrong and the generations of jazz visionaries who followed them have left us. And I was fortunate to hear and converse with many of them during the second half of the jazz century and well into the next.

All of which begs the question, implied throughout this book: What makes Chicago jazz unique? What exactly is the majesty of Chicago jazz?

Generalizing is perilous, of course, but, if pressed, I'd have to say that Chicago always has been a nurturer of "fabulous eccentrics"—artists who go their own way, regardless of musical fashion or commercial pressure. Think of how startlingly original Jelly Roll Morton's New Orleans inspired, meticulously orchestrated ensemble compositions must have sounded to Chicagoans in the rough-and-tumble Roaring '20s. Or how jolting Louis Armstrong's string of high C's would have struck Chicagoans—or anyone else—who had never heard a jazz trumpet reach into the stratosphere. Ditto the sublime poetry and seemingly effortless elegance of Armstrong's solos.

Yet Chicago audiences embraced these groundbreaking musical expressions, propelling these visionaries to global fame and laying the groundwork for subsequent generations of local jazz revolutionaries. Pianist Ahmad Jamal's stop-start musings, the Sun Ra Arkestra's incendiary eruptions, tenor saxophonist Fred Anderson's vast and thunderous soliloquies and the uncounted innovations of the AACM—among others documented in these pages—challenged expectations yet found audiences willing to come along for the ride.

After well over half a century of attending jazz performances in Chicago, I can attest that, to this day, Chicagoans continue to seek out fresh, idiosyncratic thinking in music.

The city's sound, then, is kaleidoscopic—not relegated to a single style or school or method but, quite the contrary, a seemingly unending array of iconoclastic music-making. All of it delivered without apology or pretense. Straight, no chaser.

As the great food writer Anthony Bourdain famously said of this city: "You wake up in Chicago, pull back the curtain, and you KNOW where you are. You could be nowhere else. You are in a big, brash, muscular, broad shouldered" city. "Pomposity, pretentiousness, putting on airs of any kind . . . and lack of a sense of humor will not get you far in Chicago. . . . Chicago is a town, a city that doesn't ever have to measure itself against any other city. Other places have to measure themselves against it."

That always has been the attitude of the city's jazz musicians, who—stylistically speaking—answer to no one but themselves.

Even the venues in which Chicago's jazz musicians work tend to shun ostentation and affectation. Unlike many clubs across the country, for instance, most Chicago jazz spots offer no food; only the music matters. Thus, the rambunctious character of the Green Mill (presenting music since 1907), the zero-frills ambience of Constellation (an experimental music room) and the somewhat grungy setting of the long-gone Bop Shop, Velvet Lounge, Birdhouse and others exemplify the classic Chicago jazz club. There's a palpably proletarian esthetic to these places, emblematic of the city's working-class esthetic. And though Andy's Jazz Club serves food, its boisterous atmosphere obviates any sense of pretension.

Even snazzier downtown rooms such as the Jazz Showcase and Winter's Jazz Club conceive of themselves as serious listening rooms rather than haughty nightspots or booze-it-up hangs.

The miracle of Chicago jazz, though, lies not just in its storied past but also in its perpetually emerging voices. Perhaps only a city that has been launching jazz musicians for more than a century could continue to produce uninterrupted waves of young talent. This despite an imploded record industry and a nation that marginalizes the music by keeping it off TV and nearly nonexistent on radio. Nevertheless, Chicago continues sending into the world innovators such as Thaddeus Tukes, who brings profoundly soulful expression to the vibraphone; Isaiah Collier, a saxophonist who boldly fuses sound, dance and spectacle; trumpeter Marquis Hill, who intertwines jazz with far-flung musical languages; vocalist Alyssa Allgood, who reinvents jazz standards with extraordinary sensitivity; bassist Matt Ulery, who somehow finds the place where jazz, contemporary classical and Eastern European folkloric music meet; pianist Jahari Stampley, who revels in a boundless harmonic imagination; reedist Greg Ward, who makes complex improvisation unexpectedly accessible; Kevin King, who brings currents of heavy metal into his work on woodwinds; drummer, composer and self-described "beat scientist" Makaya McCraven, who fearlessly merges genres and technologies; and on and on.

All the while, veterans such as genre-defying singer-songwriter-pianist Patricia Barber, vocal adventurer Dee Alexander, multi-instrumentalist Kahil El'Zabar, protean reedist-bandleader Ken Vandermark and others fearlessly continue to transcend musical boundaries.

The majesty of Chicago jazz, then, rings out not just in the past century's music but in the present moment and, I fiercely believe, in the century yet to come.

If so, once again it will be impossible to imagine jazz without Chicago.

ACKNOWLEDGMENTS

This book would not have been possible without the help of many generous musicians, journalists, agents, book editors, jazz impresarios and others:

First, the artists whose music I've savored in Chicago's jazz clubs and concert halls for more than 55 years.

My colleagues at the University of Chicago Press, especially Elizabeth Branch Dyson, who instantly saw the potential of this book and helped me conceive and shape it; Mollie McFee, who was indispensable in turning a vision into reality; Leslie Keros, who edited my words with a keen eye and a gentle touch; Jenni Fry, who elegantly kept all of us on the same page; Meredith Nini and Carrie Olivia Adams, who trumpeted this project to the world; and so many more.

My splendid, longtime literary agent, Jennifer Joel, and her extraordinary assistant Sindhu Vegesena at Creative Artists Agency.

Howard S. Dubin, who has been championing and supporting my work since I was a teenager, right up to and including this book.

My former Chicago Tribune colleagues, who nurtured and promoted my jazz writing, including Pam Becker, Linda Bergstrom, Robert Blau, Geoff Brown, Zbigniew Bzdak, Bob Carr, Richard Christiansen, Robin Daughtridge, R. Bruce Dold, Jennifer Fletcher, Janet Franz, Jack Fuller, William Gaines, Gerould Kern, Rick Kogan, Ann Marie Lipinski, Colin McMahon, James O'Shea, George Papajohn, William

Parker, Tom Popson, Scott Powers, Howard Tyner, Phil Velasquez, Jan Woelffer and Owen Youngman.

The club owners who welcomed me into their singular spaces, including Dave Jemilo at the Green Mill, Joe and Wayne Segal at the Jazz Showcase, Scott Stegman at Winter's Jazz Club, the Chisholm family at Andy's Jazz Club, Mike Reed at Constellation and Marguerite Horberg at HotHouse.

The guiding lights at the Hyde Park Jazz Festival, including Kate Dumbleton, Sam Lewis, Judith Stein, Almarie Wagner and the late James Wagner.

The founders of the Chicago Jazz Philharmonic, Orbert Davis and Mark Ingram.

The indefatigable forces at the Jazz Institute of Chicago, especially Lauren Deutsch, Heather Ireland Robinson, Zakiya Fola, Maggie Fouche, Mashaune Hardy and Diane Chandler-Marshall.

The staff at WDCB 90.9 FM, including Paul Abella, Dan Bindert, Leslie Keros, Bruce Oscar, Ken Scott and Gary Zidek.

The leaders of the much-missed Jazz Unites, Inc., Geraldine de Haas and the late Eddie de Haas.

The driving forces at Symphony Center Presents Jazz, especially James Fahey and Eileen Chambers.

My former professors at Northwestern University's Bienen School of Music, primarily pianist Wanda Paul, critic Thomas Willis, historian-theorist Arrand Parsons and composers Alan Stout and M. William Karlins.

The programming visionary Michael Orlove.

Philip Beck, who joined me on those first forays into Chicago's jazz clubs when we were still underage.

And readers of the Chicago Tribune, whose impassioned correspondence with me during my four-plus decades at the paper proved that listeners yearn to learn about music of great sophistication and complexity.

DISCOGRAPHY

Most of the visionaries discussed in this book have recorded prolifically and command extensive discographies. Here I've limited my choices to two recordings for each one, selected to emphasize different aspects of the artist's work.

Muhal Richard Abrams

Rejoicing with the Light (Black Saint). Abrams' restlessly inventive pianism dovetails with adventurous, uncategorizable orchestral colors.

Levels and Degrees of Light (Delmark). Here's vintage Abrams, from 1967, in which the master improviser-composer spans genres in tandem with like-minded luminaries: reedist Anthony Braxton, violinist Leroy Jenkins, tenor saxophonist Maurice McIntyre and drummer Thurman Barker, among others.

Dee Alexander

Wild Is the Wind (Blujazz). This vocal tour de force spotlights Alexander's copious melodic invention, novel sonic effects and, above all, profound expressivity.

Songs My Mother Loves (Blujazz). Alexander reimagines standards and illuminates obscurities via a vocal arsenal that will not quit.

Fred Anderson

The Missing Link (Nessa). Anderson's craggy, magisterial statements find empathetic collaboration from drummer Hamid Drake, percussionist Adam Rudolph and bassist Larry Hayrod.

Live at the Velvet Lounge (Okka Disk). There's nothing like hearing Anderson crafting vast solos in his own club, as he does here with percussionist Hamid Drake and bassist Peter Kowald.

Louis Armstrong

The Complete Hot Five and Hot Seven Recordings (Columbia/Legacy). Armstrong established the template for the jazz soloist in these recordings, thanks to his unmatched virtuosity, tonal brilliance and irrepressibly creative phrase-making.

Ella Fitzgerald and Louis Armstrong: Porgy and Bess (Verve). A dream duo: Armstrong's raspy vocals and clarion trumpet solos find poetic response from Fitzgerald's supremely luxuriant instrument.

Art Ensemble of Chicago

A Jackson in Your House/Message to Our Folks (Fuel 2000). The two landmark albums, recorded in Paris in 1969, document the ensemble's visionary conflation of ancient and contemporary, American and European, jazz and classical and more.

The Sixth Decade: From Paris to Paris (RogueArt). The Art Ensemble perpetually reinvents itself here, as veterans Famoudou Don Moye and Roscoe Mitchell are joined in 2020 by cellist Tomeka Reid, flutist Nicole Mitchell and trumpeter Hugh Ragin, among others.

Patricia Barber

Modern Cool (Premonition). The singular singer-pianist asserts her voice as songwriter with distinctive originals, such as "Touch of Trash" and "Winter," while shedding new light on well-known repertoire, including "You and the Night and the Music" and "She's a Lady."

Mythologies (Blue Note). Who but Barber would write a song cycle inspired by Ovid's "Metamorphoses"? And who but Barber could crystallize its sentiments via jazz?

Oscar Brown Jr.

Sin and Soul . . . and Then Some (Columbia). Brown's stunning debut spills over with his classic songs, including "Work Song," "Bid 'Em In," "Signifyin' Monkey" and "Afro Blue."

Mr. Oscar Brown, Jr. Goes to Washington (Verve). Brown enthralls in live performance, delivering bristling originals such as "Forty Acres and a Mule" and "Summer in the City."

Kelan Phil Cohran

Meditation (Katalyst Entertainment). Cohran conjures otherworldly tones on a variety of instruments, including the Frankiphone he invented, in collaboration with Malik Cohran on guitar, bass and keyboards.

Armageddon (Katalyst Entertainment). Cohran presides over oration, vocal chant and Afrocentric instrumental improvisation, recorded live at Cohran's Affro-Arts Theater in Chicago in the 1960s.

Orbert Davis

Priority (3Sixteen). A breakthrough recording for trumpeter Davis, "Priority" ranges from the sharp edge of his hard-bop playing to the seductiveness of his balladry.

Chicago Jazz Philharmonic: Havana Blue (3Sixteen). Davis' Chicago Jazz Philharmonic famously champions a Third Stream intertwining of jazz and classical idioms, nowhere more persuasively than in its embrace of Cuban music.

Dorothy Donegan

Dorothy Romps: A Piano Retrospective, 1953–1979 (Rosetta). This compilation documents the breadth of Donegan's pianism, from classical virtuosity to rugged boogie and blues.

Live at the 1990 Floating Jazz Festival (Chiaroscuro). Only a live performance can capture the pianist's outsized personality and keyboard brilliance.

Kurt Elling

Close Your Eyes (Blue Note). Elling makes a spectacular recording debut with this recording, which documents his technical acuity and musical fearlessness.

Live in Chicago (Blue Note). Though Elling's discography has been quite uneven, he conjures fire in a live setting, as in this date at the Green Mill in Chicago.

Kahil El'Zabar

Ritual Trio: Renaissance of the Resistance (Delmark). El'Zabar's profound partnership with bassist Malachi Favors and saxophonist Ari Brown yields illuminating homages to Ornette Coleman and John Coltrane, as well as a celebration of world music influences.

Ethnic Heritage Ensemble: Freedom Jazz Dance (Delmark). The band has shifted personnel in more than half a century of music-making; this time around, Chicago guitarist Fareed Haque partners felicitously with El'Zabar's percussion, Joseph Bowie's trombone and Ernest "Khabeer" Dawkins' reeds.

Von Freeman

Serenade and Blues (Nessa). The great Vonski stretches out with pianist John Young and drummer Wilbur Campbell—frequent foils—and bassist Dave Shipp.

The Improvisor (Premonition). Freeman summons ferocious bebop wizardry and sublime balladry in one of his last recordings.

Johnny Griffin

Introducing Johnny Griffin (Blue Note). And what an introduction, Griffin in 1956 proving volcanic on up-tempo tunes and charismatic on ballads, in the company of pianist Wynton Kelly, bassist Curly Russell and drummer Max Roach.

Chicago, New York, Paris (Verve). Griffin shows extraordinary harmonic erudition and melodic sophistication in tracing the trajectory of his long career.

Herbie Hancock

Takin' Off (Blue Note). Never was an album better named, Hancock's debut notable for his signature single "Watermelon Man" and his inspired partnering with trumpeter Freddie Hubbard, tenor saxophonist Dexter Gordon, bassist Butch Warren and drummer Billy Higgins.

Herbie Hancock and Wayne Shorter: 1 + 1 (Verve). The title refers to a duo setting of Hancock with reedist Wayne Shorter, the two conversing musically like the old friends they are, undistracted and undisturbed by anyone or anything else.

Johnny Hartman

John Coltrane and Johnny Hartman (Impulse!). This classic recording pairs Hartman's inimitably plush instrument with Coltrane's sublimely responsive tenor saxophone.

I Just Dropped By to Say Hello (Impulse!). Hartman excels with one of the greatest ensembles to join him on record: saxophonist Illinois Jacquet, pianist Hank Jones, drummer Elvin Jones, bassist Milt Hinton and guitarists Jim Hall and Kenny Burrell.

Art Hodes

Friar's Inn Revisited (Delmark). The master pianist nimbly delivers early jazz standards in the company of veterans George Brunis on trombone, Volly De Faut and Barney Bigard playing clarinet, and Barrett Deems on drums.

Pagin' Mr. Jelly (Candid). In one of the last recordings of his career, Hodes plays Jelly Roll Morton as if Hodes had been in Chicago when Morton was king—which, indeed, he was.

Ahmad Jamal

Ahmad Jamal Trio at the Pershing: But Not for Me (Argo). The recording that ignited Jamal's career, in 1958, its breakthrough singles including "Poinciana" and the title tune.

Chicago Revisited: Live at Joe Segal's Jazz Showcase (Telarc). In 1992, Jamal returns to the town that launched him, sounding as inventive as ever.

Ramsey Lewis

The In Crowd (Chess). The live recording that put Lewis on the pop culture map, thanks to the title cut and his seemingly nonchalant musical partnership with bassist Eldee Young and drummer Redd Holt.

Ramsey Lewis/Billy Taylor: We Meet Again (CBS). Anyone who doubted Lewis' keyboard dexterity and invention needs to hear him facing off with pianist Taylor.

Jelly Roll Morton

Jelly Roll Morton (JSP). Morton's recordings with various versions of His Red Hot Peppers created the template for jazz ensemble composition, arrangement and performance, luminously remastered in this five-CD box set.

Last Sessions: The Complete General Recordings (Commodore). Recorded in 1939 and 1940—near the end of Morton's life—his aptly named "Last Sessions" stands as a bittersweet final artistic statement.

Anita O'Day

Anita Sings the Most (Verve). O'Day's high-flying vocal virtuosity holds its own alongside formidable pianist Oscar Peterson, guitarist Herb Ellis, bassist Ray Brown and drummer John Poole.

Anita O'Day at Mister Kelly's (Verve). Here's a chance to hear O'Day live, recorded at the fabled Chicago nightspot.

Willie Pickens

It's About Time (Southport). Picken's belated debut as leader—in 1997—documents his volcanic power as pianist.

Marian McPartland and Willie Pickens: Ain't Misbehavin'—Live at the Jazz Showcase (Concord Jazz). McPartland's elegance and Pickens' muscularity dovetail in one of Chicago's most revered jazz rooms.

Sun Ra

Sound Sun Pleasure!! (Evidence). Here's early Sun Ra, from the mid-1950s, his Astro Infinity Arkestra staffed with luminaries such as tenor saxophonist John Gilmore and reedist James Spaulding.

At the Village Vanguard (Rounder). In one of his last recordings, from 1991, Ra takes the sounds down to chamber music level, with featured work from saxophonist John Gilmore and the singular but tragically under-recorded pianist Chris Anderson.

Reginald Robinson

Man Out of Time (88 PM; reginaldrrobinson.com). A pinnacle in the ragtime piano genius' oeuvre, the album includes such Robinson classics as the title track, "Four Horsemen of the Apocalypse" and arguably the greatest contemporary piano ragtime composition of our time, "The 19th Galaxy."

Reflections (88 PM; reginaldrrobinson.com). For the Robinson devotee, this anthology features two CDs of solo recordings (including previously unreleased compositions) and a DVD of live performances.

Ken Vandermark

Big Head Eddie (Platypus). The reedist's explosive recording debut as bandleader chronicles a vast stylistic range, in tandem with bassist Kent Kessler, drummer Michael Zerang and guitarist Todd Colburn.

Acoustic Machine (Atavistic). Vandermark dedicates each composition to a composer-arranger who influenced him, with cohesive performances from his ensemble with trombonist Jeb Bishop, reedist Dave Rempis, bassist Kent Kessler and drummer Tim Mulvenna.

INDEX

Figures are indicated by "f" after the page number. Titles of articles and reviews by Howard Reich included in this collection are given in italics.